ANNUAL REVIEW OF NURSING RESEARCH

VOLUME 30, 2012

SERIES EDITOR

Christine E. Kasper, PhD, RN, FAAN
Department of Veterans Affairs
Office of Nursing Services, Washington, DC
and
Professor, School of Nursing
Uniformed Services University of the Health Sciences,
Bethesda, MD

VOLUME EDITORS

Mary Pat Couig, MPH, RN, FAAN
Program Manager,
Emergency Management
Office of Nursing Services
Veterans Health Administration
Department of Veterans Affairs
Washington, DC

Patricia Watts Kelley, PhD, RN, FNP, GNP, FAANP
Health Sciences Officer,
Department of Veterans Affairs
Associate Professor, Uniformed Services
University of the Health Sciences,
Bethesda, MD

Annual Review of Nursing Research

Disasters and Humanitarian Assistance

VOLUME 30, 2012

Series Editor

CHRISTINE E. KASPER, PhD, RN, FAAN

Volume Editors

MARY PAT COUIG, MPH, RN, FAAN
PATRICIA WATTS KELLEY, PhD, RN, FNP, GNP, FAANP

SPRINGER PUBLISHING COMPANY
NEW YORK

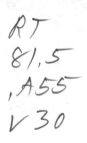

Springer Publishing Company, LLC
11 West 42nd Street
New York, NY 10036
www.springerpub.com

Acquisitions Editor: Allan Graubard
Composition: Absolute Service, Inc.

ISBN: 978-0-8261-1030-5
E-book ISBN: 978-0-8261-1033-6
ISSN: 0739-6686
Online ISSN: 1944-4028

12 13 14/ 5 4 3 2 1

The author and the publisher of this Work have made every effort to use sources believed to be reliable to provide information that is accurate and compatible with the standards generally accepted at the time of publication. Because medical science is continually advancing, our knowledge base continues to expand. Therefore, as new information becomes available, changes in procedures become necessary. We recommend that the reader always consult current research and specific institutional policies before performing any clinical procedure. The author and publisher shall not be liable for any special, consequential, or exemplary damages resulting, in whole or in part, from the readers' use of, or reliance on, the information contained in this book. The publisher has no responsibility for the persistence or accuracy of URLs for external or third-party Internet Websites referred to in this publication and does not guarantee that any content on such Websites is, or will remain, accurate or appropriate.

Special discounts on bulk quantities of our books are available to corporations, professional associations, pharmaceutical companies, health care organizations, and other qualifying groups.

If you are interested in a custom book, including chapters from more than one of our titles, we can provide that service as well.

For details, please contact:
Special Sales Department, Springer Publishing Company, LLC
11 West 42nd Street, 15th Floor, New York, NY 10036-8002
Phone: 877-687-7476 or 212-431-4370; Fax: 212-941-7842
Email: sales@springerpub.com

Printed in the United States of America by Hamilton Printing

Contents

About the Volume Editors

Mary Pat Couig, MPH, RN, FAAN, is currently a Program Manager/Emergency Management for the Office of Nursing Services (ONS), Department of Veterans Affairs. She advises the Veteran's Health Administration (VHA) chief nurse officer on public health emergency preparedness and represents the chief nurse officer and ONS on related committees and initiatives. She also works collaboratively with VHA program offices, Veterans Integrated Service Networks, facility leadership teams, and nurse executives to address complex health care delivery and nursing practice issues at a national level with a focus on public health emergency preparedness.

From 2000 to 2005 she served as the Chief Nurse Officer (assistant surgeon general/rear admiral) in the U.S. Public Health Service (PHS). As a senior health care executive, she developed policy and provided leadership to both the Commissioned Corps and civil service nurses in the PHS. She worked closely with the Office of the Surgeon General and senior leadership in the Department of Health and Human Services and was actively engaged in the development and implementation of national and global public health initiatives. During her time as the chief nurse officer, she was a member of the Federal Nursing Services Council, composed of the nurse directors of the Air Force, Army, Navy, PHS, VA, and the American Red Cross. Her collaborative efforts with the Federal Nursing Services Council and local, state, national, and international colleagues focused on strengthening nursing's role and preparation for public health preparedness. The Secretary of Health and Human Services appointed her as the lead for the Secretary's Emergency Response Team for Emergency Support Function #8, public health and medical during Hurricane Rita in 2005.

She received her BSN from Fitchburg State College in Fitchburg, MA and her master's in public health from Johns Hopkins School of Hygiene and Public Health, Baltimore, MD. She is a doctoral candidate in the graduate school of nursing at the Uniformed Services University of the Health Sciences in Bethesda, MD.

Dr. Patricia Watts Kelley, PhD, RN, FNP, GNP, FAANP, holds the position of Health Sciences Officer, Department of Veterans Affairs, Office of Research & Development. Prior to her navy retirement, she held the position of Deputy Director of Nursing and Allied Health Research, Navy Medicine Research and Development Center, Navy Headquarters, Bureau of Medicine and Surgery. She continues to hold an associate professor appointment at the Uniformed Services University of the

Health Sciences, Graduate School of Nursing, Bethesda, MD. Dr. Kelley has held several military research positions. She served as the first Navy executive director of the TriService Nursing Research Program and director of Nursing Research Services, National Naval Medical Center, Bethesda, MD. Her research interests are in the areas of clinical knowledge development and continuity of care of wounded service members, evidence-based practice, health promotion and diabetes self-care management, and nursing retention and recruitment. She served as the specialty consultant to the U.S. Navy surgeon general for nursing research. Capt. Kelley had maintained a part-time nurse practitioner practice at the National Naval Medical Center, Bethesda, MD specializing in diabetes and military health up until her recent retirement.

Dr. Kelley received her Doctor of Philosophy in Nursing from the Catholic University of America, a postmaster certificate in family primary care from Northeastern University, a Master of Science from Boston University School of Nursing with a specialty in gerontology, a Bachelor of Science in Nursing from American University, and an associate degree in science from Northeastern University. Dr. Kelley is board certified as a Family and Gerontological Nurse Practitioner and a Fellow of the American Academy of Nurse Practitioners.

Capt. Kelley entered Naval Service as family nurse practitioner in 1990 and since then, has held various clinical research, operational, staff and leadership positions overseas and within the United States. She was recognized for her service with various awards, among them are Defense Meritorious Service Medal, Meritorious Service Medal, the Navy and Marine Corps Commendation Medal two gold stars, Navy and Marine Corps Achievement Medal one gold star, and the National Defense Medal two awards.

Prior to entering into Naval Service, Dr. Kelley held a number of civilian nursing positions including serving as executive director, assistant executive director, and gerontological nurse practitioner at Windsor House Adult Day, Cambridge, MA and director of nursing senior care management nursing home corporation, Boston, MA; head nurse and staff nurse of Boston City Hospital. Dr. Kelley was responsible for several innovative geriatric programs while serving at Windsor House Adult Day Care programs, among them were the dementia dual program at Windsor House Watertown and the facilitation of the community Alzheimer's support services.

Dr. Kelley also currently serves on the board of directors for the Navy Safe Harbor Foundation and the Redeemer House Project serving veterans.

The professional associations in which Dr. Kelley participates are Sigma Theta Tau International Honor Society, the American Academy of Nurse Practitioners, the American College of Nurse Practitioners, Eastern Nursing Research Society, American Nurses Association, Maryland Nurses Association, and the Association of Military Surgeons of the United States.

Dr. Kelley resides in Silver Spring, Maryland, with her husband Stephen M. Kelley.

Contributors

Susan Bulecza, DNP, RN, CNS, PHCNS-BC
Preparedness Director, Bureau of
    Preparedness and Response
Florida Department of Health
Tallahassee, FL

Mary Pat Couig, MPH, RN, FAAN
Program Manager, Emergency
    Management
Office of Nursing Services
Veterans Health Administration
Department of Veterans Affairs
Washington, DC

Bobby A. Courtney, MA, MPH, JD
Director of Policy and Planning
MESH
Indianapolis, IN

Molly Frommelt-Kuhle, PhD, RN
Assistant Professor
Department of Nursing and Health
Clarke University
Dubuque, IA

Kristine M. Gebbie, DrPH, RN
Adjunct Professor
Flinders University
Adelaide, Australia

Sameer Vali Gopalani, MPH
College of Public Health
Kent State University
Kent, OH

Alison Hutton, PhD, RN
Senior Lecturer
Flinders University
Adelaide, Australia

Ann R. Knebel, DNSc, RN, FAAN
Deputy Director, Preparedness
    Planning
Rear Admiral, U.S. Public Health Service
U.S. Department of Health and Human
    Services
Office of the Assistant Secretary for
    Preparedness and Response
Office of Preparedness and Emergency
    Operations
Washington, DC

Roberta Proffitt Lavin, PhD, APRN-BC
Chair and Professor of Nursing and
    Health
Department of Nursing and Health
Clarke University
Dubuque, IA

Mark Libby, RN
Regional Emergency Coordinator,
    Region 1—New England
U.S. Department of Health and Human
    Services
Office of the Assistant Secretary for
    Preparedness and Response
Office of Preparedness and Emergency
    Operations
Boston, MA

Virginia Plummer, PhD, RN
Senior Lecturer
Monash University
Melbourne, Australia

Chad Priest, MSN, RN, JD
Chief Executive Officer
MESH
Adjunct Assistant Professor
Indiana University School of Nursing

Paul Root
MESH
Law student, Indiana University.
Indianapolis, IN

Lisa Schemmel-Rettenmeier, EdD, RN
Assistant Professor
Department of Nursing and Health
Clarke University
Dubuque, IA

Michaela R. Shafer, PhD, RN
Colonel, U.S. Air Force
Assistant Professor
Graduate School of Nursing
Uniformed Services University
Bethesda, MD

Lynn A. Slepski, PhD, RN, CCNS
CAPT, U.S. Public Health Service
Senior Public Health Advisor
Office of Intelligence, Security and
    Emergency Response
U.S. Department of Transportation
Washington, DC

Sharon A. R. Stanley, PhD, RN, RS
Chief Nurse
American Red Cross
Washington, DC

Andrew C. Stevermer, MSN, RN
Regional Emergency Coordinator Program
    Supervisor (Acting)
Office of Preparedness and Emergency
    Operations
Office of the Assistant Secretary for
    Preparedness and Response
U. S. Department of Health and Human
    Services
Washington, DC

**Laurel Stocks, MSN, RN, FNP, CCRN,
    CCNS**
Colonel, U.S. Air Force Reserve
Graduate School of Nursing
Uniformed Services University
Bethesda, MD

Lauren Toomey, MIS, RN
Senior Program Analyst
U.S. Department of Health and Human
    Services
Office of the Assistant Secretary for
    Preparedness and Response
Office of Preparedness and Emergency
    Operations
Washington, DC

**Elizabeth Weiner, PhD, RN-BC, FACMI,
    FAAN**
Senior Associate Dean for Informatics
Centennial Independence Foundation
    Professor of Nursing
Professor of Biomedical Informatics
Vanderbilt University School of
    Medicine
Nashville, TN

Preface

This 30th volume in the *Annual Review of Nursing Research* (ARNR) series depicts the most current research and knowledge in the rapidly expanding field of disaster preparedness and humanitarian assistance. Prior to September 11, 2001, few organizations outside of the International Red Cross and selected governmental agencies considered that planning for and response to a mass casualty event should be a fundamental item embedded in their strategic and operational plans. Humanitarian assistance has long been a focus of many local, national, and international organizations where nursing care of the victims of disaster and the nursing profession form the core of their mission. The past decade has unfortunately been a witness of international communities awash in disaster from both natural and man-made events. In this issue, Mary Pat Couig, MPH, RN, FAAN, Rear Admiral (ret.) of the U.S. Public Health Service and Patricia Watts Kelley, PhD, RN, FNP, GNP, FAANP—well-known scholars, researchers, and international leaders in the field of disaster preparedness and humanitarian assistance—have served as the volume editors. Content for the chapters was carefully chosen and edited by them into this review of nursing research in the field. Uniquely, the chapter authors represent not only the scholars of cutting-edge research but also international leaders in disaster and humanitarian work. Together, they present a clear picture of the current research and what is needed to move this field into the future.

This volume is composed of 10 chapters examining the key areas of nursing research. Roberta Proffitt Lavin and her team address conducting research during disasters in Chapter 1. In Chapter 2, the important role of leadership during disasters is detailed by Ann R. Knebel, Lauren Toomey, and Mark Libby. Michaela R. Shafer and Laura Stocks discuss the important topic of conducting ethically sound disaster nursing research in Chapter 3, whereas Bobby A. Courtney and colleagues examine the legal issues in emergency response in Chapter 4.

An in-depth review on the psychological impact of disasters on communities is led by Sharon A. R. Stanley, Susan Bulecza, and Sameer Vali Gopalani in Chapter 5. Roberta Proffitt Lavin and her team tackle the oft-neglected needs of special populations during crises in Chapter 6. In Chapter 7, Betsey Weiner and Lynn A. Slepski review the literature on nursing informatics research issues during disaster and humanitarian response. Given the complexity of delivering nursing care in times of crises, Kristine M. Gebbie, Alison Hutton, and Virginia Plummer provide an update on research in competencies and education in Chapter 8. This is followed by a discussion of willingness and the ability to respond to disaster in Chapter 9 by Mary Pat Couig.

The complexity of international disaster response and associated research is addressed by Andrew C. Stevermer in the final chapter, Chapter 10.

As series editor, it is my hope that these topically based chapters will be used not only by those conducting research studies but also as texts and supplements to nursing curricula for both the undergraduate and graduate students studying emergency management. In addition, it is important to also examine the state of research in the area to look for new and important research questions that need to be addressed so that the best possible research can be applied in times of dire human need. This would be in the best traditions of the nursing profession and our founding greats Florence Nightingale and Clara Barton.

Christine E. Kasper, PhD, RN, FAAN
Series Editor

Acknowledgments

The editors would like to acknowledge the support of the Department of Veterans Affairs, Veterans Health Administration, Office of Nursing Services and the Health Services Research and Development Service. They would also like to acknowledge their prior services, the U.S. Public Health Service and the U.S. Navy.

ANNUAL REVIEW OF NURSING RESEARCH

VOLUME 30, 2012

CHAPTER 1

Conducting Research During Disasters

Roberta Proffitt Lavin, Lisa Schemmel-Rettenmeier, and
Molly Frommelt-Kuhle

ABSTRACT

The potential for man-made or natural disasters is a reality that exists within
the confines of the global setting. Man-made and/or natural disasters, although
devastating to the human population, offers researchers the ability to explore and
advance current preparedness, response, and recovery practices. When conducting research, consideration must be given to the ethical treatment of vulnerable
populations and the protection of privacy for those affected by the disaster.

The conduct of research in a crisis or disaster situation presents many challenges to overcome barriers. Some of the most significant barriers evidenced in
the literature include time constraints, institutional review board (IRB) approval,
informed consent, sampling strategies that do not overrepresent the poor, data
collection methods from individuals that may move frequently in the days following a disaster, perceptions of doing research in the midst of suffering, and
researcher bias. To overcome these and many other challenges, prior planning
is essential, including having a research team that is ready to respond when the
conditions are right to study the research question.

© 2012 Springer Publishing Company
http://dx.doi.org/10.1891/0739-6686.30.1

CONDUCTING RESEARCH DURING DISASTERS

Ethical issues while conducting research in a crisis situation comprises both the need to protect the rights of the research participants while safeguarding research quality and accurately disseminating findings (Barron Ausbooks, Barrett, & Martinez-Cosio, 2009). Ethical considerations must be given to everyone, inclusive of the moral treatment of vulnerable populations and the protection of privacy for those affected by the disaster. Although much research occurs within the internationally accepted regulations, at times, vulnerable populations end up being exploited (Sumathipala et al., 2008). More specifically, unethical research may exploit culturally diverse populations by not taking into context the cultural morals, beliefs, and values. The National Commission for the Protection of Human Subjects of Biomedical and Behavioral Research, The Belmont Report: Ethical principles and guidelines for the protection of human subjects research (1979) reported "from an ethical perspective, research endeavors should be governed by the principals of respect for persons, beneficence, and justice" (as cited in Daugherty & White, 2010).

Health Insurance Portability and Accountability Act

The Health Insurance Portability and Accountability Act (HIPAA) of 1996 was enacted to address two significant issues: (a) insurance portability with job changes or loss and (b) protection of individuals from threats to their privacy, especially from electronic health information. The Department of Health and Human Services (HHS) implemented the Privacy Rule, a subsection of HIPAA, in 2003. The Privacy Rule resulted in significant changes in the requirements to maintain and disclose health information. The rule requires that it is necessary to inform patients of their right to review their health records for accuracy and to obtain their written approval before sharing protected health information (PHI) with anyone who does not have a legitimate reason to see the information (Lavin, 2006).

Researchers, while conducting studies, should be cognizant of the rules and regulations regarding privacy and confidentiality of all participants especially as they apply to covered entities. Covered entities include any of the following: health care providers, health plans, and health care clearinghouses. Those that are not covered entities do not have to comply with the HIPAA Privacy Rule (HHS, 2012). Individual consent must be obtained from each participant prior to using any information that comes from a covered entity even if the researcher does not work for the covered entity. Although this may seem impractical during a disaster, there are only a few exemptions to the privacy rule that may apply because it is related to disaster research and response: (a) minimum necessary information may be released for health research and specifically public health;

(b) with prior IRB approval, a waiver for individual authorization provided that conditions are met that the information is de-identified, and thus poses no significant risk to the privacy of the individual and that there are security measure in place to ensure that PHI is not released; and (c) some information may be released to public health authorities and representatives for surveillance purposes (Lavin, 2006; Nordin, Kasimow, Levitt, & Goodman, 2008). Researchers must be aware of the established rules and regulations to ensure that breaches in confidentiality do not occur (see Table 1.1). An additional challenge for the researcher includes security breaches because of the researchers' presence within the confines of the population being studied. Furthermore, local researchers are more likely to breach confidentiality because of previous knowledge of individuals participating in the research (Barron et al., 2009).

RESEARCH ISSUES

Vulnerability of Participants
Vulnerable populations include children, prisoners, and pregnant women, adults who are cognitively or mentally impaired and prospective participants who may be considered economically or educationally disadvantaged. Limitations of using the aforementioned populations for research would be a consideration for determining the acceptable level of risk versus benefit to the subjects without providing just compensation (Fleischman & Wood, 2002). This may be considered as part of the double effect, that is, when a good effect (improved patient care from the research findings) also results in a bad effect (undue coercion of a group that may be willing to take added risks to help his or her family).

In the past, researchers deliberately withheld vital information regarding participation and neglected to obtain informed consent from culturally diverse and vulnerable populations. This clear breach of trust can lead to reluctance to participate in future research. Flory, Kloos, Hankin, and Cheely (2008) outlined procedures to help build trust between researcher and participant. To promote trust, researchers used research assistants belonging to the cultural group, answered questions, and discussed participant rights prior to beginning research (Flory et al., 2008). To ensure an accurate understanding of the research agenda while addressing literacy and language issues, questionnaire items were read aloud. These actions may help to promote an atmosphere of cultural sensitivity and are an ethical responsibility of all involved in conducting disaster-related research (Flory et al., 2008).

Vulnerable populations, specifically racial and ethnic minorities, are at higher risk for experiencing greater devastation from disaster than others. This increased level of risk may be attributed to socioeconomic status, culture and

TABLE 1.1

Use of Protected Health Information in Disaster Research

Policies and Use of PHI in a Systematic Investigation

1. Determine if you or your organization is a covered entity, such as a health plan, health care clearinghouse, or a health care provider that transmits information electronically (almost everyone now does this through fax, e-mail, electronic billing, or electronic medical record).

2. The Privacy Rule does not specifically apply to research, but because the researcher may want PHI from a covered entity, it will be necessary to show how the researcher will comply with the requirements and have authorization, including the following:
   a. The name of anyone or group using the PHI.
   b. Who will disclose the PHI.
   c. A description of the information that will be used.
   d. It must state that either that it does not expire or that the authorization continues until the end of the research study (HHS, 2003).
   e. A clear statement that it will be provided to the individual upon request.
   f. The individual or their authorized representative must sign it (HHS, 2000).

3. Use of PHI without the authorization is possible under the following limited circumstances:
   a. Pursuant to a waiver from the IRB or Privacy Board and identification of the date the waiver was approved,
   b. A statement that the IRB or Privacy Board that the waiver satisfies the three criteria of the Privacy Rule (no more than minimal risk, could not practically be conducted without the waiver, and could not practically be conducted without access to PHI),
   c. A description of the PHI for which access has been determined necessary,
   d. A statement that the waiver has been reviewed by the IRB or Privacy Board and whether it was under normal or expedited review, and
   e. The signature of the chair or other member of the IRB or Privacy Board (HHS, 2003).

In addition, if the request for authorization comes from the covered entity, then the covered entity is responsible for ensuring that the individual understands the following:
1. Why the information is being requested and for what purpose it will be used;
2. That he or she may review the information before it is released and refuse to release the information;
3. The authorization to release PHI is not a requirement for treatment, payment, enrollment, or eligibility for; and
4. Whether financial compensation is being provided to the covered entity. The Privacy Rule specifies that this must be written and not merely verbal.
5. Detailed and current information on research is available through the Office of Civil Rights at the Department of Health and Human Services at http://www.hhs.gov/ocr/privacy/hipaa/understanding/special/research/index.html.

Note. HIPAA = Health Insurance Portability and Accountability Act; IRB = institutional review board; PHI = protected health information. Adapted from Lavin, R. P. (2006). HIPAA and disaster research: Preparing to conduct research. *Disaster Management Research*, 4(2), 32–37.

language barriers, level of educational preparation, lower levels of preparedness, and lack of access to appropriate relief and recovery agencies (Andrulis, Siddiqui, & Gantner, 2007; Eisenman, Cordasco, Asch, Golden, & Glik, 2007). Knowledge of culturally diverse populations is essential for conducting competent research. Familiarity with the affected cultural familial roles, responses to loss, and health care practices and beliefs promote the relationship between the participant and the researcher (Flory et al., 2008).

Barriers to Research

Research may be hindered by safety concerns, primarily related to immediate dangers founded within the crisis situation and following the disaster. The environment post disaster may be entirely unpredictable and may impede research efforts (Janssen, Lee, Bharosa, & Cresswell, 2010). Displacement of individuals, lack of communication, and emotional distress are also factors that may inhibit the research process.

Postdisaster research challenges include the inability to track displaced populations related to the rapidly changing allocation of resources, housing, and financial instability of victims (Eisenman et al., 2007; Flory et al., 2008; Hori & Schafer, 2010). Investigators conducting disaster research are encouraged to share resources and information with survivors and helping them to connect with available support services (Flory et al., 2008).

In addition, the emotional toll experienced by the disaster researchers may not be anticipated. Hearing survivor stories and visualizing physical trauma without adequate counseling knowledge may be overwhelming to the researcher. These experiences coupled with the timeliness and urgency of the research can result in burnout and fatigue (Flory et al., 2008).

Similar to the emotional toll experienced by researchers, victims may suffer retraumatization through recollection of disaster-related events and be overburdened by being subject to numerous inquiries related to the crisis event. In the recruitment of individuals for data collection, one's physical and mental health status should be considered (Fleischman & Wood, 2002).

Institutional Review Boards

The IRBs play an important role in maintaining the rights of participants in research, including crisis and disaster research. These participant's unique circumstances may put them at risk for further traumatization; therefore, IRBs and researchers should pay special attention to the selection of participants for disaster research (Fleischman & Wood, 2002).

Historically, there was no standardized IRB method for regulating disaster research and this resulted in research being conducted without prior IRB approval (Fleischman & Wood, 2002). Since September 11, the inception of accelerated IRB processes has been installed to ensure the voluntary nature and free consent of individuals participating in disaster and crisis-related research (Fleischman & Wood, 2002). During a crisis or a disaster, timely research is of the essence; delays in the IRB approval process can be prohibitive (Daugherty & White, 2010).

Researchers requiring IRB approval may want to consider collaboration with other investigators to reduce redundancy and oversampling of the populations affected by the crisis or disaster. The primary area of concern for the IRB committee, as in all research, should include keeping the research participants in the forefront of the approval process. However, IRB consideration should be given to the urgent nature of the research and not unduly hinder the investigator's attempt to collect data (Fleischman & Wood, 2002).

Compensation

Compensation for research participants may be indicative of coercion and is considered a major ethical concern. Research participants, especially monetarily disadvantaged individuals, may be likely to falsify their experiences to participate in research and gain compensation. Furthermore, the uneven representation of low-income individuals participating in the research may skew the data and affect the generalizability of the results (Barron et al., 2009). It is recommended that compensation should not be part of any disaster research and rather that when possible researchers provide helpful information and referral to resources.

Sampling and Subject Recruitment

It can be said that what impacts the participants will impact the researcher. When preparing for disaster research in an impacted area, or even when considering retrospective research that will be based on files and document produced during the disaster, one must consider the participants and the responders. Knowing that many who do research are not trained responders, does not mean that the researcher should be ignorant of what it will be like in the impacted area or the priorities of the survivors and the responders. Unless the researcher is prepared for adverse circumstances, he or she may become a burden to the responders who put saving life and property at the top of the priority list. It should come as no surprise to anyone that has responded to a disaster to find chaos in the immediate aftermath of a disaster and extending well into the recovery period. When families are dislocated, either voluntarily or involuntarily, there is little time to prepare and important documents may be left behind. In this era of electronic resources, most people still do not store their vital information in a retrievable electronic format and this is especially true with the elderly and those in poverty. Conversely, many researchers store things only in electronic format and with limited access to communications and power; this may not be retrievable. Preparation is key.

It is not uncommon to hear those that are adversely impacted by a disaster to complain of changing policies and rules that make the most basic tasks difficult and cause them to take days or weeks to accomplish. Even the routine task of making phone calls or appointments is not routine following a disaster is difficult and this is no different for the researcher (Flory et al., 2008). What adversely impacts the participant will also adversely impact the researcher so it is critical to be aware of what participants experience and plan in advance to be able to cope with such difficulties.

Completing the basic task of contacting participants following a disaster is the first and possibly the primary challenge. Many, if not most disaster survivors in a major disaster may not have easy access to a phone because both landlines and cell towers can be damaged and, depending on the extent of the disaster, can take days to weeks to repair. In hurricanes and other natural disasters, it is not uncommon for cell phone coverage to also be limited. Flory et al. (2008) had difficulty getting individuals to call in and found that some had low literacy skill that may have been an additional barrier. However, one must also consider this challenge as a potential research bias. Those most able to return, or who are most motivated to return, might be the ones that can most easily be contacted. All demographic groups do not return at the same pace and thus caution must be taken in interpreting results (Henderson et al., 2009). Researchers must identify the demographic information prior to the disaster. Most demographic information is easily available through the Census Bureau and available online. Although it may be impossible to have a representative sample, it will be possible to address any potential bias. Sampling methods and bias should be carefully considered in advance.

Finally, plan A almost always fails in a disaster so it is important for the researcher to have multiple contingency plans. Deadlines can change and chaos is a given during a disaster and recovery. This will cause difficulty in not only recruiting but also retaining study participants. Eisenman et al. (2007) reported that they would successfully recruit participants at their temporary lodgings, but when they would go to conduct the assessments, the participants would have been moved and no one could tell them the person's current location. Frequent moves while one is in temporary shelters or housing can be expected and may interfere with the research process (Flory et al., 2008). The researcher must have a plan for locating people when they do move. This can include making sure the participant has the researcher's contact information, maintaining an open line of communication with the Federal Emergency Management Agency (FEMA), the American Red Cross, and disaster case managers. This network for communication should start before the disaster. For one to be successful, the researcher needs to build a network of professional responders that he or she can call upon for advice and assistance.

The 10 "musts" of sampling during disaster research are the following:

1. Know the demographics of your population.
2. Know the sample size that is needed.
3. Know the location where sampling will occur (hospitals, clinics, shelters, assistance centers, faith-based organizations) and make contact in advance to ensure access.
4. Be prepared to explain to community leaders who are helping to identify participants how the research will benefit the community.
5. Establish a community advisory group that has input into the research. Buy-in is essential to participant recruitment.
6. All hospitals will have their own IRB. If one plans on collecting data at a hospital, there will be IRB requirements—this is a significant barrier to collecting data during the actual disaster.
7. Review the HIPAA, Privacy Rule, and Common Rule requirements—ignorance is not an excuse.
8. When approaching participants, it is helpful to have a trusted community member as a facilitator.
9. Know how to contact the participant if he or she moves. Either a backup contact or a release that will allow personnel at the current location to give you the location of the new shelter or residence.
10. Plan to address barriers—age, literacy, language, transportation, frequent moves, and other geographic, social, chaos-related incidents.

THEORETICAL PERSPECTIVE TO DISASTER RESEARCH

Many theories exist that can be used in research related to the management of natural or man-made disasters. One should select the theoretical or conceptual framework that is best related to the type of the research and the practice that one hopes the research will influence. Models that are clearly outlined can serve as a guide for implementing a detailed plan of action to enhance the response to the crisis (Herzog, 2007). Theories identified in the literature included decision theories, economic theories, and crisis theories.

Decision Theory

Decision theories such as those developed by Simon and more recently Smith are used to convey the required steps necessary to managing disasters and offer mechanisms to better understand and cope with the disaster (as cited in

Sementelli, 2007). Decision theories act as valuable frameworks for understanding crisis and disaster theory from the context of perception (Barnett et al., 2005) and are not necessarily concerned with the processes used to meet the final goal. Decision theories are also associated with the overall quality of information access (Anand & Forshner, 1995) and data collected throughout the research process (Smith as cited in Sementelli, 2007).

Economic Theory

Economic and social theories tend to have an abstract focus and offer a means for reflection and discussion. The exploration of theories assists in understanding the response and management and ethical issues of crisis and disaster. According to Sementelli (2007), economic theories tend to view crisis through the lens of economic factors. These may include loss through business productivity, damaged property, job loss, and investment in rebuilding infrastructure. Unlike decision theories, which focus on utilitarian outcomes, people think of economic theories as tending to focus on the financial aspects of the crisis and as being descriptive rather than action oriented (Sementelli, 2007).

Modern economic theory actually uses utility as an "explicit value of a function which describes human behavior in a choice-theoretic framework" (Heath, 1988; Sen, 1970). These theories are ideal for evaluation choice especially because it may relate to allocation of scarce resource or other priorities in a disaster. Utility in the von Neumann and Morgenstern economic theory is a measure of how much importance an individual assigns to goals (as cited in Sementelli, 2007). This value is a numerical representation derived from the ordering of social states based on individual choices (Dasgupta, 1993). The common characteristics of the things humans choose are utility under the condition of risk and uncertainty. This is a different interpretation than in utilitarianism where pleasure is utility.

Social Welfare Theory

Pareto's social welfare theory (McLure, 2001), which was developed to solve the problem of measuring utility, was the first notable economic theory. Pareto believed that the influence of a person's preferences on his or her conduct could be scientifically examined (McLure, 2001). For a society to achieve Pareto optimality, equilibrium must be reached so that no further exchanges of goods result in any individual being worse off. It is assumed that people are capable of ranking their preferences and that only when no one is made worse off by an individual choosing a state other than the baseline can that state be considered to be a better choice. It is hard to imagine an example where this would clearly be the case.

The two premises of the Pareto's social welfare theory are the following:

1. If everyone in the society is indifferent between two alternative social situations x and y, then the society should be indifferent, too; and
2. If at least one individual strictly prefers x to y, and every individual regards x to be at least as good as y, then the society should prefer x to y. (Sen, 1970, p. 21)

A significant problem with this approach is that "if one individual prefers x to y, and another prefers y to x, then we cannot compare them socially using the Pareto rule" (Sen, 1970, p. 22).

Pareto defined utility as ". . . the property of an action that enhances 'well-being,' and may be considered in terms of the individual (individual utility), the community (utility of the aggregate), or society broadly defined (utility of the species)" (McLure, 2001, p. 42). Improvement in utility means there is an improvement in well-being, which can be moral, physical, intellectual, or material well-being. Pareto thought that the term *utility* was far too broad to be studied scientifically and coined the term *ophelimity* or a more elementary form of utility. Essentially, Pareto did not believe that all pleasant sensations were positive. Instead, he believed that utility was the relationship of a pleasant sensation to well-being. This resulted in the ability to evaluate sensations based on individual desires whether or not the desires were legitimate. Through this approach, economic propositions can be developed that are scientifically based. Ophelimity is the pleasure that results from an exchange, and utility is the improvements in well-being that results from a change (McLure, 2001).

Over time, Pareto's definition of utility and his approach changed with his consideration of logical and nonlogical actions. Utility transitioned from its emphasis on well-being to an emphasis on the benefits of actions, which are weighted. The weight once compared produced social utility, which is the "[M]aximaxation of total happiness or satisfaction in society" (Sterba, 1980, p. 8).

Impossibility Theorem
Along the same line, Arrow's Impossibility Theorem (Sen, 1970) evolved from both Paretian welfare theory and voting paradoxes. Arrow proposed that each individual has a preference and those preferences can be ordered to produce a global preference order. If individual preferences are then used to determine social choices, it is necessary to establish when the individual preferences are relevant. This would be a useful theory for evaluating preferences for providing training to health care professions for disaster response and even evaluating how to assign who is critical during a disaster. There is always the issue of which nurses and other providers must report to work during a disaster. Ranking of choices must satisfy three

characteristics to be considered ordering: (a) transitivity—"if x is at least as good as y, and y is at least as good as z, then x should be at least as good as z," (b) reflexivity—"every alternative x must be thought to be at least as good as itself," and (c) completeness—"for any pair of alternatives x and y, either x is at least as good as y, or y is at least as good as x (or possibly both)" (Sen, 1970, p. 2).

Within Arrow's theorem, there are five properties: (a) universality or unrestricted domain—preference must work for every possible set of individual ordering; (b) Pareto principle—if everyone prefers x to y, the society should prefer x to y; (c) nondictatorship—preference is based on the choice of one individual so if he prefers x to y, then x is the choice even if it is not beneficial to society; (d) monotonicity or citizen sovereignty—if choosing x is taboo even if choosing x over y is preferred, then a social welfare function is imposed; and (e) independence of irrelevant alternatives—orderings must be related to available choices and not fictional or unavailable choices (Sen, 1970). Arrow proved that it is impossible to meet all of these properties.

Utility Theory

The process of calculating utility is difficult when attempting to make interpersonal comparisons. Sen (1970) notes that individual utility does not come in cardinal units. Cardinal units can only be determined through experimentation and then it is limited. Several issues arise, beginning with the need for a scale on which to base utility. A standard scale is linear from 0 to 1. Even then, how does one measure preferences based on pleasure or happiness? For example, how does one measure the mother being required to report to work and leaving an infant at home as opposed to the daughter being required to report to work and leaving the fragile elder parent at home? Next, the inability of individuals to make fine comparison means that measures may be made based on discrimination levels. Utility would be measured based on the difference between two alternatives resulting in a cardinal scale. This method has its own difficulties, the most prominent of which assumes that all individuals have the same discrimination levels.

Another approach to measurement of utility is seen in the approach of von Neumann and Morgenstern. As long as an individual conforms to a set of postulates, utility numbers can be determined for a set of alternatives (Sen, 1970). There are multiple ways of determining utility and different sets of postulates. Heath (1988) summarized the postulates developed by Jacob Marshak, which are considered to be the easiest to understand, as:

1. An individual's preferences are completely ordered. Any two prospects can be ordered in the sense that prospect A is preferred to B, B is preferred to A, or the individual is indifferent between them.

2. If A is preferred to B and B to C, then there exists a probability p between 0 and 1 such that the gamble A with probability p and C with probability $1 - p$, which can be stated as [pA + $(1 - p)$C], will then be indifferent (i.e., equally preferred) to B.

3. For any object of choice or "prospect" A and for any probability p one can specify another prospect B such that A will not be indifferent to the probability combination [pA + $(1 - p)$B]. The specifics of this is that a gamble in which the probability of a given prospect of A is not 1, however close to 1 it may be, cannot be regarded as the equivalent of A with certainty.

4. If A and B are indifferent and p is between 0 and 1, then [pA + $(1 - p)$C] is indifferent to [pB + $(1 - p)$C]. (p. 359)

Some conclude from this that the utility functions of different persons can be compared; however, this is not a generally accepted belief because it is not possible to know the exact amount of utility. There is no scale that can measure preferences for reporting to work like there is for measuring height.

It is also possible to get false utility when an individual makes an irrational choice. Therefore, utility must be based on rational choices that are made during normal conditions with all the necessary information to make an informed choice. For example, drug addicts prefer to service their addiction. This clearly is not a rational choice. A corrected preference would be the preference that results from full knowledge of the consequences of servicing the addiction. However, under this belief, rational choice must always rule. This raises serious concerns about personal freedom of choice and as is well documented, health care professionals have limited choice in reporting to work especially those that are federal or state employees.

Theory of Justice

The theory of justice is built on the same basic premise as utilitarianism with the exception that inequality is accepted as long as it benefits the worst off. Imagine making decisions on the allocation of scarce so that the worst off is benefited. Rawls (1971) adds the concept of primary goods to utility. Interestingly, health is not considered a primary good because it is not something one can distribute (Olsen, 1997). Rights are used to distinguish states in which the utility consequences are equal (Dasgupta, 1993). Rawls holds that if preferences are based on a veil of ignorance, individuals will always choose to maximize their primary goods because they will not know if they may someday be the person who is worst off. This approach is based on lexical ordering of the following two principles:

1. Each person is to have an equal right to the most extensive total system of equal basic liberties compatible with a similar system of liberty for all.

2. Social and economic inequalities are to be arranged so that they are both: (a) to the greatest benefit of the least advantaged, consistent with the just savings principle, and (b) attached to offices and positions open to all under conditions of fair equality of opportunity. (Rawls, 1971, p. 302)

The Rawlsian approach does not allow for anything less than very complex numerical calculation of utility and, although an interesting approach, may be more difficult to apply scientifically. Specifically, if actions should benefit the least advantaged, it will be difficult to determine how to prove which actions result in the least advantaged not being made worse off. In theory it is the most moral, but in practicality for research, it is difficult to implement.

Approaches to Utility

A quick review of utility then will show some basic differences based on the theory within which it is used. Utility is, "the basic unit of desirability in much decision theory, game theory, and economics" (Blackburn, 1994, p. 388). Utility is equivalent to individual welfare and it is assumed that individuals will allocate their resources in a manner that will maximize their utility (Black, 2002), whereas in utilitarianism, the goal is to maximize the total happiness of society or maximize social utility. And with the theory of justice, as proposed by Rawls (1971), the principle of utility is that the proper arrangement of a society occurs when its institutions maximize their satisfaction. Imagine how different our emergency response plans would look if they were based on the Rawlsian approach rather than a basic utilitarian approach.

Crisis Theory

Caplan believed that individuals in crisis are more able to accommodate an intervention and that the intervention is important. Caplan identified three stages of a crisis: (a) a perceived change in a person's state of mental equilibrium, (b) the inability to solve the problem through one's normal problem-solving techniques, and (c) that a person's mentality returns to a state of equilibrium if the crisis is successfully resolved (as cited in Murphy & Fawcett, 1983). However, Caplan does not address a person holistically.

Further expansion of the crisis theory includes the crisis in context theory (CCT). This model is reflective of not only the individual experiencing the crisis but also includes an ecological perspective. This perspective is inclusive of the concepts of cultural and social contexts in which the crisis occurred, that is, families and communities (Deiter & Pearlman; van der Kolk & McFarlane; as cited in Myer & Moore, 2006). Gist and Lubin (1989) support the CCT by similarly reflecting on the notion that communities and external factors play an important role in understanding and responding to a crisis. "CCT presents an ecological perspective for understanding the impact of crises on individuals and organizations by integrating results of research with personal observations. The model is a departure from the more traditional perspective used in crisis intervention of focusing attention solely on individuals" (Meyer & Moore, 2006, p. 145).

Haddon's Matrix
Another method that falls within the context of a crisis theory is Haddon's matrix. William Haddon (1972) introduced a conceptual framework for categorizing highway safety phenomena. His approach drew from his background in epidemiology by using the epidemiologic principles of "(1) an external agent, (2) a susceptible host, and (3) an environment that brings the host and agent together . . ." (Butler, Panzer, Goldfrank, & Institute of Medicine [IOM], 2003). By applying these principles to public health concepts, he believed it was possible to introduce a pathway to systematically analyze strategies for loss reduction and resource allocation (Haddon, 1973). Haddon (1973) specifically looked at the host, agent/vector, physical environment and social environment. These can then be divided among preevent, event, and postevent periods and any cost-cutting feasibility value criteria.

Crisis Conceptual Nursing Model
The faculty of the University of Connecticut School of Nursing proposed a final crisis model. The crisis conceptual nursing model (CCNM) was derived from the crisis theory with adaptations for nursing so that it addressed the person holistically. Lindemann was a psychiatrist who had firsthand experience with the Coconut Grove fire of 1942. Lindemann's goal was to move beyond the medical model by drawing on aspects of public health and social science (Murphy & Fawcett, 1983). If a person experienced a disaster, which overwhelmed his or her ability to cope effectively, then a crisis ensued. Murphy and Fawcett (1983) viewed crisis as an opportunity flowing from "any event that challenges the assumed state and forces the individual to change his view of, or readapt to, the world, himself, or both" (p. 47). Although Haddon's matrix has decades of research supporting it, little has ever been done with the CCNM and very little exists in the literature. However, combining the two models makes one ideal model for disaster nursing research (see Table 1.2).

Whichever theoretical framework a researcher chooses, it should be recognized that it will guide the way the researcher approaches analysis of the information. Although some models are ideal for retrospective research, the combined Haddon's matrix and CCNM allows the researcher to better define the target population. That analysis will then influence practice and future research. All health care providers should be in the forefront of developing the science of both planning and response.

TABLE 1.2
The Crisis Conceptual Nursing Model

Factor/Stage	Agent/Vector Hazardous Event	Person	Environment	Nursing	Health
Precrisis (Preparedness)	Goal: Health promotion and disease prevention				
Crisis (Response)	Goal: Amelioration or cure				
Postcrisis (Response & recovery)	Goal: Rehabilitation, maintenance of an optimal level of health and support of dying				

Cross Cutting—Nursing Process

Assessment	Planning	Implementation	Evaluation
• Identification of biophysical, psychosocial, and spiritual factors	• Priority setting and identification of goals	• Ego strengthening or general support • Mobilizing environmental sources of support	• Considers the state of dynamic equilibrium between the person and the environment • Current coping mechanisms reassessed after an intervention

Adapted from Lavin, R. P., Slepski, L., & Rettenmeier, L. (2012). Direction for nursing research and development. In T. F. Veenema (Ed.), *Disaster nursing and emergency preparedness for chemical, biological, and radiological terrorism and other hazards* (3rd ed.). New York, NY: Springer Publishing.

FUTURE NURSING RESEARCH AGENDA

In an era of diminishing budgets and a lessened focus on disaster response both nationally and at the state level, there must be a unified research agenda that sets priorities for research (see Table 1.3). The priorities should be based on addressing the needs of the least among us; the vulnerable and those with limited ability to speak for themselves. For too long, the focus has been on doing the greatest good for the greatest number of people. The result has been that preparedness, response, and recovery activities have focused on those that are actually best able to care for themselves. The same has been true of research. In examining

TABLE 1.3

Top 10 Areas for Disaster Research for Rectifying Neglected Areas

---

1. Needs of vulnerable/special needs populations during a disaster response and recovery.
2. Real-time communication and methods to enhance the effectiveness of communication between providers and with the public.
3. How to best collaborate between government, nongovernmental, and faith-based organization.
4. Geospatial Information System prepopulated for public health use during a disaster.
5. Necessary skills and competencies for all providers examined from a multidisciplinary perspective.
6. Health policy research focused on the ethical issues of decision making and the allocation of scarce resources.
7. Health policy research on the impact of disaster on the existing health care delivery system and how the system to be enhanced to improve resiliency.
8. Necessary standards of care during a disaster and treatments that may be more appropriate with mass casualties especially when the current standard of care is impractical.
9. Psychosocial impact of being part of a disaster and/or part of the disaster response.
10. The impact of spiritual distress and spiritual care during a disaster and how it influences resiliency.

---

the majority of the published nursing research, it addresses the needs of the elderly—most of whom, while frail, do have financial means—and the needs and feelings of nurses and other health care providers. The research on disaster-related care is benignly neglectful of children, those in poverty, and those with functional limitations. Most decisions for these groups are made by consensus of people who have never walked in their shoes or conducted research on the populations. Based on the evidence presented in this chapter, Table 1.3 lists the research priorities that will rectify the benign neglect.

Continued health care–related disaster research needs to be sensitive regarding the interventions provided to those in the immediate crisis, while keeping in mind the need to gather context-rich data during the crisis and reflective experiences postcrisis (Myer & Moore, 2006). More qualitative research designs may provide valuable information on the contextual factors related to crisis (Myer & Moore, 2006). It is easier to carry out and requires fewer participants. Moreover, it can provide the foundation for identification of future research.

To the extent, possible all future research should be multidisciplinary. There is little doubt that future federal grants will require a multidisciplinary approach. There is much work to be done to identify and understand how to use the differing knowledge and expertise of health care responders during a mass casualty event or natural disaster. It is well documented that volunteers who are not trained to respond frequently are burdens during the disaster. Although they mean well, they can take resources away from the actual response. Most of the currently existing information on training levels, competencies, and volunteer preparedness is anecdotal or based on retrospective accounts.

There are no identified nursing or health care–related research on the spiritual needs of disaster survivors and how spiritual distress impacts their disaster recovery. Nursing, and more recently medicine, promotes the importance of the approaching individuals holistically rather than from a reductionist perspective; yet in disaster research, a time of crisis, researchers look at the pieces rather than the whole person or the whole community.

Finally, future research on real-time communication may be beneficial because it provides mechanisms to understanding crisis and crisis interventions as they occur in the natural setting (Myer & Moore, 2006). Much of the existing field research discusses environments of chaos. Chaotic environments are inherently stressful and result in inefficiency. As health care providers, clear, concise, and effective communication is essential to patient care. It is also essential to effective disaster responses. It therefore is logical that the first step in an adequate response is improving crisis communication.

CONCLUSION

"History teaches that inadequate disaster reduction awareness and preparation repeatedly leads to preventable loss of life and damage in all major disasters" (Kaklauskas, Amaratunga, & Haigh, 2009, p. 121). Any disaster research is going to face challenges and barriers, but what is contributed can change the outcomes for the clients and the health care providers. Choosing a research topic begins with identifying a gap, choosing a theoretical framework, selecting a population to be studied, and developing a mechanism to carry out the research. There is no shortcut during a disaster to implementing a good research project and it largely depends on having prior approvals in place and a good network within the emergency response community. All of the prior planning that goes into disaster response must also go into disaster research.

REFERENCES

Anand, A., & Forshner, C. (1995). Of mad cows and marmosets: From rational choice to organizational behaviour in crisis management. *British Journal of Management, 6*(4), 221–233..

Andrulis, D., Siddiqui, N., & Gantner, J. (2007). Preparing racially and ethnically diverse communities for public health emergencies. *Health Affairs, 26*(5), 1269–1279.

Barnett, D. J., Balicer, R. D., Blodgett, D., Everly, G. S., Jr., Omer, S. B., Parker, C. L., & Links, J. M. (2005). Applying risk perception theory to public health workforce preparedness training. *Journal of Public Health Management and Practice, 11*(6 Suppl), S33–S37.

Barron Ausbooks, C., Barrett, E., & Martinez-Cosio, M. (2009). Ethical issues in disaster research: Lessons from Hurricane Katrina. *Population Research and Policy Review, 28,* 93–106. http://dx.doi.org/10.1007/s11113-008-9112-7

Black, R. (2003). Ethical codes in humanitarian emergencies: From practice to research? *Disasters, 27*(2), 95–108.

Butler, A. S., Panzer, A. M., Goldfrank, L. R., & Institute of Medicine (U.S.). (2003). Preparing for the psychological consequences of terrorism: A public health strategy. Washington, DC: National Academies Press.

Blackburn, S. (1994). *Oxford dictionary of philosophy.* Oxford: Oxford University Press.

Dasgupta, A. (1993). *An inquiry into well-being and destitution.* Oxford, United Kingdom: Oxford University Press.

Daugherty, E., & White, D. (2010). Conducting clinical research during disasters. *Virtual Mentor, 12*(9), 701–705.

Eisenman, D., Cordasco, K., Asch, S., Golden, J., & Glik, D. (2007). Disaster planning and risk communication with vulnerable communities: Lessons from Hurricane Katrina. *American Journal of Public Health, 97*(1), S109–S115.

Fleischman, A., & Wood, E. (2002). Ethical issues in research involving victims of terror. *Journal of Urban Health: Bulletin of the New York Academy of Medicine, 79*(3), 315–321.

Flory, K., Kloos, B., Hankin, B., & Cheely, C. (2008). Clinical research after catastrophic disasters: Lessons learned from Hurricane Katrina. *Professional Psychology: Research and Practice, 39*(1), 107–112.

Gist, R., & Lubin, B. (1989). Psychosocial aspects of disaster. *Journal of Traumatic Stress, 3*(2), 328–330.

Haddon, W. (1972). A logical framework for categorizing highway safety phenomena and activity. *Journal of Trauma, 12*(3), 193–207.

Haddon, W. (1973). Energy damage and the ten countermeasure strategies. *Human Factors, 15*(4), 355–366.

Heath, W. C. (1988). von Neumann/Morgenstern decision making and Harsanyi's theory of justice: After Rawls and Nozick, if it risks personal freedom and individual liberty, can it be really just? *American Journal of Economics and Sociology, 47*(3), 355–362.

Henderson, T., Sirois, M., Chen, A., Airriess, C., Swanson, D., & Banks, D. (2009). After a disaster: Lessons in survey methodology from Hurricane Katrina. *Population Research Policy Revision, 28,* 67–92. http://dx.doi.org/10.1007/s11113-008-9114-5

Herzog, R. J. (2007). A model of natural disaster administration: Naming and framing theory and reality. *Administrative Theory and Praxis, 29*(4), 586–604.

Hori, M., & Schafer, M. (2010). Social costs of displacement in Louisiana after Hurricanes Katrina and Rita. *Population and Environment, 31,* 64–86. http://dx.doi.org/10.1007/s11111-009-0094-0

Janssen, M., Lee, J., Bharosa, N., & Cresswell, A. (2010). Advances in multi-agency disaster management: Key elements in disaster research. *Information Systems Frontiers, 12,* 1–7. http://dx.doi.org/10.1007s10796-009-9176-x

Kaklauskas, A., Amaratunga, D., & Haigh, R. (2009). Knowledge model for post-disaster management. *International Journal of Strategic Property Management, 13,* 117–128.

Lavin, R. P. (2006). HIPAA and disaster research: Preparing to conduct research. *Disaster Management & Response, 4*(2), 32–37.

Lavin, R. P., Slepski, L., & Rettenmeier, L. (2012). Directions for nursing research and development. In T. F. Veenema (Ed.), *Disaster nursing and emergency preparedness for chemical, biological, and radiological terrorism and other hazards* (3rd ed.). New York, NY: Springer Publishing.

McLure, M. (2001). *Pareto, economics and society: The mechanical analogy*. London, United Kingdom: Routledge.

Murphy, E., & Fawcett, J. (1983). The crisis theory conceptual framework. In M. B. White (Ed.), *Springer series on the teaching of nursing: Curriculum development from a nursing model: The crisis theory framework* (Vol. 8). New York, NY: Springer Publishing.

Myer, R., & Moore, H. (2006). Crisis in context theory: An ecological model. *Journal of Counseling and Development, 84*, 139–147.

Nordin, J. D., Kasimow, S., Levitt, M. J., & Goodman, M. J. (2008). Bioterrorism surveillance and privacy: Intersection of HIPAA, the Common Rule, and public health law. *American Journal of Public Health, 98*(5), 802–807.

Olsen, J. A. (1997). Theories of justice and their implications for priority setting in health care. *Journal of Health Economics, 16*(6), 625–639.

Rawls, J. (1971). *The theory of justice*. Cambridge, MA: Belknap Press of Harvard University Press.

Sementelli, A. (2007). Toward a taxonomy of disaster and crisis theories. *Administrative Theory and Praxis, 29*(4), 497–512.

Sen, A. K. (1970). *Collective choice and social welfare*. San Francisco, CA: Holden-Day.

Sterba, J. (1980). *Justice: Alternative political perspective*. Belmont, CA: Wadsworth.

Sumathipala, A., Siribaddana, S. H., Hewage, S. N., Lekamwattege, M., Athukorale, M., Siriwardhana, C., . . . Prince, M. (2008). Ethical approval and informed consent: Analysis of biomedical publications originating from Sri Lanka. *BMC Medical Ethics, 9*, 3.

U.S. Department of Health and Human Services. (2000). *HIPAA Privacy Rule*. Retrieved from http://www.hhs.gov/ocr/privacy/hipaa/administrative/privacyrule/index.html.

U.S. Department of Health and Human Services. (2003). *Health information: Privacy*. Retrieved from http://www.hhs.gov/ocr/privacy/hipaa/understanding/special/research/index.html

U.S. Department of Health and Human Services. (2012). *For covered entities*. Retrieved from http://www.hhs.gov/ocr/privacy/hipaa/understanding/coveredentities/index.html

CHAPTER 2

Nursing Leadership in Disaster Preparedness and Response

Ann R. Knebel, Lauren Toomey, and Mark Libby

ABSTRACT

Nurses serve as leaders in disaster preparedness and response at multiple levels: within their own homes and neighborhoods, at disaster scenes, and the workplace, which can vary from a health care facility, in the community, or at the state, national, or international level. This chapter provides an overview on theories of leadership with a historical context for nursing leadership; setting the context for nursing leadership in disaster preparedness and response. Although few research studies exist, there are numerous examples of nurses who provide leadership for disaster preparedness and response. To define the current state of the science, the research studies cited in this chapter are supplemented with case studies from particular disasters. The major finding of this review is that nursing leadership in disaster preparedness and response is a field of study that needs to be developed.

INTRODUCTION

The purpose of this chapter is to review the research literature regarding nursing leadership in disaster preparedness and response. A literature search was conducted in July 2011 using the databases MEDLINE/PubMed, CINAHL Plus, Web of Science/Social Sciences Citation Index, and Scopus. The search terms used were either used alone or in combination: *leadership, leader, disaster, preparedness, emergencies*, and *nursing and nurses*, which yielded 106 articles after excluding those not in English and not specific to nursing leadership during a disaster. A subsequent search was conducted in September 2011 to sharpen the focus to center on crisis leadership. The databases searched were PsycINFO, MEDLINE/PubMed, CINAHL Plus, and the Center for Creative Leadership's (CCL) Website. The search terms used included *crisis leadership, disaster*, and *emergencies and nursing*, which resulted in 44 articles published in English. Additional articles were identified by hand searching the bibliographies of the articles included in this review. Most articles reviewed were not research studies. Relevant nonresearch studies are summarized to provide context for nursing leadership in disaster preparedness and response. There were only two relevant research studies and five doctoral dissertations. Articles that evaluated nursing leadership lessons learned for specific events were also included.

To set the context for nursing leadership in crisis situations, this chapter begins with an overview of the theories of leadership. Nursing leadership in disaster preparedness and response from a historical context is briefly described. The articles included in this review incorporate nursing leadership both in the United States and internationally. Figure 2.1 shows graphically that nurses provide leadership at multiple levels, whether that is at the disaster scene or in their own homes, in a health care facility or in a community in which they work, or at other levels (state, national, or international). Although there are few research studies, there are many examples of nurses who provide leadership for disaster preparedness and response. The research studies cited in this chapter are supplemented with case studies and anecdotal information to define the current state of the science for nursing leadership during disasters. The major finding of this review is that nursing leadership in disaster preparedness and response is a field of study that needs to be developed.

LEADERSHIP THEORIES AND CRISIS LEADERSHIP
Definition of Leadership
Definitions of leadership vary, but there are certain components that are central to the concept of leadership. Leadership, first and foremost, involves a *process* that occurs between the leader and his or her followers. The second component of leadership involves *influence*, which is concerned with how a leader affects his or her followers. The third component is that it occurs in *groups*. Groups are made up of individuals that have a common purpose. The fourth and final component of leadership is concerned with accomplishing *goals*. It is the leader that is responsible for directing a group of individuals toward accomplishing some task or outcome (Cotton, 2009; Stogdill, 1974).

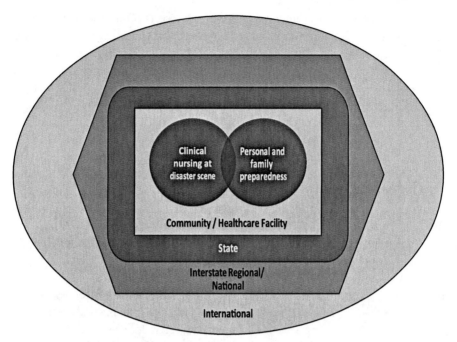

FIGURE 2.1 This outlines the various ways in which nurses provide leadership during disasters. Nurses are leaders within their own homes assuring that their families have a disaster supply kit and a plan. As the largest health care workforce, nurses provide leadership in clinical care for disaster victims at the scene of an emergency and their places of employment in the community, the hospital, or other locations. Nurses provide leadership at multiple levels including state, regional, national, and international.

Theories of Leadership

The earliest research about leadership was based on the study of men who were considered great leaders and who arose from aristocracy. This *great man theory* argues that a few people are born with the necessary characteristics to be great, and they can be effective leaders in any situation (Marriner-Tomey, 2009). The *trait theory* of leadership became popular in the mid-1940s and was based primarily on the "great man" theory, but it differed by taking the position that leadership qualities can be identified and taught (Marquis & Huston, 2005). *Situational theory* rose to prominence during the 1950s, expanding on "trait theory" with the caveat that leader traits vary and are determined by the particular situation (Sullivan, 1995). What was lacking in these early theories of leadership was the ability to predict which leadership behaviors would be most effective in specific situations.

In *situational leadership theory*, the leader looks at the different variables surrounding the situation to make the best choice of leadership style (Marriner-Tomey, 2009). The leader will alter the style of leadership based on an analysis of the follower's readiness, meaning the level of motivation and competence an individual has for an assigned task. The leader assesses the follower's capacity to complete the assigned task and provides the appropriate leadership behavior that best meets the needs of the follower in the given situation.

Transformational leadership theory recognizes that for leaders to be effective, the organizational culture needs to change (Grohar-Murray & DiCroce, 2003). With this leadership style, both the leader and the followers have the same purpose, and they raise one another to higher levels of performance. The transformational leader mobilizes others and grows and develops with the followers. In practice, establishing and maintaining both organizational and personal trust with others represents the fundamental strategy of the transformational leader (Grohar-Murray & DiCroce, 2003).

Integrative leadership theory concludes that the leader, the follower, and the situation all influence leadership effectiveness (Marriner-Tomey, 2009). Leaders need to be aware of their own behavior and influence on others, they need to recognize the individual differences of their followers (characteristics and motivations), they need to understand the structures available to perform specific tasks, and they need to analyze the situational variables that impact the ability of followers to complete tasks, including environmental factors. With integrative leadership, the leader considers all of these factors using a "wholistic" approach to oneself and others, and adjusts his or her leadership style through adaptive behavior (Marriner-Tomey, 2009).

Similar to the evolution seen in the general theories of leadership, there has also been an evolution in the literature specific to nursing leadership. No longer is a "born" nurse leader viewed as effective in all situations (Sullivan, 1995). There is growing consensus that different styles of nursing leadership are needed depending on the situation. As an example, in a crisis situation in which the followers have little or no knowledge or experience (e.g., patient in cardiac arrest), an autocratic style of nursing leadership may be most appropriate, where the leader takes total control, issues directives, and excludes group decision making (Sullivan, 1995). Alternatively, in noncrisis situations, less autocratic styles may be appropriate. The thoughtful study and implementation of transformational leadership is recommended for implementation in health care organizations because it is congruent with nursing's values and organizational requirements (Grohar-Murray & DiCroce, 2003). Accountability for practice is a hallmark of these organizations. Decision making and communication are shared equally in institutions that support transformational leadership (Sullivan, 1995).

Crisis Leadership

Large-scale disasters starting in the late 1970s gave rise to much of the available literature on crisis leadership. These disasters included

- Tylenol's cyanide poisonings,
- National Aeronautics and Space Administration's Challenger and Columbia tragedies,
- Metropolitan Edison's Three Mile Island nuclear disaster,
- Exxon's Valdez oil spill,
- 2001 terrorist attacks, and
- Hurricane Katrina.

These events established crisis leadership as a new and rapidly developing field. A recent review found that 80% of existing literature has been published since 1985, establishing crisis leadership as a relatively new area of inquiry (Pauchant & Douville, 1993). Because of its recent development, the study of crisis leadership lacks an overall conceptual paradigm, is highly fragmented, covers a wide range of complex variables, and has been studied through the lens of numerous disciplines including economics, history, psychology and philosophy (Pauchant & Douville, 1993). Few data-based studies exist, and more analytical works result from attempts by researchers to synthesize anecdotal information. These analytic works are practitioner oriented rather than theoretical and are derived primarily from consultants hired to resolve crises for large corporations and governmental entities (Jones, 2010).

The definition of *crisis leadership* identifies three essential components: communication, clarity of vision and values, and caring relationships (Klann, 2003). Leaders who develop, pay attention to, and practice these qualities are better able to handle the important human dimension of a crisis. *Crisis management* focuses on planning; controlling; leading; organizing; and motivating prior to, during, or after a crisis. Crisis management is different than crisis leadership. With crisis leadership, the leader provides vision and influence in a noncoercive manner to provide strategic decision making and guidance across the phases of the crisis. Crisis leadership includes crisis management but extends beyond to cultivate the followers' desire to achieve a vision and mission in a time of crisis (Porche, 2009; Weiss, 2002).

When a disaster strikes, crisis leaders need to remind people of their strengths despite the fear and anxiety provoked by the event (Bandura, Caprara, Barbaranelli, Gerbino, & Pastorelli, 2003; Seeger, Sellnow, & Ulmer, 2003). By quickly offering information that is needed to make decisions, the crisis leader will empower people to help themselves and their loved ones survive. In a crisis, the crisis leader will be judged by the content of official messages, the speed of the communication, and the perception of their credibility (Peters, Covello, & McCallum, 1997; Seeger et al., 2003). Leaders strongly influence the ability of individuals, organizations, communities, and nations to cope with and recover from crises (Mitroff, 2004). Crisis leaders approach the public as equals in the disaster situation by empowering their health-risk decision making (Fischer, 1998; Reynolds, 2009; Sandman & Lanard, 2004; Seeger et al., 2003; Ulmer, Sellnow, & Seeger, 2007).

Effective crisis leadership boils down to responding to the human needs, emotions, and behaviors caused by the crisis (Klann, 2003). Effective crisis leaders respond to the emotional needs perceived by those experiencing the crisis. People are more apt to follow a leader who is reassuring and who can meet their primary needs (Reynolds, 2009). Crisis leaders use integrative leadership and adapt the style of leadership to the given situation to ensure success (Hersey & Blanchard, 1969; Xavier, 2005). Comprehensive emergency management requires leaders to consider not only the immediate crisis response but also leadership for hazard mitigation and disaster preparedness and recovery. These components are intertwined and require a flexible leadership approach that is different than the approach needed during the actual emergency response (Waugh & Streib, 2006). What this means is that a crisis leader needs to be cognizant of the possibility that other leadership approaches may be more effective during the different phases of a crisis (Cotton, 2009).

NURSING LEADERSHIP AT MULTIPLE LEVELS

Figure 2.1 outlines the various ways in which nurses provide leadership during disasters. From a preparedness perspective, nurses are leaders within their own homes for *personal and family preparedness*, assuring that their families have a disaster supply kit and a plan for responding to the threats that are likely to occur in their community. As the largest health care workforce, nurses provide leadership in caring for disaster victims whether that is caring for disaster victims at the *scene of a disaster*, providing care to the broader *community*, or caring for victims at their place of employment such as a *health care facility*. Nurses are increasingly providing leadership at the *state, regional, national*, and *international* levels where they lead planning and policy efforts to enhance the preparedness of the nation to respond to disasters. The history of nursing leadership in crises provides the context for understanding the ways in which nurses provide leadership at multiple levels.

History of Nursing Leadership in Crises
Pioneer Nurse Leaders
Nurses have served as crisis leaders during wars, disasters, and epidemics; demonstrating vision, courage, and endurance in managing some of the worst

circumstances imaginable. A discussion of nursing leadership in crises would be incomplete without mentioning the pioneer nurse leaders.

At the request of the British government, Florence Nightingale and a corps of 38 trained nurses cared for sick and injured soldiers during the Crimean War (a conflict between the Russian Empire and an alliance of Britain, France, and the Ottoman Empire in the mid-1800s). Nightingale's clinical work is often cited as heroic, but it was her employment of statistics and her skills as a leader, advocate, and administrator that led to a dramatic decline in mortality during this war (Cohen, 1984).

At the beginning of the American Civil War (1861–1865), teacher and nurse Clara Barton cared for wounded soldiers. As the war continued, she demonstrated tremendous political leadership and willpower, developing innovative systems of care such as moving nursing to the front lines. Over the span of 17 years, she went on to organize the American Red Cross in 1881. She was instrumental in the U.S. Senate adopting, in 1882, the first Geneva Convention to protect the sick and wounded in wartime (Barton, 1922).

Recognizing the leadership role of clinical nurses in saving lives on the battlefield, the Surgeon General, in 1901, requested that the nurse corps become a permanent corps of the U.S. Army Medical Department (Army Reorganization Act, 31 Stat. 753). Jane A. Delano, who served as the second superintendent of the U.S. Army Nurse Corps, expanded the capability of the nation to respond to disasters by founding the American Red Cross Nursing Service in 1909. She also served as the first president of the American Nurses Association, an organization created to represent the interest of the growing profession of nursing. As a result of Delano's leadership, there were more than 8,000 registered nurses available to meet the needs of wounded soldiers when the United States entered World War I in 1917.

Disasters Where Nurses Demonstrated Individual Clinical Leadership
In 1918 and 1919, the Spanish influenza outbreak sickened one of every four Americans, caused more than 500,000 deaths in the United States, and more than 40 million deaths worldwide. The U.S. Public Health Service (PHS) and the Red Cross appealed to nurses—retired, private, and students, and women with any type of nursing experience—and they responded, leading efforts to mitigate this public health emergency and risking their lives to care for those who were ill (Schoch-Spana, 2001).

During World War II (1941–1945), more than 59,000 American nurses served in the U.S. Army Nurse Corps. Using systems of care similar to those developed by Clara Barton, these nurses worked closer to the front lines than they ever had before. Within the "chain of evacuation," these nurses served under fire in field and evacuation hospitals, on hospital trains and ships, and as flight nurses on medical transport planes. Because of the personal risks assumed by these nurses and the clinical leadership they demonstrated, they contributed to the extremely low postinjury mortality rate among American military forces in every theater of the war. Fewer than 4% of the American soldiers who received medical care in the field or underwent evacuation died from wounds or disease (Tomblin, 1996).

During the Cold War period after World War II, the primary national threats concerned the advent of nuclear weapons, fallout, and the possibility of bacteriological and chemical warfare. In 1954, the U.S. Department of Health, Education, and Welfare (DHEW) was given responsibility for developing requirements, plans, and operating procedures for an emergency medical stockpile program and for preparing national emergency plans and preparedness programs for health services and civilian health manpower (Federal Civil Defense Act of 1950). These responsibilities included development of national plans for coordinating with professional organizations to prepare and mobilize nurses to serve in clinical leadership roles during health emergencies.

The Disaster Relief Act of 1974 directed the Secretary of the U.S. Department of Health and Human Services (HHS, formerly DHEW) to provide medical response capability (including nursing care) for catastrophic disasters. In 1980, the Department of Defense initiated the Civilian Military Contingency Hospital System through which civilian hospitals were enlisted to provide reserve beds to treat American military casualties if military capacity proved inadequate (Beary, Bisgard, & Armstrong, 1982). The program began to recruit hospitals but ran into resistance from groups concerned that the government was preparing for nuclear war (Day & Waitzkin, 1985).

At the same time, HHS planners became increasingly concerned that the nation did not have sufficient capacity to deliver a medical response during catastrophic disasters. This concern led to a recommendation to establish a single national system for military and civilian response. In 1981, President Ronald Reagan established the Principal Working Group on Health. This led to the formation of the National Disaster Medical System (NDMS) in 1984, a partnership among HHS, the Department of Defense, the Veterans Administration, and the newly formed Federal Emergency Management Agency (Brandt, Mayer, Mason, Brown, & Mahoney, 1985).

In 1989, Hurricane Hugo struck the Caribbean, hitting St. Croix especially hard. The NDMS was activated for the first time, deploying two disaster medical assistance teams (DMATs), including a full complement of nurses who staffed a 106 bed field hospital. Providing care in these austere conditions, volunteer nurses demonstrated clinical leadership in treating 294 victims, admitting 38 patients, and airlifting 8 patients (Bern, 1998). The first domestic use of NDMS was in 1992 when Hurricane Andrew hit South Florida as a Category 4 hurricane. Over the course of a few weeks, 15 DMATs from 11 states were deployed to South Florida. These teams included nearly 600 federal volunteer nurses, physicians, and support staff. They provided primary health care, emergency medical services, mental health services, and outreach to more than 17,000 patients (Burkholder-Allen, Rega, & Budd, 1994).

Nurses rose to the occasion to care for the victims of terrorism on U.S. soil. In 1995, domestic terrorists bombed the Murrah Federal Building in Oklahoma City, killing 167 people, including children at the on-site day care center (Anteau & Williams, 1997). Even though the World Trade Center in New York City was attacked with a truck bomb in 1993, it was the act of terrorism which occurred on September 11, 2001 that changed the nation. On that date, Al-Qaeda terrorists hijacked commercial airliners and flew them into both World Trade Center towers in New York City and the Pentagon in Arlington, Virginia. A fourth aircraft crashed in Shanksville, Pennsylvania, short of its intended target. The NDMS and U.S. PHS Commissioned Corps nurses officers responded to the events of September 11, setting in motion the broadest emergency response conducted by HHS to date (Babb & Beck, 2001). Although PHS nurses participated in many deployments before September 11 (Debisette, Martinelli, Couig, & Braun, 2010), this particular deployment accelerated the transformation of the PHS Commissioned Corps because people came to realize the tremendous leadership potential of a uniformed service of 6,000 health care professionals (Knebel et al., 2010).

Soon after the terrorist attacks of September 11, letters laced with anthrax began appearing in the U.S. mail. Five Americans were killed and 17 were sickened in what became the worst biological attacks in U.S. history (Gursky, Inglesby, & O'Toole, 2003). Nurses demonstrated clinical leadership, working alongside epidemiologists and investigators to protect and inform the public. For example, PHS nurses were called upon to dispense postexposure prophylaxis to U.S. Postal Service employees and congressional staff who had been exposed to anthrax spores.

In 2005, Hurricane Katrina made landfall as a powerful Category 3 storm in the Gulf Coast, with its greatest impacts in Louisiana and Mississippi. Hurricane Katrina was followed within weeks by hurricanes Rita and Wilma. These disasters will long be remembered for the disruption of whole communities, the loss of life, and the chaos that ensued. Most of New Orleans' hospitals and other health care resources were destroyed or inoperable. Nurses in hospitals and nursing homes did the best they could to protect their patients until help arrived (Bernard & Mathews, 2008; Franco et al., 2006; Laditka et al., 2008). Nurses and other health care providers were deployed to the Gulf Coast through NDMS, PHS, American Red Cross, and countless other avenues to provide medical assistance. These nurses provided leadership in the face of substantial challenges, making triage and treatment decisions for patients whose numbers far exceeded supplies and personnel (Debisette et al., 2010; Klein & Nagel, 2007). This was the most massive patient assessment, stabilization, and evacuation operation in U.S. history (U.S. Government Accountability Office, 2006).

In the spring of 2009, a new flu virus (H1N1) spread quickly across the United States and the world. The U.S. government coordinated a public health emergency response within the states that helped limit the impact of the outbreak. Considerable planning had already been done for a potential H5N1 flu pandemic. Despite differences in the H5N1 planning scenarios and the actual H1N1 pandemic, many of the systems established through pandemic planning were used and useful for the 2009–2010 pandemic response. Through planning, administering programs, providing bedside care, and organizing immunization clinics, nurses demonstrated leadership and were engaged at the local, regional, and national level (Lessler et al., 2009).

Nursing Leadership in the Community and Beyond

Public health nurses provide leadership in the community to improve disaster plans and response activities. The Association of State and Territorial Directors of Nursing published a position paper that provides policy guidance describing the roles and actions public health nurses must assume to protect the health and safety of communities, families, and individuals during emergencies (Jakeway, LaRosa, Cary, & Schoenfisch, 2008). Public health nurses serve as leaders to develop policy and preparedness plans and provide frontline disaster health and core public health services during disasters. They also serve in leadership and management roles in emergency operations centers. Competencies for public health nursing leaders have been defined (Gebbie & Qureshi, 2002).

Because public health nursing leaders could be faced with health threats of catastrophic proportions like an influenza pandemic, they should consider best practices in leadership, successful leader influences on followers, and the communication processes involved. If leading is the exercise of influence on others to accomplish a goal (Yukl, 2002), leadership in public health may be challenging to influence people to take the actions recommended. For public health leaders who do not have reward or coercive power over the public to obtain behavioral compliance, they must rely on transformational leadership skills.

Crises are emotion-laden events, and managing these emotions will be critical. In a community setting, a lack of transformational leadership will make it more difficult for public health leaders to mobilize the community to do more with less self-interest (Sivanathan & Fekken, 2002). Interventions are needed to optimize the leadership and communication styles employed by public health nursing leaders during a crisis. A first step may be to analyze transformational leadership and rhetorical sensitivity levels (concern for self and others without being rigid; Reynolds, 2009). Through this analysis, expectations of public health nursing leaders during crises could be explored.

At the *health care facility level*, nurse executives provide leadership to assure that the needs are met for both existing patients and those who require care because of the consequences of a disaster. During disasters, increased stress levels, information overload, situational chaos, disruption of services, casualties, and distractions with crowds and media all hamper lines of communication. It is the responsibility of the nurse executive to be assertive and take the lead in these situations.

Building on lessons from the 2001 terrorist attacks, Fahlgren and Drenkard (2002) discuss the leadership role of the health care system nurse executive in preparing for and responding to disasters. These authors believe that by maintaining a state of readiness through assessment, planning, implementation, and constant evaluation (a framework built on the nursing process), nurses are providing leadership and service to their community. In a companion article, Drenkard, Rigotti, Hanfling, Fahlgren, and LaFrancois (2002) apply the nursing process (assessment, planning, implementation, and evaluation) as an organizing framework for an all-hazards approach to disaster planning in health care facilities. Many process improvements were implemented in a large not-for-profit health care system following the terrorist attacks in the National Capital Region in 2001. The nurse executive was a key partner in the improvements that were made (Drenkard et al., 2002).

The Department of Veterans Affairs (VA) Office of Nursing Services chartered a collaborative effort with the VA Emergency Management Strategic Healthcare Group (EMSHG) and the National Nurse Executive Emergency Preparedness Workgroup to review disaster-related staffing procedures. One of the initial tasks of the group was to delineate disaster deployment activities and competencies to ensure quality nursing care. Core competencies were developed for nursing leaders and clinical staff (Coyle, 2007). The competencies were designed to prepare VA nurse leaders to respond to disasters in the communities they serve and to prepare staff nurses to safely deploy in support of disaster operations. The nurse leader competencies are consistent with excellence in nursing care and improved patient outcomes.

The next level where nurses provide leadership is the *state*, where nurses manage grant programs to promote preparedness for public health and hospitals.

For example, many nurses serve as the coordinators for the Public Health Emergency Preparedness (PHEP) and Hospital Preparedness Program (HPP) grants. The Centers for Disease Control and Prevention's (CDC) PHEP cooperative agreements provide funding to states, territories, and eligible municipalities to strengthen health departments' abilities to respond to all types of public health incidents (CDC, 2012). The HHS Office of the Assistant Secretary for Preparedness and Response's (ASPR) HPP funding supports building more resilient communities and to improve surge capacity and enhance community and hospital preparedness for public health emergencies (ASPR, n.d.a). For fiscal year 2010, PHEP provided nearly $700 million in funding to support public health preparedness (CDC, 2010) and HPP provided $390.5 million to help hospitals and other health care organizations strengthen the medical surge capability across the nation (ASPR, n.d.a).

At the *national* level, nurses serve in key leadership roles in disaster preparedness and response. ASPR was created when the Public Health Service Act was amended by the Pandemic and All-Hazards Preparedness Act (PAHPA) of 2006 after Hurricane Katrina. Its mission is to lead the country in preparing for, responding to, and recovering from the adverse health effects of emergencies and disasters by supporting communities, strengthening health and response systems, and enhancing national health security (ASPR, n.d.c). There are several senior nurses within ASPR who are leaders in policy, preparedness planning, response, and recovery.

Military nursing has evolved beyond the army nurse corps to include other armed forces. At the national level, these military nurse corps are joined by nonmilitary Federal nurses and the American Red Cross to comprise the national nursing workforce. The national nursing workforce is represented by the Federal Nursing Service Council (FNSC). The FNSC includes the nurse leaders of the air force, American Red Cross, army, VA, navy, and PHS, representing more than 125,000 nurses with a beneficiary population exceeding 8.5 million. The Council brings together its collective leadership to advance and strengthen professional nursing practice among federal agencies and the American Red Cross (U.S. PHS, n.d.). One of the Council's priorities is to determine ways to maintain the readiness of federal nurses to fill clinical roles during domestic disaster deployments.

At the *regional* level, ASPR has Regional Emergency Coordinators (RECs) stationed throughout the nation who provide leadership for preparedness and response, facilitating the work of state and tribal colleagues in public health emergency preparedness. They serve as ASPR's foremost regional leaders to represent ASPR in support of community resiliency and regional integration of public health and medical preparedness, response, and recovery. Nine of the 34 RECs are nurses (ASPR, n.d.b).

The HHS Office of the Assistant Secretary for Health (ASH) has Regional Health Administrators (RHAs) who serve as the senior federal public health officials and scientists in the region to foster all-hazards preparedness activities for the department (ASH, n.d.). In actual public health emergencies, ASPR and the ASH may request an RHA to serve as a senior consultant to the response. Several of the RHAs are nurses.

Nursing leadership in disaster preparedness and response is evident internationally as well. The Lillian Carter Center for International Nursing in Atlanta brought together chief nursing officers and chief medical officers from 70 countries to foster partnerships among key national health leaders (Salmon, 2005). The focus of the meeting was biological threats to health with one of the purposes being to create a joint plan for advancing preparedness against these threats.

In 2006, the World Health Organization (WHO), in collaboration with the International Council of Nursing (ICN), hosted a consultation regarding the contributions of nursing and midwifery in emergencies (WHO, 2007). Because nurses are the comprehensive primary health care providers in most countries, they may also be the first responders during emergencies. The attendees at the consultation recommended that WHO advocate for the inclusion of nurses and midwives in disaster planning activities within ministries of health. In the United States, this is already occurring within HHS; but in many countries, nurses are not often at the table to influence policy and planning (WHO, 2007).

Recognizing the urgent need to accelerate efforts to build the capacities of nurses in the midst of continued health threats and disasters, the ICN and WHO published a "Framework of Disaster Nursing Competencies" (ICN & WHO, 2009). The ICN and WHO (2009) aptly wrote: "The sporadic nature of disaster nursing education has resulted in a workforce with limited capacity to respond in the event of a disaster, develop policy, educate or accept leadership roles" (p. 28). Graduate programs have been developed in the United States, Europe, and Asia to prepare nurses as experts in disasters, addressing issues such as leadership, education, and policy roles. However, more programs are needed to prepare and sustain an international workforce of nurses to undertake education and leadership roles (WHO, 2007). A focal point for these efforts is the WHO Collaborating Center for Nursing in Disasters and Health Emergency Management. The Center promotes research on disaster preparedness, response, and recovery and plays a leading role in developing a network for nursing and other health professionals involved in health emergency management (WHO, n.d.).

SUMMARY OF RESEARCH STUDIES

Research Findings

Although nurses serve as leaders in many aspects of disaster preparedness and response, there are few studies of nursing leadership in crises. Articles were identified as research if they evaluated nursing leadership as part of postevent after action analyses or lessons learned or used research methods to investigate aspects of nursing leadership in disasters. There were five doctoral dissertations (Cotton, 2009; Foster, 2007; Jones, 2010; Porche, 2009; Reynolds, 2009), eight lessons learned analyses (Demi & Miles, 1984; Dennis, 2007; Drenkard et al., 2002; Fahlgren & Drenkard, 2002; Hynes, 2006; Johnson, 2002; Priest, 2009; Sheetz, 2010), two qualitative research studies (Peltz et al., 2006; Shih et al., 2009), and one facilitated discussion (Rego & Garau, 2008).

Dissertation Research

The findings from the dissertations by Cotton (2009) and Reynolds (2009) are described in earlier sections of this manuscript and will not be repeated here. The dissertations by Foster (2007), Jones (2010), and Porche (2009) will be described here. Foster conducted a study of the Top Officials Exercise 2 (TOPOFF2) in 2003, at which the exercise scenario was a bioterrorism attack in Chicago. The exercise involved more than 100 federal, state and local agencies and institutions, and provided an opportunity to examine leadership, communication, and conflict resolution issues among multijurisdictional crisis response agencies.

Although the study is not specific to nursing, it examined leadership, communication, and conflict management processes in emergency events as they relate to the effectiveness of multijurisdictional crisis teams. The main findings of this study are that by having a better understanding of how emergency response groups are led, how they communicate with each other, and how they manage conflict, there will be a greater probability of saving lives and reducing property loss in the future (Caro, 1999; Dynes & Warheit, 1969; Foster, 2007; Lindell & Perry, 1992; Quarantelli, 1988, 1995). Identifying the type and nature of an emergency helps define the scope of leadership required among responding agencies. An emergency can be a single catastrophic event, such as hurricane Katrina or may grow and be identified slowly such as an outbreak of a contagious disease (Quarantelli, 1987). An example of a slowly developing emergency was the anthrax attacks of 2001. In this event in which several people died from anthrax exposure, it took weeks before authorities determined the source (Argenti, 2002). Regardless of the type of emergency, effective leadership is a critical component of the response effort (Foster, 2007).

The dissertations by both Porche (2009) and Jones (2010) examined leadership during Hurricane Katrina. Porche conducted interviews of 14 formal and informal leaders from a private acute health care facility. The narrative analysis identified the following crisis leadership characteristics: ability to leverage knowledge, skills, practical experience, and leadership acumen, irrespective of hierarchy or authority, to provide effective crisis leadership to manage the emergency response, plan during the crisis aftermath, and resume the provision of health care services. Once individuals emerged as crisis leaders, these leaders displayed behaviors and characteristics of a crisis leader, engaged in crisis management, promoted teamwork, and maintained communication throughout the situation.

Crisis leaders were described as critically thinking and being *decisive* even when there was limited factual information. They maintained a personal *calm* manner, which also had a calming effect on others. The crisis leader was highly *visible and accessible* throughout the institution; they were everywhere from the board room to the front line engaging in multiple activities—*multitasking*. Their continual presence assisted with maintaining a central mission to maintain safety, meet basic needs, and evacuate everyone from the crisis situation. Through their *decisive manner, focused mission, and positive attitude*, they presented a vision that everyone was going to be evacuated and remain safe. The crisis leader was not appointed. The role assumption of crisis leader was *autonomous*.

As the organizational conditions continued to deteriorate, the leadership challenges changed. To endure this situation, the crisis leaders had to have the *physical strength* and *stamina* to withstand the long hours of work, lack of rest, continual heat, and lack of hydration and nutritional support. The dedication of the crisis leaders was evident in their *selfless commitment*. These leaders were present until the end and were the last individuals to be evacuated. These individuals placed the needs of others above their personal needs. Throughout the crisis, the crisis leaders maintained a positive attitude (Porche, 2009).

Jones (2010) conducted interviews with seven high-ranking leaders of local, state, and federal organizations that were in positions of leadership prior to, during, and following Hurricane Katrina. Again, the findings are not specific to nursing but have implications for nursing leadership in crises. The findings suggest that individuals aspiring to leadership roles should learn about the situational leadership model, and because it is frequently used to train leaders within organizations, it should be made available for all to study. As for crisis leadership, research shows that there is not necessarily a certain style of leadership best suited for a crisis but rather a combination of styles. The leadership style used by leaders during a crisis should be the style, manner, and approach needed to provide direction, implement plans, and motivate people.

When leaders need to be authoritarian, they should be. The same is true when they need to be participative and/or delegative, using the needed style when they have to. Although good leadership uses all three styles, with one of them normally being dominant, bad leadership tends to stick with one style (Clark, 1997). Using a combination of styles was found to be true with the high-ranking leaders who were interviewed for this study because they all spoke of changing and using leadership styles based on the situation and what needed to be accomplished (Jones, 2010).

Postevent Lessons Learned

Of the eight "lesson learned" manuscripts, Drenkard et al. (2002) and Fahlgren and Drenkard (2002) are described in earlier sections of the manuscript and will not be repeated here. Demi and Miles (1984) present data from the July 1981 skywalk collapse that occurred at the Hyatt Regency Hotel in Kansas City. The authors identify the leadership functions needed during disasters. They suggest a model for integrating these leadership functions with the nursing process functions of assessment, planning, intervention, and evaluation, an approach similar to what Drenkard and colleagues proposed. They apply this proposed model as a framework to organize data in the case study of the Hyatt disaster. The authors conclude that nurses provide leadership in all phases of a disaster and at all organizational levels. The nurses who were most effective leaders were those who held formal roles in the disaster response plan and who had disaster training. Gaps in effective use of resources were identified (e.g., air medical evacuation and use of some area hospitals). They also noted that nurses were not invited to participate in disaster planning and evaluation committees outside of hospitals and were not invited to participate in the follow-up evaluation program held on the first anniversary of the disaster.

The article by Johnson (2002) provides practical leadership lessons learned at one health care institution in the National Capital Region following the terrorist attacks on the Pentagon in 2001. Specific lesson learned are described. For example, the leadership of the disaster committee is crucial for success, and checklists were indispensable in helping to bring order to chaos.

Hynes (2006) discusses her observations during the severe acute respiratory syndrome (SARS) outbreak and the need for leadership competencies within the critical care setting. The crisis was managed most effectively when interdependence and group cohesion were valued and present. Hynes recommends that critical care nurses who are involved in pandemic influenza planning should advocate for education and training to support them in assuming clinical leadership roles, especially conflict management. The benefits of computerized simulation technology are described.

Following Hurricane Katrina, the campus of a small, private, historically black institution was completely destroyed (Dennis, 2007). Dennis (2007) provides an anecdotal description of how information gleaned from the Leadership Enhancement and Development (LEAD) project assisted her as the university worked to create a new organizational structure and return to New Orleans.

Also within the context of Hurricane Katrina, Priest (2009) discusses the role nurse leaders can play in planning for catastrophic events. He emphasizes the importance of nurse leaders helping nurses understand the core values and ethics that will apply in disaster situations. What he identified as most important was having conversations about what constitutes a catastrophe, what nurses might expect in such an event, and how they would be expected to respond. Legal liability is briefly discussed. Priest states that a nurse leader must ask, "How should I apply my limited resources so that they can have the greatest impact and save the most lives?" (p. 50). To make such decisions requires a focus on core values. If nurse leaders focus on these core values when making decisions, those decisions will be made more effectively and consistently. The nurse leader must continue to be an advocate for his or her staff in this situation, ensuring that nurses have water, food, and rest to the extent possible.

Research Studies

From the literature searches and secondary sources reviewed, there were only two manuscripts that could be categorized as research in disaster leadership, both using qualitative research methods. The first article by Peltz et al. (2006), although not specific to nursing leadership, does focus on the Israeli Defense Forces Home Front Command's research team sent to study the response of the Thai medical system to the 2004 tsunami disaster (Peltz et al., 2006). The analysis of the Thai disaster management response was based on Quarantelli's (1987) 10 criteria for evaluating the management of community disasters. The research team met with Thai officials from the Ministry of Public Health and Air Force, the provincial governors and health officials, and provincial and district hospital staff and directors. The delegation also visited prehospital facilities, reviewed patient logs, and interviewed officials, health care workers, foreign volunteers, and injured victims. The three most important elements identified by the research team for effective disaster management were (a) the flow of information, (b) overall coordination, and (c) leadership. Examples of good leadership were identified within the ministry of health, the governor of the province, a clinical physician, the manager of one hospital and the royal family. In the hospitals in which leadership was less outstanding, doctors often lacked information and felt that the chaotic situation was not being controlled. Hospitals that conducted recent exercise drills performed better than those who did not. Peltz et al. identify several prerequisites for successful emergency management including equipping the team leaders with leadership tools to enhance resilience and improve the response to their personal needs.

The second research study did focus specifically on nursing leadership. Shih and colleagues (2009) explored Taiwan's nurse leaders' reflections and experiences of the difficulties they encountered and the survival strategies they employed during the response to the SARS epidemic. The authors conducted in-depth focus group interviews with 70 nurse leaders from four Northern Taiwan hospitals involved in the SARS epidemic, and participants completed an open-ended questionnaire. Content analysis was undertaken and themes were generated. Five stages of the event were identified: facing shock and chaos, searching for reliable sources to clarify myths, developing and adjusting nursing care, supporting nurses and clients, and rewarding nurses. The qualitative data were further analyzed using Hobfall's concepts of conservation of resources. Additional themes were identified: (a) nurse leaders are important executors of interventions in health disasters; (b) emotional intelligence is required to effectively manage one's internal conflicts and interpersonal relationships; (c) sociopolitical and analytical skills are needed to foster participation, seek sanctions and support, marshal resources and facilitate decision making; and (d) building a support system to help manage conflicts between familial and professional roles. Adequate support from important persons (families, colleagues, and friends) and metaphysical strength (spiritual or religious beliefs) in times of intense strain and stress helped sustain the morale and motivation of nurses fighting SARS.

Facilitated Discussion

The final article analyzed was a facilitated discussion. The CCL brought together a small group of "frontline" leaders—people who were involved in the crisis response during Hurricane Katrina in either formal or informal roles (Rego & Garau, 2008). These frontline leaders shared their stories with people who have expertise in public health, terrorism, and disaster-related crises. These discussants helped the group to put the Katrina experiences into a broader context of leadership in times of crisis. The design coupled right-brain activities such as storytelling and mind mapping with left-brain thinking to log insights and rank key lessons.

The findings suggest that organizations with adaptable and empowered cultures are likely to adapt well to the challenges inherent in a crisis. According to Rego and Garau (2008),

> when standard operating procedures and protocols no longer make sense and the chain of command is broken, or formal leadership is unable to absorb and make sense of a rapidly evolving situation, the leadership capability embedded in the organizational DNA is the reserve that is left to count on. (p. 48)

The authors point out the strong relevance of the field of complexity (e.g., "wicked problems") to crisis leadership. In times of crisis, people want to help. The challenge is to enable the connectivity that makes assistance more possible and more effective. A thread throughout the report is the importance of creative leaders implementing creative leadership solutions in times of crisis. The report emphasizes the importance of leadership development (vs. training) to support creativity and empowerment (Rego & Garau, 2008).

SUMMARY OF RESEARCH

The background on leadership theories and the historical context for nursing leadership across multiple levels (individual, community, facility, state, regional, national, and international) provides the framework from which to review the literature on nursing leadership in disaster preparedness and response. The literature review identified few research studies specific to the topic. Several of the general leadership theories—situational, integrative, and transformational—provide a useful way of conceptualizing disaster leadership. Crisis leadership is a relatively new field of study that incorporates the integrative leadership style. The central theme of the analysis is that leaders in disasters must be able to adapt their leadership style to the specific circumstances. Case studies from disasters describe nurse leaders as needing sociopolitical skills and emotional intelligence to be effective. Nurse leaders use values-based decision making to bring order to chaos, focus on the most important tasks, and maximize available resources to save lives. Ensuring the health and safety of the people you lead is crucial for success. Nurses will be a major component of the frontline response to any disaster, so nursing involvement and leadership in preparedness planning can reap benefits during the actual crisis. Crisis leadership skills can and must be developed to ensure that the nation has the crisis leaders we need to respond to the inevitable natural disasters and the increased risk of terrorism. To advance the science of nursing leadership in disaster preparedness and response requires going beyond synthesis of anecdotal information to more rigorous research methodologies.

RECOMMENDATIONS FOR FUTURE RESEARCH

The recommendations for future research fall into three areas: leadership training and development, theory development, and research methods and measures. Effective response to disasters requires strong leadership, strategic planning, and interprofessional collaboration (Littleton-Kearney & Slepski, 2008). Several schools of nursing have developed master's degree programs and postmaster's certificates in emergency planning and disaster response. Many of these programs focus on helping nurses develop leadership skills for emergency response and disaster preparedness. Incorporation of disaster nursing leadership content in curricula of more programs is needed.

In addition to providing leadership training in graduate nursing curriculum, there is a need for crisis training for all professions that support the societal infrastructure which includes nurses (Austin, Martin, & Gregory, 2007; Carrel, 2005; Flin & Slaven, 1995; MacFarlane, Joffe, & Naidoo, 2006; Reynolds, 2004; Schoch-Spana, Franco, Nuzzo, & Usenza, 2007; Ulmer et al., 2007). Beyond classroom training, there is a need to study the effectiveness of alternative educational strategies such as scenario training, simulation technology, and field exercises. For example, in 2004, CDC's crisis and emergency risk communication (CERC) for leaders course was created to quickly fill a gap in public health crisis leadership training (Courtney, Cole, & Reynolds, 2003). The course used case studies and included taped interviews with leaders who had experienced major crises such as the 1995 Oklahoma City bombing and the September 11, 2001 World Trade Center attack (Reynolds, 2004). There is a need to develop and test innovative leadership development approaches that look beyond typical leadership theory to include chaos theory, solving "wicked problems," emotional intelligence, political skills, and creativity.

Attention should be given to testing theories of leadership in disasters, with particular focus on testing crisis leadership theory. As a new area of inquiry, the theory of crisis leadership requires better conceptual definition. A central tenet of disaster leadership is that no one leadership theory will allow leaders to be effective in all situations and they must be able to adjust their leadership style to the situation. Future theoretical development should investigate the effectiveness of different leadership styles in a range of disaster situations. Typical methodologies for theory development may not be adequate, so methodologies like the ones employed by the CCL will be needed (Rego & Garau, 2008).

Finally, there is a need to develop the research agenda for nursing leadership in disaster preparedness and response. Currently, the literature focuses primarily on anecdotal "lessons learned" and corrective action planning. More rigorous research methodologies need to be applied to questions that investigate nursing leadership during disasters across the multiple levels identified in Figure 2.1. Nursing leadership across all components of emergency management (mitigation, preparedness, response, and recovery) needs to be examined. There is a need to develop valid and reliable measures of leadership styles. With valid and reliable measures, it will be possible to investigate the styles that are most effective in specific scenarios. Nurses serving in disaster leadership roles in the United States should engage in collaborative research with their counterparts internationally.

Leaders influence the ability of the nation to cope with and recover from crises. By focusing on leadership skill development, theory generation, and more rigorous research methods, it will be possible to develop the science of nursing leadership in disasters, so nurses on the front lines of disasters will be better able to assume a leadership role.

ACKNOWLEDGMENT

The contributions of Alicia Livinski, MPH, MA, biomedical librarian, National Institutes of Health Library, are gratefully acknowledged.

DISCLAIMER

The views expressed in this manuscript do not necessarily represent the views of the U.S. Department of Health and Human Services, U.S. Public Health Service, Office of the Assistant Secretary for Preparedness and Response, or the U.S. Government.

REFERENCES

Anteau, C. M., & Williams, L. A. (1997). The Oklahoma bombing. Lessons learned. *Critical Care Nursing Clinics of North America*, 9(2), 231–236.

Argenti, P. (2002). Crisis communication: Lessons from 9/11. *Harvard Business Review*, 80(12), 103–109.

Austin, Z., Martin, J. C., & Gregory, P. A. (2007). Pharmacy practice in times of civil crisis: The experience of SARS and the blackout in Ontario, Canada. *Research in Social & Administrative Pharmacy: RSAP*, 3(3), 320–335.

Babb, J., & Beck, D. (2001). The US Public Health Service providing care and leadership. *The Officer*, 77(10), 15–17.

Bandura, A., Caprara, G. V., Barbaranelli, C., Gerbino, M., & Pastorelli, C. (2003). Role of affective self-regulatory efficacy in diverse spheres of psychosocial functioning. *Child Development*, 74(3), 769–782.

Barton, W. E. (1922). *The life of Clara Barton: Founder of the American Red Cross*. Boston, MA: Houghton Mifflin.

Beary, J. F., III, Bisgard, J. C., & Armstrong, P. C. (1982). The civilian-military contingency hospital system. *The New England Journal of Medicine*, 306(12), 738–740.

Bern, A. I. (1998). The National Disaster Medical System (NDMS) is activated for Hugo! *American College of Emergency Physicians Disaster Medicine Section Newsletter*, 1(1). Retrieved from http://www.acep.org/content.aspx?id=41252

Bernard, M., & Mathews, P. R. (2008). Evacuation of a maternal-newborn area during Hurricane Katrina. *MCN The American Journal of Maternal Child Nursing*, 33(4), 213–223.

Brandt, E. N., Jr., Mayer, W. N., Mason, J. O., Brown, D. E., Jr., & Mahoney, L. E. (1985). Designing a National Disaster Medical System. *Public Health Reports*, 100(5), 455–461.

Burkholder-Allen, K., Rega, P., & Budd, C. A. (1994). An analysis of patient satisfaction with one DMAT's performance during Hurricane Andrew relief efforts. *Prehospital and Disaster Medicine*, 10, 92.

Caro, D. H. J. (1999). Towards integrated crisis support of regional emergency networks. *Health Care Management Review, 24*, 7–19.

Carrel, L. F. (2005). "Epidemic in Switzerland": Description of a strategic leadership exercise by the Swiss government. *Journal of Contingencies and Crisis Management, 13*(4), 170–175.

Centers for Disease Control and Prevention. (2010). *Public health emergency preparedness cooperative agreement budget period 10 extension (FY 2010) funding.* Retrieved from http://www.cdc.gov/phpr/documents/Revised_PHEP_BP10_Extension_Funding_Table_Aug2010.pdf

Centers for Disease Control and Prevention. (2012). *Funding and guidance for state and local health departments, public health emergency preparedness cooperative agreements.* Retrieved from http://www.cdc.gov/phpr/coopagreement.htm

Clark, D. R. (1997). *Leadership styles.* Retrieved from http://www.nwlink.com/~donclark/leader/leadstl.html

Cohen, I. B. (1984). Florence Nightingale. *Scientific American, 250*(3), 128–137.

Cotton, G. L. (2009). *Hurricane Katrina: An evaluation of governmental leadership and the disaster surrounding the city of New Orleans.* Retrieved from PsycINFO database. (UMI No. AAI3350239)

Courtney, J., Cole, G., & Reynolds, B. (2003). How the CDC is meeting the training demands of emergency risk communication. *Journal of Health Communication, 8*, 128–129.

Coyle, G. A., Sapnas, K. G., & Ward-Presson, K. (2007). Dealing with disaster. *Nursing Management, 38*(7), 24–29.

Day, B., & Waitzkin, H. (1985). The medical profession and nuclear war. A social history. *The Journal of the American Medical Association, 254*(5), 644–651.

Debisette, A. T., Martinelli, A. M., Couig, M. P., & Braun, M. (2010). US Public Health Service Commissioned Corps Nurses: Responding in times of national need. *The Nursing Clinics of North America, 45*(2), 123–135.

Demi, A. S., & Miles, M. S. (1984). An examination of nursing leadership following a disaster. *Topics in Clinical Nursing, 6*(1), 63–78.

Dennis, B. P. (2007). Leadership—the journey continues. *The ABNF Journal: Official Journal of the Association of Black Nursing Faculty in Higher Education, Inc, 18*(4), 109–111.

Drenkard, K., Rigotti, G., Hanfling, D., Fahlgren, T. L., & LaFrancois, G. (2002). Healthcare system disaster preparedness, part 1: Readiness planning. *Journal of Nursing Administration, 32*(9), 461–469.

Dynes, R. R., & Warheit, G. (1969). Organizations in disasters. *EMO National Digest, 9*, 2–13, 19.

Fahlgren, T. L., & Drenkard, K. N. (2002). Healthcare system disaster preparedness, part 2: Nursing executive role in leadership. *Journal of Nursing Administration, 32*(10), 531–537.

Fischer, H. W. (1998). *Response to disaster: Fact versus fiction & its perpetuation: The sociology of disaster* (2nd ed.). New York, NY: University Press of America.

Flin, R. H., & Slaven, G. N. (1995). Identifying the right stuff: Selection and training on-scene emergency commanders. *Journal of Contingencies and Crisis Management, 3*(2), 113–123.

Foster, S. C. (2007). *Leadership, communication and conflict resolution in emergency situations: A case study of the TOPOFF 2 exercise.* Retrieved from PsycINFO database. (UMI No. 3259657).

Franco, C., Toner, E., Waldhorn, R., Maldin, B., O'Toole, T., & Inglesby, T. V. (2006). Systemic collapse: Medical care in the aftermath of Hurricane Katrina. *Biosecurity and Bioterrorism: Biodefense Strategy, Practice, and Science, 4*(2), 135–146.

Gebbie, K. M., & Qureshi, K. (2002). Emergency and disaster preparedness: Core competencies for nurses. *American Journal of Nursing, 102*(1), 46–51.

Grohar-Murray, M. E., & DiCroce, H. R. (2003). *Leadership and management in nursing* (3rd ed.). Upper Saddle River, NJ: Prentice Hall.

Gursky, E., Inglesby, T. V., & O'Toole, T. (2003). Anthrax 2001: Observations on the medical and public health response. *Biosecurity and Bioterrorism: Biodefense Strategy, Practice, and Science, 1*(2), 97–110.

Hersey, P., & Blanchard, K. H. (1969). Life-cycle theory of leadership. *Training and Development Journal, 23*(2), 26–34.

Hynes, P. (2006). Reflections on critical care emergency preparedness: The necessity of planned education and leadership training for nurses. *Dynamics, 17*(4), 19–22.

International Council of Nurses & World Health Organization, Western Pacific Region. (2009). *ICN framework of disaster nursing competencies.* Geneva, Switzerland: World Health Organization.

Jakeway, C. C., LaRosa, G., Cary, A., & Schoenfisch, S. (2008). The role of public health nurses in emergency preparedness and response: A position paper of the Association of State and Territorial Directors of Nursing. *Public Health Nursing, 25*(4), 353–361.

Johnson, J. E. (2002). Leadership in a time of disaster. Being prepared for new age threats. *Journal of Nursing Administration, 32*(9), 455–460.

Jones, J. E. (2010). *The challenge of leadership in times of crisis: A case study of Hurricane Katrina.* Retrieved from PsycINFO database. (UMI No. 3398721)

Klann, G. (Ed.). (2003). What is crisis leadership? In *Crisis leadership: Using military lessons, organizational experiences, and the power of influence to lessen the impact of chaos on the people you lead.* Greensboro, NC: Center for Creative Leadership.

Klein, K. R., & Nagel, N. E. (2007). Mass medical evacuation: Hurricane Katrina and nursing experiences at the New Orleans airport. *Disaster Management & Response, 5*(2), 56–61.

Knebel, A. R., Martinelli, A. M., Orsega, S., Doss, T. L., Balingit-Wines, A. M., & Konchan, C. L. (2010). Ground Zero recollections of US Public Health Service nurses deployed to New York City in September 2001. *Nursing Clinics of North America, 45*(2), 137–152.

Laditka, S. B., Laditka, J. N., Xirasagar, S., Cornman, C. B., Davis, C. B., & Richter, J. V. (2008). Providing shelter to nursing home evacuees in disasters: Lessons from Hurricane Katrina. *American Journal of Public Health, 98*(7), 1288–1293.

Lessler, J., Reich, N. G., Cummings, D. A., Nair, H. P., Jordan, H. T., & Thompson, N. (2009). Outbreak of 2009 pandemic influenza A (H1N1) at a New York City school. *New England Journal of Medicine, 361*(27), 2628–2636.

Lindell, M. K., & Perry, R. W. (1992). *Behavioral foundations of community emergency planning.* Washington, DC: Hemisphere.

Littleton-Kearney, M. T., & Slepski, L. A. (2008). Directions for disaster nursing education in the United States. *Critical Care Nursing Clinics of North America, 20*(1), 103–109, viii.

MacFarlane, C., Joffe, A. L., & Naidoo, S. (2006). Training of disaster managers at a masters degree level: From emergency care to managerial control. *Emergency Medicine Australasia, 18,* 451–456.

Marquis, B. L., & Huston, C. J. (2005). *Leadership roles and management functions in nursing: Theory and application* (5th ed.). Philadelphia, PA: Lippincott Williams & Wilkins.

Marriner-Tomey, A. (2009). *Guide to nursing management and leadership.* St. Louis, MO: Mosby Elsevier.

Mitroff, I. I. (2004). *Crisis leadership: Planning for the unthinkable.* Brookfield, CT: Rothstein Associates.

Nursing Emergency Preparedness Education Coalition. (2003). *Educational competencies for registered nurses responding to mass casualty incidents.* Retrieved from http://www.nursing.vanderbilt.edu/incmce/competencies.html

Office of the Assistant Secretary for Health, Department of Health and Human Services. (n.d.). *Regional health administrators.* Retrieved from http://www.hhs.gov/ash/rha/index.html

Office of the Assistant Secretary for Preparedness and Response, Department of Health and Human Services. (n.d.a). *Hospital Preparedness Program (HPP).* Retrieved from http://www.phe.gov/preparedness/planning/hpp/pages/default.aspx

Office of the Assistant Secretary for Preparedness and Response, Department of Health and Human Services. (n.d.b). *Regional emergency coordinators overview.* Retrieved from http://www.phe.gov/preparedness/responders/rec/pages/default.aspx

Office of the Assistant Secretary for Preparedness and Response, Department of Health and Human Services. (n.d.c). *Vision, mission, values*. Retrieved from http://www.phe.gov/about/aspr/strategic-plan/Pages/vision.aspx

Pauchant, T. C., & Douville, R. (1993). Recent research in crisis management: A study of 24 authors' publications from 1986 to 1991. *Organization & Environment, 7*, 43–66.

Peltz, R., Ashkenazi, I., Schwartz, D., Shushan, O., Nakash, G., Leiba, A., & Bar-Dayan, Y. (2006). Disaster healthcare system management and crisis intervention leadership in Thailand— lessons learned from the 2004 tsunami disaster. *Prehospital and Disaster Medicine, 21*(5), 299–302.

Peters, R. G., Covello, V. T., & McCallum, D. B. (1997). The determinants of trust and credibility in environmental risk communication: An empirical study. *Risk Analysis, 17*(1), 43–54.

Porche, D. J. (2009). *Emergent leadership during a natural disaster: A narrative analysis of an acute health care organization's leadership.* Retrieved from PsycINFO database. (UMI No. 3378903)

Priest, C. (2009). Catastrophic conditions, tough decisions: The roles and responsibilities of nurse leaders in disaster settings. *Nurse Leader, 7*(3), 48–50.

Quarantelli, E. L. (1987). *Criteria which could be used in assessing disaster preparedness planning and managing* (Paper No. 122). Newark, DE: Disaster Research Center, University of Delaware.

Quarantelli, E. L. (1988). Assessing disaster preparedness planning. *Regional Development Dialogue, 9*, 48–69.

Quarantelli, E. L. (1995). *Disaster planning, emergency management, and civil protection: The historical development and current characteristics of organized efforts to prevent and respond to disasters* (Paper No. 22). Newark, DE: Disaster Research Center, University of Delaware.

Rego, L., & Garau, R. (2008). *Stepping into the void: Reflections and insights from a forum on Crisis Leadership convened at the Center for Creative Leadership March 13–15, 2007.* Greensboro, NC: Center for Creative Leadership.

Reynolds, B. J. (2004). *Crisis and emergency risk communication: By leaders for leaders.* Atlanta, GA: Centers for Disease Control and Prevention.

Reynolds, B. J. (2009). *An exploration of crisis experience and training as they relate to transformational leadership and rhetorical sensitivity among U.S. public health officials.* Retrieved from PsycINFO database. (UMI No. 3344533)

Salmon, M. E. (2005). Global biological threats to health: An imperative for collaboration. *Research and Theory for Nursing Practice, 19*(1), 9–13.

Sandman, P., & Lanard, J. (2004). *Misleading toward the truth: The U.S. Department of Agriculture mishandles mad cow risk communication.* Retrieved from http://www.psandman.com/col/madcow.htm

Schoch-Spana, M. (2001). "Hospital's full-up": The 1918 influenza pandemic. *Public Health Reports, 116*(Suppl. 2), 32–33.

Schoch-Spana, M., Franco, C., Nuzzo, J. B., & Usenza, C. (2007). Community engagement: Leadership tool for catastrophic health events. *Biosecurity and Bioterrorism: Biodefense Strategy, Practice, and Science, 5*(1), 8–25.

Seeger, M. W., Sellnow, T. L., & Ulmer, R. R. (2003). *Communication and organizational crisis.* Westport, CT: Praeger.

Sheetz, A. H. (2010). The H1N1 pandemic: Did school nurses assume a leadership role? Some thoughts on leadership. *NASN School Nurse, 25*(3), 108–109.

Shih, F. J., Turale, S., Lin, Y. S., Gau, M. L., Kao, C. C., Yang, C. Y., & Liao, Y. C. (2009). Surviving a life-threatening crisis: Taiwan's nurse leaders' reflections and difficulties fighting the SARS epidemic. *Journal of Clinical Nursing, 18*(24), 3391–3400.

Sivanathan, N., & Fekken, G. C. (2002). Emotional intelligence, moral reasoning, and transformational leadership. *Leadership & Organizational Development Journal, 23*(3/4), 198–204.

Stogdill, R. M. (1974). *Handbook of leadership: A survey of theory and research.* New York, NY: Free Press.

Sullivan, M. P. (1995). *Nursing leadership and management* (2nd ed.). Spring House, PA: Springhouse.

Tomblin, B. (1996). *G.I. Nightingales: The Army Nurse Corps in World War II.* Lexington, KY: The University Press of Kentucky. Retrieved from http://books.google.com/books?id=hQ950vkOhY8C&

Ulmer, R. R., Sellnow, T. L., & Seeger, M. W. (2007). *Effective crisis communication: Moving from crisis to opportunity.* Thousand Oaks, CA: Sage.

U.S. Government Accountability Office. (2006). *Disaster preparedness: Preliminary observations on the evacuation of hospitals and nursing homes due to hurricanes—briefing for congressional committees* (GAO-06-443R). Washington, DC: Author. Retrieved from http://www.gao.gov/new.items /d06443r.pdf

U.S. Public Health Service Nursing, U.S. Public Health Service. (n.d.). *Federal Nursing Service Council.* Retrieved from http://phs-nurse.org/federal-nursing-service-council.html

Waugh, W., & Streib, G. (2006). Collaboration and leadership for effective emergency management. *Public Administration Review, 66,* 131.

Weiss, R. P. (2002). Crisis leadership. *Training and Development, 56*(3), 28–33.

World Health Organization. (2007). *The contribution of nursing and midwifery in emergencies. Report of a WHO consultation. WHO headquarters, Geneva, 22–24 November 2006.* Geneva, Switzerland: Author.

World Health Organization. (n.d.). *WHO Collaborating Center for Nursing in Disasters and Health Emergency Management.* Retrieved from http://www.coe-cnas.jp/who/eng/about_center/ index.html

Xavier, S. (2005). Are you at the top of your game? Checklist for effective leaders. *Journal of Business Strategy, 26*(3), 6–13.

Yukl, G. (2002). *Leadership in organizations* (5th ed.). Upper Saddle River, NJ: Prentice Hall.

CHAPTER 3

Conducting Ethically Sound Disaster Nursing Research

Michaela R. Shafer and Laurel Stocks

ABSTRACT

Health care professionals have always faced the threat of catastrophic disaster and pandemic infectious illness but have continued to practice without adequately considering the ethical consequences of many of the decision-making tools we currently have in place. Lack of research on these ethical decisions in the face of disasters regarding the 3Rs—rationing (triage and allocating scarce resources), restrictions (quarantine and the denial of care based on some criteria or the magnitude of the disaster), and responsibility (duty to treat and duty to report for work)—will leave nurses to make decisions in the throws of disaster rather than before the crisis occurs. This chapter focuses on conducting ethically sound nursing research in disasters. A survey of the literature on the topic to include current research on the 3Rs, frameworks, and methodological problems will be examined. This chapter concludes with a call to action for the nursing profession to accept their role as patient advocates and drive the research necessary to avoid the ethical pitfalls seen in recent disaster decisions and scenarios.

© 2012 Springer Publishing Company
http://dx.doi.org/10.1891/0739-6686.30.47

INTRODUCTION

The focus of this chapter is to define ethical decision making, and explore nursing research on ethical decision making in disasters. For purposes of this work, humanitarian assistance without a precipitating natural or man-made disaster will not be addressed here. To understand this topic, it is important to define ethical principles and to understand the context and methodological challenges inherent in nursing ethics research pertaining to disasters. These challenges will become evident as we discuss the paucity of disaster-related research done by nurses. This chapter has two goals: to review current nursing and health-related research in the literature on ethics and disaster and to determine areas for future research on ethical dilemmas for nurses created by disaster scenarios. First, ethical principles will be defined and potential frameworks for decision making in ethically sound disaster nursing research will be discussed. Several issues regarding methodological challenges of disaster research will be identified. A review of nursing and health-related disaster management research will examine the duty to treat the ethical soundness of triage protocols, the allocation of scarce resources, and finally the nurses' duty to report to work during a disaster. Each of these presents ethical dilemmas for the nurse and decisions must be based on ethical principles, not historical or common practice. Finally, strategies for overcoming the challenges of ethics in disaster nursing research will be presented, with implications for conducting this research and expanding the knowledge base in this ever-growing field.

Prior to discussing research regarding the ethics of disaster nursing, it is essential to review the ethical principles that apply to disaster response. Holm (2007) argues that choice is the factor that creates the ethical questions in disaster relief. He believes that the ethical dilemma arises from the fact that people choose to live in areas prone to disaster and that people can choose to participate in relief or not. Choice is framed by one's personal and professional ethics. Most professional organizations, like nursing, have a written professional code of ethics. The American Nurses Association (ANA) Code of Ethics for Nurses provides guidance on ethical behaviors expected of nurses in their practice. However, ambiguity in the standards regarding behaviors during a disaster and conflicting standards regarding one's duty to self and the patient may create dilemmas. Ethical principles are "basic and obvious moral truths that guide deliberation and action" (Burkhardt & Nathaniel, 2007, p. 53). Adherence to these moral principles is important for ethical nursing practice. The ANA (2010) issue brief "Who will be there? Ethics, the law, and a nurse's duty to respond in a disaster" identifies the lack of a coherent strategy in determining the ethical and legal protections and requirements for nurses during a crisis situation. This represents a gap in the nation's disaster preparedness and response systems.

The primary ethical principles that guide nursing practice are autonomy, beneficence, nonmaleficence, veracity, confidentiality, justice, and fidelity (Winland-Brown, 2009). *Autonomy* implies freedom of choice, and the ability to decide how one will interact with and use the health care system. It also implies the freedom to make choices about one's own life and death. Bioethics describes autonomy in terms of a patient's ability to receive adequate information to make an informed decision about whether to participate and comply with the treatment being proposed. Patient autonomy can be compromised in disaster scenarios when decisions about resources are based on triage systems that may or may not be ethically sound.

The principle of *beneficence* implies the doing of good. Most would argue that in everyday clinical situations and in disaster scenarios, nurses attempt to do good for the most people. However, what is our responsibility to do good for all, and can that be achieved in an overwhelming disaster or public health emergency? How is the decision to treat determined? Do we betray this principle in making those decisions during triage, and when deciding whether to expend scarce resources on one individual or not? As many as nine different triage protocols appear in the literature dealing with disasters and public health emergencies such as a pandemic. Research into the ethical soundness of those protocols is required.

Nonmaleficence simply means to avoid harm. Most nurses would believe that they would never intentionally induce harm to a patient. Yet, during disasters, health professionals are challenged by situations of euthanasia veiled as doing the best for victims (Fink, 2009; Priest & Bahl, 2008). Is the nursing profession willing to accept those decisions in times of extreme duress and lack of resources?

Veracity means to tell the truth. This is an important principle in disaster nursing as we determine whether to tell a patient that we have chosen to place him or her in a category that will ensure his or her death even though under normal circumstances, we would be able to save him or her. During disaster triage, are we honest with the patients and their family about the choices we have made? More importantly, have we determined that the systems used are the most ethical and truly the most appropriate for any given scenario? Are we willing to present and solicit public support for the decisions that will affect their lives in the event of a disaster and declare authorship to the community? Only then, can the nurse avoid the lingering fear that decisions were not made equitably and based on the principles that withstand the most egregious event.

Confidentiality assures the nondisclosure of patient information without prior approval. This principle is challenged throughout a disaster. Health care providers value confidentiality, but it appears that patients are more likely to relinquish this principle when disaster strikes at least during the early stages of triage and treatment.

Justice relates to the equitable distribution of, and fair, appropriate treatment for patients. The literature is replete with the recognition that in a disaster, giving care to some may require denying it to others. But how are those decisions made? Are they congruent with societal norms and based on fact or history? Is the health care system transparent in their decisions and have they validated and communicated them to the public they serve?

The final principle is *fidelity*. Fidelity refers to promise-keeping and faithfulness. It is particularly relevant in the duty to care and in allocating scarce resources. Do we ever abandon the care of those to whom we have established a professional relationship? Do we sacrifice the sick and dying to care for those that can be saved? And finally, is our duty to the patient or to self and family? Which has priority?

These ethical principles all have great relevance in responding to disasters. Understanding how or if the principles are used to make decisions in disaster nursing is important. The nursing profession's code of ethics from the ANA that guides nursing practice is lacking on direction for the complex issues that arise during the enveloping chaos around a disaster (Grimaldi, 2007). This chapter will examine the research in disaster nursing to determine if these principles have been applied or studied and recommend areas for future research in the ethics of disaster nursing.

METHODOLOGY

The breadth of disaster research in general, and by nurse researchers and ethicists in particular, is sparse. The nature of a disaster immediately places limitations on doing research that might be perceived as unethical; so to study nursing ethics in disaster is a complex problem. Multiple processes were undertaken in the preparation of the content for this chapter and literature review. Initially, the key terms *medical ethics* and *disaster research* (delimiters: English, humans) were used to conduct a search of MEDLINE in the last 10 years. This search yielded 146 citations. In the second search, the key words *nursing ethics* and disaster research (delimiters: English, humans) were used and yielded 47 articles. Additional searches of CINAHL using the same key words yielded 50 new results, PsycINFO yielded 10 new results, and EMBASE yielded 17 additional results. It was determined to review research articles in all databases (total of 223 articles) to access areas of concern for disaster nursing research. Of these 223 articles, 31 were White Papers, policy or addressed legal aspects of disaster; 114 articles were editorials, news articles, or journals providing opinion and education on ethics in disaster; 10 described frameworks that could be used to make ethical decisions during a disaster; and 43 covered a wide variety of topics including humanitarian assistance. Forty-one articles had relevance to this chapter on research in ethical decision making during a disaster, and these will be reviewed in the subsequent discussion. Although the search was restricted to English language articles, there were articles from around the world. Despite this wide net, most studies used a qualitative or mixed methods design, underscoring some of the methodological challenges of research in this area. The paucity of this research has left the nursing community without adequate guidance for making ethical decisions during a disaster. Suggestions for strategies to study ethical decision making in disasters will be provided based on needs highlighted by this literature review.

LITERATURE REVIEW
Overview of Ethics and Disaster Research

Two issues in *The Journal of Clinical Ethics* (Fall, 2010; Spring, 2011) were dedicated to ethics in disaster. They provide an excellent backdrop to the numerous ethical dilemmas that arise within medicine and nursing during a natural disaster or pandemic. One article by Caro, Coleman, Knebel, and DeRenzo (2011) recounts ethical decisions made by the project on the allocation of scarce resources following a nuclear detonation, which was commissioned by the Office of the Assistant Secretary for Preparedness and Response in the U.S. Department of Health and Human Services. This committee, which included physicians, nurses, and ethicists, provided decision-making guidance to those that would be expected to make ethical decisions regarding the care and treatment of those exposed to an improvised nuclear device (IND). Although the IND was the focus of the paper, the committee grappled with how to provide care in a system overwhelmed by patients in an ethical manner. The commonly held notion of "the greatest good for the greatest number"—meaning saving the most lives—was challenged. This public health model is widely recognized as necessary during a large-scale event. It implies that reductions in resources would force a change in normal clinical decision making to benefit the most people, not necessarily those who come first or those who are the sickest (Christian et al., 2006; Kraus, Levy, & Kelen, 2007; Rubinson & O'Toole, 2005; White, Katz, Luce, & Lo, 2009). This posits the ethical principle of utilitarianism whose aim of action should be the largest possible balance of pleasure over pain, or the greatest happiness for the greatest number. Some individuals on the task force disagreed with this ethical platform and asked questions such as "Why is saving lives the only good to be considered?" and "Are all steps towards efficiency to be tolerated, regardless of how unfair they are?" (Caro et al., 2011, p. 35). They also questioned whether these decisions were made on clinical outcomes or historical precedent. Based on gathering of data and group consensus, the task force agreed to pull back along the ethics continuum toward a more egalitarian approach that emphasized fairness in decision making.

The task force recognized that it would be impossible to allocate resources to everyone who needed them and realized that beneficence would be compromised because health care professionals would not be able to act in the best interest of each individual patient. Autonomy would also be compromised because resources will not be offered to everyone, but only those with the highest priority. In determining that priority, the principle of justice must be garnered. This prioritizing of patients must not be discriminatory to those with disabilities, chronic illness, or other conditions that define worth in a society such as age. Fairness must remain the foundation upon which ethical decisions are made about care. However, the dissonance between the egalitarian and utilitarian views needs to be addressed; and currently, there is no consensus in the literature on which is preferable, or if there are times when one is preferred over the other. This will become evident in the research reviewed.

The following sections are examined based on Wynia's (2007) model, which states that there are three primary ethical challenges for health care professionals in preparing for disasters. Each must be studied to determine the most prudent and ethical way to address the challenge. First is a question of rationing, which entails decisions about triage and rationing of scarce resources such as mechanical ventilators, vaccines, and medications. Next is the question of restrictions, which implies that there will be restrictions on a person's liberties (quarantine) and access to health care services (denial of care based on some criteria or the magnitude of the disaster). Finally and probably the most difficult to predict and plan for is responsibilities, which refers to the health care professional's ability or willingness to continue to provide care even at great personal risk to themselves and their family (Johnstone, 2009). The review of the literature will be guided by these ethical challenges because most of the current research falls into one of these three categories.

Rationing
Triage
A *New York Times* article discusses the unimaginable decisions that had to be made in the aftermath of Hurricane Katrina (Fink, 2009). Multiple triage protocols have been designed addressing how health care professionals will prioritize care during an overwhelming disaster. They describe how painful triage will be when those decisions may make the difference between life and death.

Good (2008) conducted a study on nurses' triage decision making in a disaster by applying virtue-based ethics. An analysis of the primary ethical principles linked to disaster decision making and nursing decision making were reviewed in the literature. The author found that the five principles of fidelity, veracity, autonomy, justice, and beneficence were primary in disaster triage decision making and must be taught in schools of nursing and hospitals and reinforced with guidelines and protocols. Despite extensive planning, especially for the possibility of an influenza pandemic, there is little information on the ability of health care professionals to ethically and effectively handle an onslaught of disaster victims.

One study conducted by Rottman et al. (2010) queried emergency physicians and nurses, hospital nursing supervisors and administrators, and infection control personnel on their attitudes and expectations concerning clinical care during a pandemic influenza outbreak. They conducted qualitative interviews with 46 respondents from 34 randomly selected emergency departments in Los Angeles County. The interviews highlighted the adequacy of supplies and resources, availability of an adequate triage protocol and ability to make triage decisions, quality of the care delivered, and decision making throughout the process. Contrary to the consensus in the literature, they found "little salience that an influx of variably ill patients with influenza would force stratified healthcare decision-making" (p. 99).

Similar results were found by Sztajnkrycer, Madsen, and Baez (2006). This article collated information in the literature on the ethical values upon which triage decisions are based. Research is presented that shows significant variability in triage decisions by personnel trained in triage. In a disaster, personnel will be called upon that may or may not have that skill and be completely outside their comfort zone. Even when personnel committed to using a stable triage system, highly variable results were obtained. The implications are that people apply their own values to triage systems and therefore, the principles of justice and fairness may be compromised. These authors also challenge the notion that scarce resources only occur during a disaster. Often, resources are stretched and must be allocated. These decisions occur daily in hospitals and on the battlefield. So the following question was posed: Are resources truly limited in a disaster? If not, then the utilitarian, public health model of triage may be inappropriate.

A similar review of the literature was done to determine if there were clear guidelines on how to triage effectively in a disaster scenario. This review revealed that there was no consensus on how to triage and no uniform decisions were made about whether utilitarianism or egalitarianism was best as an ethical framework for triage decision making (Tannsjo, 2007).

Only these four studies listed earlier, with nurses as study participants or authored by nurse researchers, were found in the literature. Two were qualitative and two were reviews of the literature. Despite the very real possibility of nurses providing triage during a disaster, no experimental, quasi-experimental, or outcome-based studies on ethical decisions in triage by nurses were found. Multiple papers were found written by physicians on the various triage protocols, but even then few, if any, were based on research findings. Payne (2007) posits that science alone will not be able to adequately resolve decision making in these scenarios. Nursing is obliged to articulate the ethical underpinnings for triage and resource allocation that contribute to any methodology used for rationing. This is an area ripe for nursing research in the future because the ethical basis and understanding of the impact of triage cannot be delayed until the disaster is upon us.

Scarce Resources

Scarce resources during a disaster may include everything from vaccines to mechanical ventilators. In response to a potential pandemic influenza outbreak, the Ontario health care system projected that the demand for critical care beds during a pandemic will peak at 171% of capacity, whereas demand for mechanical ventilators will reach 118% of capacity. These projections are over and above those already in use by current inpatients (Christian et al., 2006). Impact models have clearly shown that our current surge protocols will fail in the face of a widespread catastrophe (Farrar, 2010). Those projections have obligated nursing leadership to tackle the problem prior to any such disaster. Nurses must be at the table to ensure "an ethical, just, and legal distribution of scarce resources while protecting against racial, ethnic, socioeconomic, or other forms of inequity" (Farrar, 2010, p. 2). However, the literature is absent of studies regarding the allocation and use of scarce resources by health professionals, and particularly by nurses. The literature is replete with opinions and commentary by nurses, physicians, public health officials, and bioethicists, but little has been done to validate those opinions.

One study provided recommendations based on an extensive review of the literature that are wholly utilitarian, claiming that allocation decisions should be based on a patient's chance of survival to discharge (White et al., 2009). They analyzed ethical principles and an allocation strategy that included saving the most lives overall while prioritizing care to those that had had the least chance to live a long life. This phenomenon relates to maximizing the number of "life-years" saved. They put forth that certain groups such as the elderly and the functionally impaired will be denied access to care. This is an area for future study because others wholeheartedly disagree with this premise.

Peterson (2008) argues that the utilitarian model, adopted by most governments in response to a potential pandemic, is morally unacceptable and places too much emphasis on a person's ability to contribute to society. This author advocates for a lottery system. This is based on a consequentialist (the moral value of an act should be judged by the value of its consequences) view of moral-ity and states that an action is right if and only if it has an optimal outcome. Strictly deciding one's worth based on a happiness quotient or preference list of attributes is unacceptable. He believes that the mere chance of getting some scarce resource matters morally, even if it is never realized.

The only nursing research found on the topic was a study by Bailey et al. (2011). More than 5,200 undergraduate students, support staff, and academicians at a large university completed a web-based questionnaire that asked them to rank access to scarce resources for 11 different groups. Then, they were provided seven different access plans and asked to pick the access plan that most align with their ethical values. Participants ranked health care workers the highest priority (89%), followed by emergency personnel (85%). The participants gave the high-est priority (39.9%) to the access plan that stated, "save the most lives." Although this was certainly the highest scoring access plan, there was significant disagree-ment among the participants on how to ethically allocate scarce resources.

There are a multitude of articles that propose models for studying alloca-tion of scarce resources. Downar and Seccareccia (2010) state there are several substantive values that have relevance, including (a) protection of the public from harm, (b) proportionality, (c) duty to provide care, (d) reciprocity, (e) equity, and (f) trust. Rosoff (2010) states that when scarce resources are not afforded to some, it is the duty of the health care professional to adhere to the principle of relief of suffering and provide comfort or palliative care especially to the dying. Nurses need to be at the table because they are the ones who will be expected to care for the dying when resources are withheld. What does that conversation look like to a patient in this scenario? When should that conversation occur? Nurses need to participate in the discussion with the community about how these decisions will be made and whether they actually need to be made or not.

One final paper by Trotter (2010) believes that an ethically defensible approach to the allocation of scarce resources is the "sufficiency of care" model, which is (a) adaptive, (b) resource driven, and (c) responsive to the values of the populations being served. He argues that most expert disaster planners make assumptions that are not true such as respiratory failure will always (a) require mechanical ventilators, (b) occur in hospitals, and (c) be able to be planned in advance without sophisticated consultation about the ethical dilemmas that will ensue. He and others execute a call to action to study how these decisions should be made and by whom.

Kraus et al. (2007) discuss lifeboat ethics and urge nursing leaders to col-laborate and determine standards and key interventions of sufficient care for all patients. These altered standards must address whether a treatment is futile or provides some or any benefit to the patient. To accomplish that, a set of minimum criteria for survival must be established, and then a maximum number of resources to be expended on any single patient must be determined before the disaster strikes. These are areas uniquely relevant to nursing and nursing decision making.

The review of the current information revealed a plethora of opinion papers based on various ethical principles. No consensus is evident. Only one study was found that peripherally involved nurses in a survey study. Nurses cannot continue to practice in a vacuum where these decisions have such extensive ramifications for the public's health. As emergency room, critical care, and public health nurses are all bound by the decisions society deems reasonable for rationing supplies during a catastrophic event, the profession is in the position to begin the research required to develop ethical, evidence-based practice guidelines, and initiate the conversation with the public to explain those guidelines.

Restrictions

Restrictions on a person's liberty (quarantine) and access to health care services (denial of care based on some criteria or the magnitude of the disaster) will be discussed here. Restrictions may be required, particularly if there is a pandemic, that will force quarantine of those infected to protect the public. In this country, where individual freedom is paramount, there is little consensus on how we will address this type of quarantine and whether the public will be willing to accept the decisions made by health care professionals. Public health models are utilitarian and attempt to save the most people. Society may agree in theory, but this concept severely restricts patient autonomy.

Canadian officials were compelled to institute quarantine measures during the severe acute respiratory syndrome (SARS) epidemic for the first time in generations. Upshur (2003) discusses the ethical issues arising out of a quarantine to control the spread of a communicable disease. He defines quarantine as the "separation of those exposed individuals who are not yet symptomatic for a period of time (usually the known incubation period of the suspected pathogen) to determine whether they will develop symptoms" (para. 3). In a related article by Upshur (2001), he describes four principles that must be met to institute such an extreme autonomy-limiting strategy by public health officials. First, the *harm principle* must be met, which implies that the harm to others is so significant that it warrants the restriction of individuals who could spread that infection (or harm). Second, the *proportionality principle* should be observed. Public health officials need to use the least restrictive measures available to achieve disease control. He advocates that quarantine be voluntary before any mandated restrictions are implemented. He notes that in Toronto during the SARS outbreak, more than 30,000 persons were actually quarantined, but the Toronto Public Health Department only wrote mandatory detainment orders for 22 people, which shows an impressive understanding or compliance by the public to voluntarily restrict movement in an attempt to control transmission of the disease. Third, *reciprocity* must be upheld. This is a very important concept as will be seen in the duty to report in the following section. When individuals are asked by a society to curtail their personal liberty for the greater good, then there is a mutual obligation by society to assist them with their responsibilities. This implies that society as a whole cannot discriminate against those that have voluntarily taken up quarantine and that there must be means to provide these individuals with basic necessities such as food, water, and mental health services. They should not suffer a penalty for having honored an obligation to society. The last principle—*transparency*—must be upheld that obligates public health officials to communicate their justification for any restrictive action, and allows for an appeal process. Once these conditions are met, then there is a "prima facie justification for the use of quarantine" (Upshur, 2003, p.1). These principles provide an ethical framework from which to view quarantine and other public health initiatives that impose restrictions.

Other frameworks have been offered by Kass (2001) and Childress et al. (2002) that address the notion of quarantine. Both of these frameworks require that the effectiveness of the intervention play a role in determining whether to institute quarantine or not. Some argue that waiting to know exactly how that would work would place society in danger.

One of the most comprehensive overview articles covers every different type of ethical dilemma that might be encountered in a pandemic. It is a short article distributed by the University of Toronto Joint Centre for Bioethics (Collins, 2005). The myriad of ethical dilemmas inherent in a pandemic are enormous, but little research is available to determine how to best deal with these dilemmas. Nurses are called upon by the ANA Code of Ethics Provision 3 "The nurse promotes, advocates for, and strives to protect the health, safety, and rights of the patient" (ANA, 2008, p. 23). Nurses will need to step up to provide answers via tested theories and models for how to best ensure the public safety and ensure those solutions are ethically sound.

Responsibilities
Duty to Treat
Wynia (2007) states that the duty to treat must be delineated by considerations such as the level of risk versus benefit to the employee, the degree to which society depends on health care professionals to mediate the public health threat, and each professional's acceptance of risk that is over and above what is normal. The author poses four important questions to consider when evaluating the duty to treat. First, how sound are ethical obligations during a catastrophe? Second asks

the question, to whom do these principles apply? Third, should the responsibilities be left to the individual and therefore be less constrained, or should they be explicit, with a definite set of rules set by a body of professionals? Finally, how can the policies in public health actually encourage responsible actions? These questions are fundamental to determine how health care professionals will determine their ethical duty to treat. There were several research articles that dealt with nurse's duty to treat and they are reviewed here.

Tzeng (2004) studied 172 nurses' sense of professional duty to provide care for SARS patients despite the obvious risk to their own health. A conceptual model was developed and tested using ordinal logistic regression modeling which revealed two significant findings. First, a statistically significant predictor of nurses fulfilling their professional care obligations was related to whether they agreed with the level of infection control protection provided during the SARS epidemic. They believed that if their organization provided the necessary tools and protections, the nurses were more likely to fulfill their professional obligations. The second finding showed that not requiring quarantine of health care workers was also a statistically significant predictor of nurses' willingness to fulfill their duty to treat, meaning that if they were not subjected to a mandatory quarantine and kept away from their families, they were more likely to fulfill their professional obligations.

Kane-Urrabazo (2007) completed a review of the literature to identify contributing factors to a nurse's sense of duty and the resultant consequences of such during a disaster. The author found that nurses almost unanimously feel a duty to treat, but that sense of duty is enhanced if they feel their nursing administrators commit to and have a moral obligation to protect the staff, particularly in disaster scenarios where nurses encounter extremely high risk.

The two previous studies demonstrate that an institution's moral obligation to protect health care workers to the extent possible affects a nurse's ability to focus on and care for patients during a time of catastrophe. This duty to treat is also linked to a duty to report to work.

Duty to Report or Respond

A retrospective review on disaster nursing by Strangeland (2010) showed that there were very few studies that focused on nurses' intent to report in the event of a future disaster. Nurses are expected to respond during a catastrophic event, but lost in those expectations are the trepidations of nurses who will be required to provide care despite potentially being significantly affected by the disaster. The author suggests that research needs to be done to understand the motivations and concerns of those who decide to respond to the call of duty during disasters. This information must be addressed prior to implementing plans that expect a full complement of nurses to be present for work. A few studies were found that attempted to look at just such issues.

An integrative review of the literature was conducted by Chaffee (2009), which examined both qualitative and quantitative studies from 1991 to 2007. This review found that each of the 27 studies showed some individuals that would remain on duty during both a natural disaster and a chemical, biological, radiological, nuclear, and high-yield explosives (CBRNE) event. However, the numbers significantly dropped between the responders to natural disasters and CBRNE events. Four studies cited safety as their primary concern and would be more likely to report if provided protective gear and vaccinations. In addition, three studies identified family obligations as the limiting factor to reporting. However, three cited increased training and knowledge would improve their willingness to report and one study found that financial incentives would also improve their report to duty numbers. These findings were found in similar articles after 2007 and are reviewed in the following discussion.

A study by Grimes and Mendias (2010) looked at nurses' sense of duty and intent to report to work. They concede that nurses have historically responded without concern for their personal safety in times of disaster, yet little is known about whether nurses would continue that trend during a pandemic emergency or bioterrorist attack where they and their families may be at risk. A survey of 292 nurses was done immediately after completing a bioterrorism course. They completed a personal professional profile (PPP), a test of bioterrorism knowledge (TBK), and an intention to respond (IR) instrument. The IR instrument measured participant's scores (0 = *extremely unlikely*, 10 = *extremely likely*) on the prospect of caring for patients that present with 1 of 10 infectious diseases. These scores were correlated with the PPP and TBK scores. The IR is higher if the infection risk is lower. Overall, the IR score was positively related to a better knowledge of bioterrorism and participating in a previous disaster scenario. Those who were found to be less likely to respond were those with more years in nursing and those with children. The results showed that nurses determined risks that were acceptable based on different infectious diseases and made their decision to respond depending on that information. This is valuable information for nursing administrators and implies that a duty to respond in an emergency is not universal and is qualified by several factors.

In 2008, Draper et al. conducted a multimethod study using focus groups and a survey. The focus groups determined the range of factors nurses identified that would improve the likelihood of them working through an influenza pandemic. Phase 2 collated the focus group information and a review of the literature to design a questionnaire that would ascertain the generalizability of these factors. They hoped the survey would estimate the proportion of health care professionals affected by each factor and how likely they would be to work during the pandemic. Individuals had concerns about infecting family members and friends and the need to be the primary caregiver for those individuals if they fell ill. The authors concluded that it was vital to determine how motivated health care professionals would be to work throughout a pandemic and how factors such as personal and professional values and adherence to ethically sound decision making would influence that behavior.

Two studies with nursing students as participants looked at their inclination to volunteer during a pandemic. Tzeng and Yin (2006) measured the willingness of baccalaureate nursing students to remain on the job and care for patients with avian influenza. Nearly 42% were concerned with insufficient infection control measures in the hospital and the lack of equipment readily available to prevent nosocomial infections. Despite that, about 57% indicated they were willing to care for avian influenza patients. Yonge, Rosychuk, Bailey, Lake, and Marrie (2010) examined 484 nursing students' knowledge, risk perception, and their likelihood of volunteering in a pandemic using a cross-sectional survey. The responses on the web-based questionnaire showed that in a pandemic, 67.9% were likely to volunteer, if they were able to do so. If they were provided adequate protective gear to prevent infection, 77.4% said they would volunteer. Finally, 70.7% of students believed they had a professional obligation to volunteer during a pandemic. These two studies along with the one by Grimes and Mendias (2010) seem to give credence to the notion that the younger the nurse, who may have fewer outside responsibilities and a higher sense of duty to the profession, may be more likely to respond in a disaster. This concept will need to be studied further.

The U.S. Department of Homeland Security (2007) strategy for pandemic influenza implementation plan suggested that up to 40% of health care workers may be absent from work for a period of up to 2 weeks during the height of a pandemic. Irvin, Cindrich, Patterson, and Southhall (2008) conducted a confidential survey to determine the number of staff who would report to duty in a pandemic. One hundred sixty-nine participants in a 600-bed, Level II trauma center were asked to answer a series of questions with a *yes*, *maybe*, or *no*. If they answered "maybe," they were asked to choose one of four potential reasons for their answer. A scenario was presented where there was a 50% mortality rate with treatment and 10% of the general population would be at risk. Overall, 54% of the sample responded "yes" when asked if they understood the avian influenza threat. Nurses responded 22% of the time that they did not understand the threat. When participants were asked if they would come to work during a pandemic, 50% answered "yes," 42% answered "maybe," and 8% said "no." When stratified, physicians were most likely to report to work (74%), and nurses were most unlikely to come in (15%). There was virtually no difference between those with children and those without children. When an incentive of triple pay was added to the scenario, 52% said "yes" and 19% said it would not make a difference in their decision.

A survey of 644 health care professionals at a university hospital was done looking at ethical issues that arose during an influenza pandemic (Ehrenstein, Hanses, & Salzberger, 2006). The study examined the relationship between professional duty and the conflict arising from the possible transmission of influenza virus to family members. Of the 644 participants, 182 (28%) believed it was acceptable for health care workers to forsake their jobs during a pandemic to keep themselves and their families safe. Another 337 (52%) disagreed and 125 (19%) had no opinion. Most (58%) did not think that this decision should be left to the employee, and a large majority (77%) did not believe health care professionals should be permanently dismissed for abandoning the workplace during a pandemic. Very few (21%) believed that those without children should be the primary health care workers responsible for the care of influenza patients. The results showed that a small majority of health care workers believed they had a professional obligation to treat patients despite any potential risk. The researchers were concerned that professional ethical guidelines have not adequately addressed this tension between duty to self and duty to others and suggest that research must be done to develop guidelines that take into account these ethical dilemmas.

Ehrenstein et al. (2006) recommended guidelines but do not state specifics for those guidelines. Many have stated that the duty to treat or duty to report must be tempered with the duty to self as proclaimed by the ANA Code of Ethics which states, "The nurse owes the same duties to self as to others, including the responsibility to preserve integrity and safety, to maintain competence, and to continue personal and professional growth" (ANA, 2008, p. 55). If examined, there are three interpretive statements that guide this provision. First is moral self-respect, which states that "what I owe to others as moral duties, I likewise owe to myself" (ANA, p. 57). Second is the duty for professional growth and the need to remain competent. Finally, the interpretive statements look at the wholeness of character of the nurse (ANA, 2008). It would be the first interpretive statement that many argue would allow the nurse to abandon her duty to treat or report in an effort to remain well and honor familial obligations. The duty to remain well enables the nurse to perform her duties. It does not relieve her of the moral duty to care for patients. The literature often discusses the fact that nurses enter the profession with the understanding that there are inherent dangers and accepting those dangers is part of the moral obligation to which they have committed. However, it is important to note that some groups are more apt to abandon their own personal well-being to care for patients. It is imperative to study and understand what drives that sense of duty and if it can be taught or instilled.

NURSING AND HEALTH CARE PROFESSIONALS' CONCERNS IN DISASTER-RELATED ETHICAL RESEARCH

Nurses continue to have concerns over how they will need to function in the case of a disaster. A case study by Priest and Bahl (2008) discussed the challenges for health care institutions to build individual capacity. They used case studies to stimulate discussion among nurses around the issues of preparedness and ethical response to disasters. They used the exemplar case study of alleged euthanasia at Memorial Hospital Medical Center in New Orleans to illustrate the myriad of ethical dilemmas that will need to be faced by health care professionals.

Ethical themes also arose out of a qualitative study by Giarratano, Orlando, and Savage (2008). They used semistructured interviews with 16 perinatal nurses between 9 and18 months after they worked on an obstetrical unit in New Orleans during Hurricane Katrina. Themes included (a) duty to care; (b) duty conflicts; (c) uncertain times: chaos after the storm (evacuation: routes through uncertainty, hopelessness, abandonment, and/or fear); (d) strength to endure; (e) grief: loss of relationships, identity, and place; (f) anger; and (g) feeling right again. Many of these confirm the dissonance encountered between preserving one's own life and the duty to care and also the need to feel supported by the facility if they are to remain and perform their duties.

What is the best way to conduct ethical research in times of disaster? Several authors have provided guidance. Dobalian, Claver, and Fickel (2010) applied a conceptual model to guide the development of hypotheses related to decision making that occurred in Veterans Affairs nursing homes after hurricanes Katrina and Rita. They determined that ethical dilemmas arose and influenced the decisions made about evacuation. They found a lack of outcome data relevant to these types of disasters. This information is necessary when decisions are being made about vulnerable populations but it is often difficult to obtain.

O'Mathuna (2010) warns that conducting disaster research is fraught with ethical implications. Over and above normal concern for human subject research, disaster research must consider the degree of devastation that the participants themselves experience. The highest priority in disaster research must remain protecting the participants from harm. Other ethical issues include participant recruitment to include the role of compensation and potential coercion, the ability to adequately obtain informed consent, and the notion of balancing burdens and benefits. These issues are similar to human subjects' research in general, but disaster research also includes cross-cultural collaboration and communication, addressing participant vulnerability related to the degree of devastation, and protecting researchers and victims from exploitation and will have to be addressed to ensure that ethically sound research is being conducted during catastrophes.

Austin (2008) suggested using Callaghan's framework for thinking ethically and Taylor's "worries" of modern life framework for studying disaster nursing research. The author argues that current public health frameworks used in disasters rely heavily on moral reasoning and that may be inadequate to guide nurses' ethical decision making. The authors suggest the use of relational ethics, which "situates ethics within relationships and our commitment to one another, and which recognizes that context matters in ethical decision-making" (Austin, 2008, p.10) as a better alternative for studying ethical decision making during a disaster.

CONCLUSIONS AND A CALL TO ACTION

The frequency of devastating natural disasters and the potential for catastrophic injury or harm during a CBRNE event will continue to test the health care profession's ability to respond quickly and adequately to contain and reduce pain and suffering. Surge capacity will continue to be a challenge and decisions based on tested ethical guidelines will need to be outlined for all professionals to understand. Based on the findings of the studies previously discussed, it appears that ensuring provider safety with vaccinations for both the provider and their family, providing protective equipment, decreasing the need for quarantine, and education on the risks associated with caring for patients in a disaster are strategies that can significantly improve health care provider adherence to guidelines during a disaster.

Several nursing textbooks related to disaster nursing (Adelman & Legg, 2009; McGlown, 2004; Powers & Daily, 2010; Veenema, 2007) devote entire chapters to ethical dilemmas and research in disasters but rarely are the two discussed together. Research is focused on education, clinical decision making in light of current frameworks, and policy. Yet, each of those by necessity requires a look into the ethics of those decisions. The authors recommend that any research on nursing and disasters must include an examination of the ethical principles guiding the decisions. Decisions have been made on how health professionals, especially nurses, should conduct themselves during a disaster, but decisions about rationing, restrictions and responsibilities have rarely if ever been tested with outcomes. There is little evidence that these models truly distribute resources appropriately, or that they even save the most lives as they purport to do. Investigations must be conducted on the decisions made to ensure they are ethically sound and are palatable to the general public. Nurses have the unique opportunity, as patient care advocates, to conduct that research and challenge the status quo until ethical evidence supports the decisions being made during disasters.

DISCLAIMER

The views expressed are those of the authors and do not reflect the official policy or position of the Department of Defense or the U.S. government.

REFERENCES

Adelman, D. S., & Legg, T. L. (2009). *Disaster nursing: A handbook for practice*. Sudbury, MA: Jones and Bartlett.

American Nurses Association. (2010). *ANA issue brief: Who will be there? Ethics, the law, and a nurse's duty to respond in a disaster*. Retrieved from http://www.nursingworld.org/MainMenuCategories/WorkplaceSafety/DPR/Disaster-Preparedness.pdf

Austin, W. (2008). Ethics in a time of contagion: A relational perspective. *Canadian Journal of Nursing Research, 40*(4), 10–24.

Bailey, T. Haines, C., Rosychuk, R. J., Marrie, T. J., Yonge, O., Lake, R., . . . Ammann, M. (2011). Public engagement on ethical principles in allocating scarce resources during an influenza pandemic. *Vaccine, 29*(17), 3111–3117.

Burkhardt, M. P., & Nathaniel, A. (2007). *Ethics and issues in contemporary nursing* (3rd ed.). Clifton Park, NY: Delmar Cengage Learning.

Caro, J. J., Coleman, C. N., Knebel, A., & DeRenzo, E. G. (2011). Unaltered ethical standards for individual physicians in the face of drastically reduced resources resulting from an improvised nuclear device event. *The Journal of Clinical Ethics, 22*(1), 33–41.

Chaffee, M. (2009). Willingness of health care personnel to work in a disaster: An integrative review of the literature. *Disaster Medicine and Public Health Preparedness, 3*, 42–56.

Childress, J., Faden. R. R., Gaare, R. D., Gostin, L. O., Kahn, J., Bonnie, R. J., . . . Nieburg, P. (2002). Public health ethics: Mapping the terrain. *Journal of Law, Medicine & Ethics, 30*, 170–178.

Christian, M., Hawryluck, L., Wax, R., Cook, T., Lazar, N. M., Herridge, M. S., . . . Burkle, F. M. (2006). Development of a triage protocol for critical care during an influenza pandemic. *Journal of the Canadian Medical Association, 175*(11), 1377–1381.

Collins, T. (2005). *Ethics in a pandemic*. Retrieved from http://www.eurekalert.org/pub_releases/2005-11/uotj-eia112105.php

Dobalian, A., Claver, M., & Fickel, J. J. (2010). Hurricanes Katrina and Rita and the Department of Veterans Affairs: A conceptual model for understanding the evacuation of nursing homes. *Gerontology, 56*(6), 581–588.

Downar, J., & Seccareccia, D. (2010). Palliating a pandemic: "All patients must be cared for." *Journal of Pain and Symptom Management, 39*(2), 291–295.

Draper, H., Wilson, S., Ives, J., Gratus, C., Greenfield, S., Parry, J., . . . Sorrell, T. (2008). Healthcare workers' attitudes towards working during pandemic influenza: A multi-method study. *BMC Public Health, 8*, 192.

Ehrenstein, B. P., Hanses, F., & Salzberger, B. (2006). Influenza pandemic and professional duty: Family or patients first? A survey of hospital employees. *BMC Public Health, 6*, 311.

Farrar, J. A. (2010). Pandemic influenza: Allocating scarce critical care resources. *Journal of Nursing Administration, 40*(1), 1–3.

Fink, S. (2009). Strained by Katrina, a hospital faced deadly choices. *New York Times, 30*. Retrieved from http://www.nytimes.com/2009/08/30/magazine/30doctors.html?_r=2%pagewanted=print

Fowler, M. D. M. (Ed.). (2008). *Guide to the code of ethics for nurses: Interpretation and application.* Silver Spring, MD: American Nurses Association.

Giarratano, G., Orlando, S., & Savage, J. (2008). Perinatal nursing in uncertain times: The Katrina effect. *MCN: The American Journal of Maternal Child Nursing, 33*(4), 249–257.

Good, L. (2008). Ethical decision-making in disaster triage. *Journal of Emergency Nursing, 34*(2), 112–115.

Grimaldi, M. E. (2007). Ethical decisions in times of disaster: Choices healthcare workers must make. *Journal of Trauma Nursing, 14*(3), 163–164.

Grimes, D. E., & Mendias, E. P. (2010). Nurses' intention to respond to bioterrorism and other infectious disease emergencies. *Nursing Outlook, 58*(1), 10–16.

Holm, S. (2007). Medical aid in disaster relief. In R. E. Ashcroft, A. Dawson, H. Draper, & J. R. McMillan (Eds.), *Principles of healthcare ethics* (2nd ed., pp. 671–678). Hoboken, NJ: Wiley.

Irvin, C. B., Cindrich, L., Patterson, W., & Southhall, A. (2008). Survey of hospital healthcare personal response during a potential avian influenza pandemic: Will they come to work? *Prehospital Disaster Medicine, 23*(4), 328–333.

Johnstone, M.-J. (2009). Health care disaster ethics: A call to action. *Australian Nursing Journal, 17*(1), 27.

Kane-Urrabazo, C. (2007). Duty in time of disaster: A concept analysis. *Nursing Forum, 42*(2), 56–64.

Kass, N. E. (2001). An ethics framework for public health. *American Journal of Public Health, 91*, 1776–1782.

Kraus, C., Levy, F., & Kelen, G. (2007). Lifeboat ethics: Considerations in the discharge of inpatients for the creation of hospital surge capacity. *Disaster Medicine and Public Health Preparedness, 1*(11), 51–56.

McGlown, K. J. (Ed.). (2004). *Terrorism and disaster management: Preparing healthcare leaders for the new reality.* Chicago, IL: Health Administration Press.

O'Mathuna, D. P. (2010). Conducting research in the aftermath of disasters: Ethical considerations. *Journal of Evidence Based Medicine, 3*(2), 65–75.

Payne, K. (2007). Ethical issues related to pandemic flu planning and response. *AACN Advanced Critical Care, 18*(4), 356–360.

Peterson, M. (2008). The moral importance of selecting people randomly. *Bioethics, 22*(6), 321–327.

Powers, R., & Daily, E. (Ed.). (2010). *Disaster nursing.* Cambridge, NY: Cambridge University Press.

Priest, C., & Bahl, M. (2008). Nursing during catastrophic disaster: A case study from New Orleans. *Journal of Nursing Law, 12*(4), 157–164.

Rosoff, P. M. (2010). Should palliative care be a necessity or a luxury during an overwhelming health catastrophe? *Journal of Clinical Ethics, 21*(4), 312–320.

Rottman, S. J., Shoaf, K. I., Schlesinger, J., Selski, E. K., Perman, J., Lamb, K., & Cheng, J. (2010). Pandemic influenza triage in the clinical setting. *Prehospital and Disaster Medicine, 25*(2), 99–104.

Rubinson, L., & O'Toole, T. (2005). Critical care during epidemics. *Critical Care, 9*, 311–313.

Strangeland, P. A. (2010). Disaster nursing: A retrospective review. *Critical Care Nursing Clinics of North America, 22*(4), 421–436.

Sztajnkrycer, M. D., Madsen, B. E., & Baez, A. A. (2006). Unstable ethical plateaus and disaster triage. *Emergency Medicine Clinics of North America, 24*(3), 1–4.

Tannsjo, T. (2007). Ethical aspects of triage in mass casualty. *Current Opinion in Anaesthesiology, 20*(2), 143–146.

Trotter, G. (2010). Sufficiency of care in disasters: Ventilation, ventilator triage, and the misconception of guideline-driven treatment. *Journal of Clinical Ethics, 21*(4), 294–307.

Tzeng, H. M. (2004). Nurses professional care obligation and their attitudes towards SARS infection control measures in Taiwan during and after the 2003 epidemic. *Nursing Ethics*, *11*(3), 277–289.

Tzeng, H. M., & Yin, C. Y. (2006). Nurses' fears and professional obligations concerning possible human-to-human avian flu. *Nursing Ethics*, *13*(5), 455–470.

Upshur, R. E. (2001). Principles for the justification of public health intervention. *Canadian Journal of Public Health*, *93*, 101–103.

Upshur, R. E. (2003). The ethics of quarantine. *Virtual Mentor*, *5*(11). Retrieved from http://virtual mentor.ama-assn.org/2003/11/msoc1-0311.html

U.S. Department of Homeland Security. (2007). *National strategy for pandemic influenza*. Retrieved from http://www.flu.gov/planning-preparedness/federal/pandemic-influenza-oneyear.pdf

Veenema, T. G. (Ed.). (2007). *Disaster nursing and emergency preparedness for chemical, biological, and radiological terrorism and other hazards* (2nd ed.). New York, NY: Springer Publishing.

White, D. B., Katz, M. H., Luce, J. M., & Lo, B. (2009). Who should receive life support during a public health emergency? Using ethical principles to improve allocation decisions. *Annals of Internal Medicine*, *150*(2), 132–138.

Winland-Brown, J. E. (2009). Medical repatriation: Physicians' and nurses' responses to a dilemma. *Southern Online Journal of Nursing Research*, *9*(4). Retrieved from http://www.resourcenter.net/images/SNRS/Files/SOJNR_articles2/Vol09Num04Art01.html

Wynia, M. K. (2007). Ethics and public health emergencies: Encouraging responsibility. *American Journal of Bioethics*, *7*(4), 1–4.

Yonge, O., Rosychuk, R. J., Bailey, T. M., Lake, R., & Marrie, T. J. (2010). Willingness of university nursing students to volunteer during a pandemic. *Public Health Nursing*, *27*(2), 174–180.

CHAPTER 4

Legal Issues in Emergency Response

Bobby A. Courtney, Chad Priest, and Paul Root

ABSTRACT

During disasters, health care providers are faced with limited resources, harsh environments, and an increased amount of sick and injured patients. These conditions sometimes require health care providers to deviate from existing treatment protocols. Deviating from these protocols results in a perception of increased legal risk for health care providers. This has led to a national debate regarding the necessity of establishing altered standards of care for health care providers during crisis events. This chapter explores the development of disaster preparedness, the issue of health care provider liability, and national and local efforts to protect providers in disaster situations.

INTRODUCTION

Disasters challenge health care organizations and providers in numerous ways. Whether it is the treatment of unfamiliar injuries, unusually large numbers of patients, or delivery of care under austere conditions, disasters have the potential to suddenly, and without warning, change the delivery of health care. Given the high value attributed to systematic, evidence-based, reproducible health care interventions, change following a crisis event poses a significant challenge.

Modifying usual treatment protocols to account for an unusually large number of patients, or providing care with fewer personnel or resources in an austere environment, understandably makes competent and caring health care professionals nervous. These changes also result in a perception of increased legal risk because patients begin to receive care that is qualitatively different from that which would usually be provided.

In this chapter, we explore the individual liability of nurses and health care providers responding to disasters. We begin by describing the critical role that nurses and providers play during these types of events and because this liability is inexorably bound with larger organizational emergency preparedness issues, we also briefly trace the development of health care emergency preparedness in the United States and discuss its impact on individual provider readiness. Next, with apologies to our law school professors who might bristle at the simplistic nature of our description, we outline the legal process by which individuals are found to be liable for injuries to others. With this background, we then describe the evolution of policies regarding health care provider liability during disasters as well as existing legal protections and the opportunities and challenges they create.

This chapter relied on public health and legal institute reports, model legislation, expert commentary, medical journal articles, legal cases and statutes, and mutual aid agreements. Key search terms producing the best results included "altered standards of care" and "health care provider liability." Public health organizations and medical journals provided more literature on health care provider liability whereas legal sources on the issue were limited. This is most likely because of the legal community's stance that health care providers are protected by the existing standard of care so no altered standard of care is necessary. An example of this position is the American Bar Association's (ABA; 2011) recent support of programs to educate health care providers of the current standard of care rather than develop new standards. Primary sources including volunteer protection statutes and case law also proved valuable to this chapter.

BACKGROUND

Nurses: Born of Crisis

Health care providers, especially nurses, have a special role during disasters. Consider that nursing was born from disaster and conflict. Florence Nightingale founded the basic tenants of modern nursing while caring for soldiers during the Crimean War. In the United States, Clara Barton, founder of the American Red Cross, distinguished herself first on the battlefields of the civil war. Whether we are consciously aware of it during our daily practice, the history of nursing is managing patients during catastrophe and crisis.

Thankfully, contemporary nurses and other health care professionals rarely have the opportunity to provide care during disasters. Most health care professionals work in complex delivery systems that are dependent on technology and involve highly scripted, if not still evolving, evidence-based protocols that drive almost every health care activity. Although the controlled nature of hospitals provides an important degree of certainty and predictability to modern medical and nursing practice and is, of course, essential to reducing error and improving safety in many ways, it has diminished the ability of health care providers to respond effectively during disasters. Consider that some of the very skills required during an emergency—creativity, decisiveness without evidence, and improvisation in the face of diminished resources—are those we are systematically attempting to eliminate from controlled hospital environments.

Even as our health care systems become more controlled, and our care more tightly scripted, the world around us remains unstable. The events of September 11, 2001 served as a powerful motivator to improve preparedness for disasters in all sectors of our society.

Hospital Emergency Preparedness
Driven largely by grant programs and policies established by the federal government, modern health care emergency preparedness programs in the United States sought to build capacity in organizations and institutions to maintain basic operations to care for the sick and injured. As a result, activities such as stockpiling supplies, developing plans, and assessing the surge capacity of hospitals served as the foundation for national preparedness programs and continue to dominate most planning efforts. Because of their operational nature, many hospitals assigned responsibility for these grant-funded preparedness activities to safety personnel or, in some cases, an emerging group of professional emergency managers who were well suited to the logistical and operational tasks necessary to implement programs within hospitals, but many of whom had no clinical training or background. The result was predictable—the development of a highly refined health care emergency management process within hospitals with only minimal attention paid to ensuring the delivery of high quality clinical care during crises.

Although operationally focused, this strategy did involve significant training for health care workers. However, the major focus of the training was, and continues to be, the command and control of individuals within an institution through systems such as the Incident Command System (ICS) or the Hospital

Incident Command System (HICS). Implicit assumptions were made that clinical providers knew how to take care of patients, but that they lacked an understanding of how to integrate this care into all stages of the emergency management cycle. With some exceptions such as the clinical training programs developed by the American Medical Association's National Disaster Life Support Foundation, there have been few coordinated programs designed to prepare individual health care providers to respond effectively to disasters.

Hurricane Katrina, and the flooding in its wake, laid bare the vulnerabilities of the health care system during crisis. The failure of the health care safety net called into question the basic tenants of health care preparedness doctrine, including the idea that hospitals could ever be truly self-sustaining in a catastrophic emergency. The catastrophic loss of infrastructure rendered most hospital emergency plans useless. Operating in conditions eerily similar to those faced by Florence Nightingale and Clara Barton, hospitals and patients relied on the creativity and decisiveness of physicians and nurses to save lives. However, within a few miles inside the city of New Orleans, health care providers behaved and responded in radically different ways. The grizzly deaths of patients under suspicious circumstances at Memorial Medical Center and the callous abandonment of patients at St. Rita's Nursing Home were in stark contrast to the well-executed clinical response and heroic life-saving measures at other health care organizations in the city. Stated simply, not all health care providers were adequately prepared to make good decisions under tough conditions (Fink, 2009).

The Nature of Liability

The determination of individual civil liability and the resulting award of compensatory or punitive damages in the United States rests on a complex patchwork of laws, regulation, and court decisions going back to the founding of our country. There is rarely a "clear case" of liability because most decisions about negligent conduct are considered on a case-by-case basis. Despite apparent complexity, determining who is liable for actions or inactions in the United States is actually elegantly simple. First-year law students are taught a simple method to determine when the action (or inaction) of an individual is converted into a legal wrongdoing, or "tort." Simply put, an action is a tort if a person owes a duty to another to act (or not act) in a certain way and breaches this duty, causing damages to the person to whom the duty is owed (Prosser, Dobbs, Keeton, & Keeton, 1984). Duty, breach of duty, causation, and damages are the fundamental elements of a tort.

Health care providers can commit a tort and be liable for their actions or inactions in a myriad of ways. Consider the simple case of a nurse who gives the wrong medication to a patient resulting in the patient's death. The nurse has a broad duty to provide competent care. That duty is established by the state nursing practice act and is assumed by the registered nurse in exchange for certain privileges granted by the state (e.g., the license to independently practice within the scope of the nurse's education). That duty is breached when the nurse administers the wrong medication to the patient. Unfortunately, damages resulted to the patient that died. There is no question that the cause of the damages was directly related to the nurse's breach of duty. Therefore, we have a clear case of a duty, a breach, causation, and damages that would constitute a civil wrongdoing that could result in liability to the individual nurse.

In general, and at the risk of oversimplifying this complex topic, duties are created in three ways. First, duties can be created based on a collection of decisions from civil cases in which juries in individual cases find a duty exists even where one was not known before. For example, a jury may declare that a nurse in a particular case has a duty to double-check the orders of physicians and not to carry out potentially dangerous orders even though the nurse normally has a duty to follow physician orders (*Rowe v. Sisters of Pallottine Missionary Soc'y*, 2001). Occasionally, these duties are created by professionals through formal declarations of professional organizations (e.g., a physician's ancient duty to "do no harm"). Other times, duties are created by legislation. For example, the duty of confidentiality regarding specific forms of identifiable health information in the United States was created through the Health Insurance Portability and Accountability Act (HIPAA; 1996).

Determining a breach of duty in the United States is generally left to civil juries composed of citizens. In the health care context, a breach is typically identified when a health care provider fails to provide care to an individual patient that meets the standard of care in the community. In the State of Indiana, for example, a provider breaches a duty to the patient when he or she

> fails to exercise the degree of reasonable care and skill in providing health care to a patient as would a reasonably careful, skillful and prudent health care provider acting under the same or similar circumstances. The malpractice may consist of doing something that the health care provider should not have done under the circumstances, or the failure to do something that the health care provider should have done under the circumstances. (*Weinberger v. Boyer*, 2011)

The question left to juries in malpractice cases then is really quite simple: "Did the provider act as a reasonably careful, skillful, and prudent [provider] would act in the same situation?" In the State of Indiana, this is the standard of care to which providers are held. The standard is quite flexible by design and can change from case to case. For example, it may be a violation of the standard of care to fail to run a diagnostic test on a patient who would otherwise benefit from such a test. However, if such a test were unavailable through no fault of the provider (e.g., because the manufacturer of the test could not produce it) failure to provide the test would probably not be found to be a breach. In the latter instance, a reasonably skilled and similarly situated provider would also not have been able to administer the test.

Recently and frequently, coinciding with the rise of evidence-based medicine, the concept of "standard of care" is being confused with a medical best practice that physicians should follow. Consider, for example, instances in which a group of nurses evaluate scientific evidence and determine that a particular nursing intervention is generally the best intervention for any given constellation of symptoms. This nursing evidence is subsequently published as a "practice guideline" for other nurses to follow. Although this guideline may become evidence in the pursuit of determining whether a nurse breached a duty in any particular situation, it is not per se evidence of a duty itself. These guidelines, for example, cannot consider the individual contexts of every given nursing care situation. However, the term standard of care has frequently been used to describe these best practices. As we discuss in detail later in this chapter, this confusion of terminology between evidence-based health care practices and the legal standard of care has made a significant impact on health care liability policy, especially in the context of disasters and emergency care situations.

The process of identifying professional duties in the health care context, ruling on their breach, and determining whether that breach subsequently caused damages is frequently long, arduous, and expensive for plaintiffs and defendants alike. This is because, as discussed earlier, each individual case is decided against the relevant facts of the situation. This process requires plaintiffs and defendants to build cases with expert witnesses and results in law being created case by case, as has been done for hundreds of years in the United States, and in England prior to the founding of our country.

Much has been written about the shortcomings of this system to efficiently and adequately identify and compensate for wrongdoings committed by health care professionals. Organizations and individuals proposing reform, led largely by health care professionals, decry the current system as unfair and unjustly rewarding to plaintiffs, resulting in increased health care costs. Injured individuals, led largely by their lawyers and advocacy groups, argue that the current system disincentivizes the bringing of new cases because of caps on damages and other hurdles established by many states and creates an unsafe health care system where providers are not held accountable for their actions.

The resolution of this complex debate is beyond the scope of this chapter; however, it is important to note at the outset that a discussion of individual health care professional liability generally is substantially different from liability during disasters. The reason is simple: With the exception of the civil cases brought against a group of providers who were also accused of second-degree murder during Hurricane Katrina, there have been no recorded cases of successful civil malpractice actions brought against health care providers resulting from breaches of duties during a disaster (Annas, 2010). This is likely because reasonable juries would correctly apply the legal standard of care in such cases, taking into account that a reasonably skilled practitioner in a similarly situated disaster circumstance would likely not give care considered a "best practice." This is important because, as discussed earlier, health care malpractice cases (i.e., those cases seeking to determine whether there was a duty, breach, causation, and damage) are decided by individual cases over many years. The lack of cases arising from disaster situations is as important to the development of case law in this area as would be several cases finding individual liability for malpractice actions (Annas, 2010).

Despite a lack of malpractice actions during and following disasters, in recent years, there have been substantial efforts to provide liability protections to individual health care practitioners who undertake to serve their fellow citizens during times of crisis. Proponents of these protections argue that they are necessary to incentivize volunteer medical providers who would otherwise fail to respond to disasters. Although this may be true, there have been no significant research studies that demonstrate this phenomenon. Regardless, liability protections now exist in many parts of the United States and through the federal government. The remainder of this chapter discusses these protections and outlines their limitations. Focusing on legal issues is a common pastime in the United States, perhaps because of the complexity of our system. This preoccupation, however, may be fatally flawed in the case of disaster preparedness. Whatever the merits of providing liability protection to providers, such protection fails to prepare health care providers to perform the most important function in any crisis, to make good decisions under tough conditions.

DISASTERS AND TORT LIABILITY
Model State Emergency Health Powers Act

Concern over health care provider liability during disasters has its roots in the aftermath of September 11, 2001. Increased national attention regarding the public health response to these events led the Centers for Disease Control and Prevention (CDC) to commission the Center for Law and the Public's Health at Georgetown and Johns Hopkins universities to produce draft legislation for states to use in assessing existing laws related to catastrophic public health emergency response (Hodge & Gostin, 2002a). The resulting Model State Emergency Health Powers Act (MSEHPA), touted as a modernization of public health law, recommends a series of statutory provisions state public health emergency preparedness and response (Hodge & Gostin, 2002b).

MSEHPA was not without controversy because it recommended numerous measures affecting individual civil liberties (Hodge & Gostin, 2002c). For example, mandatory testing, treatment, and vaccination; quarantine and isolation; and certain travel restrictions have been the subject of significant criticism (Annas, 2003), notwithstanding the drafters' intention that they be exercised on a temporary or limited basis (Hodge & Gostin, 2002b, 2002c). Moreover, MSEHPA contained broad civil immunity provisions (Georgetown University & Johns Hopkins University [GU & JHU], 2001b). Specifically, sections 804(a) and 804(b)(2) exempt government and public health authorities referenced in the Act as well as private actors rendering assistance or advice at the request of the State or its political subdivisions from liability for death or injury to persons except in cases of gross negligence or willful misconduct (GU & JHU, 2001b). Section 608(b)(3) similarly exempts any out-of-state health care providers appointed to respond to a public health emergency (GU & JHU, 2001a).

Altered Standards of Care in Mass Casualty Events

Similar concerns over liability are illustrated in efforts by federal agencies to address the provision of care where resources are limited. For example, in 2004, the Agency for Healthcare Research and Quality (AHRQ) and the Office of the Assistant Secretary for Preparedness and Response (ASPR) convened a panel to examine how standards of clinical care might need to be altered during a mass casualty event; identify what planning, guidance, and tools would be needed to ensure an effective clinical response to such an event; and recommend specific action to address government, community, and health systems planners' needs relative to this topic (AHRQ, 2005a). Panelists included experts in the fields of bioethics, emergency medicine and management, health care administration, health law and policy, and public health as well as representatives from federal agencies and professional organizations (AHRQ, 2005a). The group's final report largely addressed clinical issues (e.g., triage protocols, resource allocation guidelines, and the sufficiency of human resources); however, it also identified several legal, policy, and ethical issues affecting health care delivery, most notably the need to establish clear authorization authority for use of altered standards of care and provider liability (AHRQ, 2005b). With respect to the latter, the group called for adjustments in several areas including, but not limited to, liability for care provided under stress with diminished resources; certification, licensing, and scope of practice; institutional autonomy; facility standards; patient privacy and confidentiality; documentation of care; property seizures; and protocols for quarantine or mass immunization (AHRQ, 2005c).

Institute of Medicine
Guidance for Establishing Crisis Standards of Care for Use in Disaster Situations: A Letter Report

In August 2009, the Institute of Medicine (IOM), a not-for-profit, nongovernmental organization, was called on by ASPR to convene an ad hoc committee (the Committee on Guidance for Establishing Standards of Care for Use in Disaster Situations, hereinafter referred to as the "Committee") to provide national framework guidance for public health officials, health care facilities, and clinical providers in the development of policies and protocols for standards of care during emergency events where resources are scarce (IOM, 2009b). Phase 1 of this two-phase activity called for (a) identification of key elements to be included in standards of care protocols, (b) identification of potential triggers for use by public health officials to develop standards of care protocols, and (c) creation of a template for use by public health officials when developing guidance for provider communities developing standards of care (IOM, 2009a).

The Committee published its preliminary guidance in a letter report entitled *Guidance for Establishing Crisis Standards of Care for Use in Disaster Situations* (IOM, 2009a). Noting that ethical goals in medical care are absolute and that health care professionals are obligated to provide the best possible care regardless of the circumstances, the Committee recommended "crisis standards of care" as the optimal level of care that can be delivered during a disaster (IOM, 2009c). These standards were defined as

> [A] substantial change in usual healthcare operations and the level of care it is possible to deliver, which is made necessary by a pervasive (e.g., pandemic influenza) or catastrophic (e.g., earthquake, hurricane) disaster. This change in the level of care delivered is justified by specific circumstances and is formally declared by a state government, in recognition that crisis operations will be in effect for a sustained period. The formal declaration that crisis standards of care are in operation enables specific legal/regulatory powers and protections for healthcare providers in the necessary tasks of allocating and using scarce medical resources and implementing alternate care facility operations. (IOM, 2009c, p. 18)

Based on an assessment of various state, federal and international protocols, published literature, and available guidance documents, the Committee offered several recommendations to assist states in the early stages of developing crisis standards of care including collaboration among state public health authorities and localities in the development of consistent crisis standards of care protocols

(IOM, 2009d); adherence to ethical norms when crisis standards of care are in effect (IOM, 2009e); stakeholder engagement in the development of crisis standards of care (IOM, 2009f); collaboration among state, federal, and local governments to ensure both intrastate and interstate consistency in the implementation of crisis standards of care (IOM, 2009i); and state agency and local collaboration to ensure consistent implementation of crisis standards of care (IOM, 2009j).

Citing concerns that existing emergency protections "do not provide immunity or indemnify practitioners for acts that constitute gross negligence, willful or wanton misconduct, or crimes," the Committee also recommended that appropriate agencies be given authority to institute crisis standards of care, adjust licensed or credentialed providers' scopes of practice, and alter licensure and credentialing practices to encourage provider response (IOM, 2009g). Evoking provisions outlined in the MSEHPA, the Committee also suggested that "[a]bsent national comprehensive liability protections, state and local governments should explicitly tie existing liability protections (e.g., through immunity or indemnification) for health care practitioners and entities to crisis standards of care," and that courts evaluating malpractice claims arising from emergencies should be cognizant of the legal effect of changing standards of care and consider whether adherence to the report's guidance provides "sufficient evidence" of meeting such standards (IOM, 2009h, pp. 49–50).

Controversy Following the 2009 Letter Report

The IOM Committee's immunity recommendation has generated significant debate among legal scholars, policymakers, and professional associations, particularly concerning terminology and the need for expanded provider protections. With respect to terminology, opponents of the Committee's position criticize its attempt to distinguish between medical and legal standards of care, citing three specific arguments. First, organizations seeking to develop guidelines for emergencies are addressing a need for modified standard procedures, not altered standards of care (Annas, 2010; see generally IOM, 1990). Because the standard of care is inherently flexible, it need not be "altered" during a disaster. In other words, there is no altered standard of care, only altered circumstances (Annas, 2010). Second, customary medical practice does not conform to a precisely defined concept; rather, it is variable and based on environmental and demographic factors, cultural expectations, and reimbursement patterns (Annas & Miller, 1994). Finally, critics contend that the Committee's failure to reference court cases where providers have been sued for breaching the standard of care during an emergency event undermines its premise that courts differ in their interpretation of the legal standard of care during disasters (Annas, 2010). As such, providers are "are entitled to reasonable protections for noncriminal acts of ordinary negligence, based on an appropriate standard of care in crisis situations" (Gostin et al., 2010, p. 1379).

Concerning the need for comprehensive immunity, opponents cite a lack of data to support the Committee's assertion that providers will not respond without liability protections, and specifically note the ambiguity of recent surveys and historical reviews (see Institute for Bioethics, Health, Policy, and Law, 2003; Alexander & Wynia, 2003; Annas, 2002; DiMaggio, 2005; Iserson et al., 2008; Qureshi et al., 2005) as well as various perceptual and physical barriers (e.g., providers' perception of self-efficacy in response, concerns regarding personal safety, childcare or eldercare obligations; Barnett et al., 2005). In addition, opponents reference existing mechanisms that limit provider liability during a disaster (Annas, 2010). First, certain state protections may be available to providers who act in good faith and without willful misconduct, gross negligence, or recklessness when responding to an emergency (e.g., Good Samaritan statutes, Volunteer Protection Acts [VPAs], and Tort Claims Acts; Ray, 2009; see also Nonprofit Risk Management Center, 2009). Second, the Public Readiness and Emergency Preparedness (PREP) Act allows for limitations on provider liability following the formal declaration of a disaster by the federal government (see PREP, 2005; Section 1135 of the Social Security Act, 2010). Third, formal disaster declarations by state governments often trigger statutory immunity provisions for negligent conduct on the part of emergency and public health workers (Hoffman, 2008; see also Emergency Management Assistance Compact [EMAC], 1996; Lindsay, 2008). In general, legislatures link these provisions to compliance with government instructions, contracts, or other legal requirements; public health statutes; or emergency statutes (Hoffman, 2008). Proponents of more expansive liability protections cite wide variation in these protections and claim they create confusion and uncertainty (Gostin et al., 2010).

The ABA recently weighed in on the issue by adopting a resolution opposing "laws that would alter the legal duty of reasonable care in the circumstances owed to victims of a natural or manmade disaster by relief organizations and health care practitioners," and supporting "programs to educate relief organizations and health care practitioners about their duty of care owed to victims of a natural or manmade disaster" (ABA, 2011). In its report proposing the resolution, the ABA emphasized that the legal duty owed to disaster victims was a "time-honored principle that should not be altered, especially on the basis of confusion or speculation" (ABA, 2011). Furthermore, the Association noted that victims were entitled to expect reasonable care as circumstances permit, and that it was the duty of lawyers to explain the law clearly to those whom it applies and to protect individuals' rights to "competent and accountable care, including in a disaster" (ABA, 2011).

Crisis Standards of Care: A Systems Framework for Catastrophic Disaster Response
In 2011, the IOM Committee reconvened to conduct Phase 2 of the study to examine the impact of its 2009 letter report, identify metrics to assess crisis standards of care protocol development, develop templates for crisis standards of

care planning and implementation, define terms and provide consistent language for cross-jurisdictional communication, and develop tools for engaging the public in developing crisis standards of care plans (IOM, 2012a). The Committee's Phase 2 report, published in March 2012, was designed as a multivolume resource manual that includes (a) a framework for development and implementation of crisis standards of care plans; (b) consideration of the legal, ethical, palliative care, and mental health issues that entities at each level of a disaster response should address; (c) stakeholder roles and responsibilities, operational considerations, and templates that outline functions and tasks for allocation of scarce resources during a disaster; (d) a public engagement toolkit; and (e) sample plans and lists of potentially scarce medical resources and their challenges (IOM, 2012a).

In its consideration of liability, the Committee identifies "two predominant paths to assessing and resolving potential negligence claims resulting from the implementation of [crisis standards of care]" (IOM, 2012b, p. 59). Specifically, one that is based on a flexible, evolving standard and another based on legal liability protections taking effect upon declaration of a state of emergency (IOM, 2012b). Several surveys of prospective medical reserve corps volunteers are also provided as empirical data to illustrate how liability risks may influence provider willingness to participate during a disaster (IOM, 2012c). Although informative, these studies are largely anecdotal because they do not contain representative sample populations and fail to establish the substantial evidence base necessary for informed policymaking. Finally, the Committee continues to refer to a patchwork of liability protections that contain "significant limits to liability protections overall" such as the failure of some protections to provide coverage outside of officially declared emergencies (i.e., coverage commences only on the date of an emergency declaration and ceases the moment the declaration is terminated) and failure of virtually all protections to "immunize or indemnify practitioners or entities for acts that constitute gross negligence, willful or wanton misconduct, or crimes" (IOM, 2012d, 2012e, pp. 69–70). Given these circumstances, the Committee encourages stakeholders to assess the range of existing protections in their specific jurisdictions and determine whether additional protections are required to facilitate implementation of crisis standards of care (IOM, 2012e).

EXISTING PROTECTIONS

Assuming the threat of civil liability may discourage some providers from responding during a disaster (see Hodge, 2006), several federal and state protections exist to mitigating this risk. As a caveat, providers should become familiar with the specific laws of the state where they will practice. Moreover, although all laws mentioned during this discussion provide immunity from civil liability, no statute provides complete immunity in every situation. For example, nearly every state and federal law that grants immunity to health care providers responding to a disaster contains an exception if the provider acts in a criminal manner or with "gross negligence" or "willful or wanton misconduct." During the discussion that follows, the immunity granted by such laws will simply be referred to as "limited immunity."

Federal Laws
Federal Public Readiness and Emergency Preparedness Act
Signed into law in 2005, the PREP Act provides liability protection to "covered persons" who administer "countermeasures" during a public health emergency. For PREP's liability protections to become effective, the U.S. Secretary of Health and Human Services must issue a declaration that includes "a determination that a disease or other health condition or other threat to health constitutes a public health emergency . . ." (Hodge, 2006, § 247 d-6d(b)(1)). In the declaration, the Secretary will identify certain countermeasures to be covered (i.e., drugs and vaccines; Hodge, 2006, § 247 d-6d(i)(1)). PREP provides liability protection for covered persons, which includes "qualified persons" who "prescribe, administer, or dispense" the countermeasure (Hodge, 2006, § 247 d-6d(i)(2)). Qualified persons include licensed health professionals (Hodge, 2006, § 247 d-6d(i)(8)). Therefore, if PREP is in force, health care providers who administer official countermeasures may have limited immunity from civil liability (see Hodge, 2006, § 247 d-6d(c)).

Federal Volunteer Protection Act
Congress passed the federal VPA in 1997 (2006). The federal VPA provides a lower level of protection than most state VPAs, which will be discussed in detail later. Congress intended the Act to promote volunteerism by limiting the liability of volunteers who assist nonprofit organizations or government entities for all activities, not necessarily disasters. As such, it was not intended as a means of eliminating provider liability, rather Congress sought to reduce nonprofit insurance expenses and increase the efficiency of federal funding to nonprofit entities (VPA of 1997, 2006). However, the law does provide protection for volunteer health practitioners (VHPs), defined as individuals who do not receive compensation other than reimbursement for costs (VPA of 1997, 2006).

The VPA states that no volunteer of a nonprofit organization or governmental entity shall be liable for harm that they cause while acting on behalf of the organization as long as (a) the volunteer was acting within the scope of his or her responsibilities to the organization; (b) the volunteer is properly licensed for the activities performed on behalf of the organization or governmental entity in the state where the volunteer activities occurred; (c) the harm was not caused by willful or criminal conduct, or gross negligence; and (d) the harm was not caused by operating a motor vehicle or other vehicle that requires a license (VPA of 1997, 2006). Protection under the Act is not dependent on the declaration of an emergency (VPA of 1997, 2006; see also Hoffman, 2008).

Several gaps in the VPA limit its effectiveness for VHPs and other volunteers. First, the law does not affect any legal action brought by a nonprofit or governmental organization against a volunteer (see VPA of 1997, 2006). Therefore, a VHP could become indirectly liable for money damages if the VHP injures someone who, because they are not able to sue the provider directly because of the protection of the VPA, sues the nonprofit or governmental organization where the volunteer was working. If the organization has to pay a judgment against the injured person, the organization would have the right to sue the volunteer for indemnity, making the volunteer indirectly liable. Second, the law gives states the option to opt out of the law, so that the law's protections will not apply in that state's courts (see VPA of 1997, 2006). However, the law only protects medical professionals volunteering in the state where they hold their license (VPA of 1997, 2006), so the VPA will probably not provide protection for out-of-state VHPs. The bottom line is that although the federal VPA might appear to provide some liability protection for VHPs volunteering in a disaster, it contains gaps that weaken its protections.

State Laws
State Volunteer Protection Acts
Most states have their own VPAs, some of which add protections to the federal VPA. Inconsistent state laws are overridden by the federal VPA, although more protective state laws remain in effect (VPA of 1997, 2006). For example, the Florida VPA (2011) provides limited immunity to volunteers of nonprofit organizations who act in good faith and in the scope of their official duties. The Florida VPA provides greater protection than the federal VPA because the Florida law does not allow the nonprofit organization to be able to sue the volunteer. In one case where a volunteer rear-ended a motorist and was sued for negligence, a Florida appellate court explained that the clear intent of the Florida VPA is to shift liability from the volunteer to the nonprofit organization (see *Campbell v. Kessler*, 2003). Arizona law provides another example of a volunteer protection statute that provides more protection than the VPA Ariz. (1997). The Arizona volunteer protection statute provides limited immunity from civil liability for volunteers of nonprofit organizations, hospitals, and government entities so long as the volunteer is acting within the scope of their duties (VPA, Ariz., 1997). Arizona's law, like the Florida VPA, is intended to transfer liability from the volunteer to the nonprofit organization, hospital, or government entity (VPA, Ariz., 1997). Conversely, some other states have less robust volunteer protection measures that do not add a great deal to the federal VPA as it applies to VHPs. For example, Indiana law provides limited immunity from civil liability for

volunteers of nonprofit organizations but specifically excludes health care providers (Ind. Code, 2005). Therefore, although Indiana adds protections to the VPA, it does not add protection for nurses, doctors, or other medical professionals.

Important Model Legislation Affecting Volunteer Health Practitioners: The Emergency Management Assistance Compact and the Uniform Emergency Volunteer Health Practitioners Act

Some states have adopted model laws related to emergency management that may affect liability protection for providers assisting during a disaster. The EMAC (1996) is a model law that all 50 states have adopted in some form. The EMAC is a mutual aid agreement between states that provides uniformity in liability and reimbursement issues that arise when states lend aid to other states during a disaster. One of the most fundamental aspects of EMAC is that all officers or employees of the state *providing* aid are, for purposes of liability, considered officers or employees of the state *requesting* aid (see EMAC, 1996). Federal and state governments enjoy sovereign immunity from suit but, if waived, generally immunize government employees from liability for torts committed within their scope of employment, and instead allow the government to be held liable (see Prosser et al., 1984). Therefore, officers and employees, including providers who assist pursuant to the EMAC, have limited immunity for all acts and omissions (Prosser et al., 1984). The primary caveat in EMAC is that providers must be classified as officers or employees of the state providing aid to receive liability protections under EMAC. For example, if a registered nurse travels to a neighboring state to assist in a disaster, he or she cannot rely on liability protection through EMAC unless deemed an official officer or employee of the state providing the aid. Ambiguity over who is and who is not an officer or employee means that a provider assisting in an out-of-state disaster should not rely on EMAC protections unless they are certain it applies to their particular situation.

The Uniform Emergency Volunteer Health Practitioners Act (UEVHPA; 2007) is a recent development in state model legislation that seeks to address one of EMAC's primary shortcomings. Although EMAC only applies to medical professionals who enter into agreements with their home jurisdictions to be deployed during a disaster, UEVHPA seeks to provide liability protection to a wider array of medical professionals (Uniform Law Commission [ULC], 2006). UEVHPA requires that VHPs register with a preapproved registration system (ULC, 2006), and in the case of a disaster or emergency, a volunteer who has preregistered is able to work in a state that has adopted UEVHPA and enjoy limited immunity from civil liability (UEVHPA, 2007). However, only 12 states have adopted the model legislation thus far. In addition, not every state that has adopted UEVHPA has adopted the immunity provision for VHPs. As a result, UEVHPA is not yet a reliable source of civil liability protection for most VHPs.

Good Samaritan Statutes

Most states have enacted some form of a Good Samaritan law meant to encourage assistance in the case of an emergency by removing the threat of civil liability. Good Samaritan laws vary widely from state to state. In some states, Good Samaritan laws are very similar to disaster statutes that grant some degree of immunity from civil liability to providers assisting during publicly declared disasters. In other states, Good Samaritan laws do not explicitly recognize publicly declared disasters and are therefore less clear about whether they apply during a disaster, or whether they simply apply to situations such as car accidents and heart attacks. A lack of clarity about Good Samaritan statutes in these states means that it would be unwise for a provider to rely on immunity from civil liability by invoking such a statute.

The Good Samaritan laws in some states provide explicit immunity from civil liability for providers assisting in large-scale disasters. For example, the Florida Good Samaritan Act (FGSA; 2011) provides immunity to all persons rendering aid during an emergency. Specifically, state statute notes that

> [a]ny person, including those licensed to practice medicine, who gratuitously and in good faith renders emergency care . . . related to and arising out of a public health emergency . . . or at the scene of an emergency outside of a hospital, doctor's office, or other place having proper medical equipment . . . shall not be held liable for any civil damages as a result of such care or treatment . . . (FGSA, 2011)

However, many Good Samaritan laws do not explicitly mention public health emergencies and therefore seem to confine volunteer immunity to situations where medical professionals might stumble upon an emergency (FGSA, 2011). For example, Tennessee law provides limited immunity to any person, including licensed medical professionals, who render "emergency public first aid and rescue services" (Tennessee Good Samaritan Act, 1999). The law does not specify that immunity is limited to any particular type of emergency, but it also does not explicitly mention public health emergencies. Although the Tennessee law might provide broad immunity like the FGSA, it might as easily be confined to small emergencies on which a provider might stumble. In another example, Idaho law grants limited immunity to "any person who in good faith, being at, or stopping at the scene of an accident, offers and administers first aid or medical attention to any person or persons injured in such accident . . ." (Idaho Code Ann., 2011). The Idaho law does not specifically exclude large-scale disasters, but because the law refers to "stopping at" an accident, its language implies that it might only apply to small-scale emergencies such as car accidents or heart attacks. In a final example, Mississippi law grants limited immunity to licensed medical professionals who render care at the scene of an emergency or during transit to a medical facility (Miss. Code Ann., 2007). The language of the Mississippi law, like the Idaho law, might only apply to persons who stumble upon a small-scale emergency and attempt to help rather than persons who go to an emergency or large-scale disaster to render aid.

State Public Health and Emergency Management Provisions Affecting Provider Liability

Many states have specific statutory protections for providers assisting during a disaster, although the level of protection varies widely across jurisdictions. Some currently provide broad immunity from liability for providers who assist during declared disasters or emergencies, regardless of whether the provider holds a license in that state. In Illinois, for example, state law provides limited immunity for "disaster relief volunteers," which includes physicians, nurses, and other health professionals licensed in any state, who assist during a disaster or catastrophic event or within 10 days after the end of the event (Disaster Relief Volunteers, 2007). Similarly, in Indiana, medical professionals may not be held liable for acts or omissions related to providing health care services during an officially declared disaster or emergency so long as they are licensed in Indiana or any other state and so long as the person provides services that are within the scope of his or her license and at a location where medical services are being provided during the declared disaster or emergency (Ind. Code, 2006). Delaware has a comparable provision that provides limited immunity to "qualified medical personnel engaged in emergency or disaster relief operations or activities in connection with any emergency or disaster . . ." (Del. Code Ann., 2007). "Qualified medical personnel" includes all volunteers who participate in the response to an officially declared emergency (Del. Code Ann., 2007). The Delaware law also states that qualified medical personnel shall be indemnified by the state against any expenses incurred in defending a lawsuit that occurs as a result of a disaster (Del. Code Ann., 2007). Lastly, Montana provides immunity for volunteer civil defense workers (Mont. Code Ann., 2009). The term "civil defense workers" includes "volunteer professionals," which are defined as individuals with an unrestricted license to practice a profession in Montana or any other state (Mont. Code Ann., 2009).

Other states require some act in addition to an official disaster declaration for liability protections to become available to providers. For example, California law grants immunity to medical professionals licensed in any state who assist during a disaster or emergency so long as they help at the express or implied request of a government official (Cal. Gov't Code, 2010). As such, a declaration of disaster is not sufficient to activate the immunity provision for providers without the additional request by a government official. In Missouri, providers licensed in any state who agree to assist in the case of an emergency declared by the governor are granted limited immunity from liability from any acts or omissions, but the volunteers must first be approved by the state emergency management agency (Mo. Rev. Stat., 2007). Similarly, New Hampshire grants immunity to "emergency management workers," which include any volunteers engaged in emergency management work pursuant to a request by the state government or any of its political subdivisions (N.H. Rev. Stat. Ann., 2011). In Hawaii, providers who assist in disaster response are granted limited immunity for any acts or omissions so long as any authorized person accepted such services (Haw. Rev. Stat., 2002). Although the Hawaii law does not provide a definition for "authorized person," it is clear that an additional act is necessary after the initial declaration of emergency for protection to become available.

To summarize, the federal PREP Act provides liability protection to licensed health professionals administering countermeasures during a public health emergency declared by the U.S. Secretary of Health and Human Services. The federal VPA grants limited protection to volunteers assisting nonprofit organizations or government entities during disasters, whereas state VPAs vary in the degree of protection, either by shifting liability to providers' affiliated organizations or remaining silent on the issue of health care volunteers. Model legislation also exists, namely the EMAC, which effectively makes officers or employees of states providing aid, for purposes of liability, officers or employees of the state requesting aid; and the UEVHPA, which seeks to extend the compact's reach to a wider array of medical professionals, specifically those registered with a preapproved registration system. Finally, some state Good Samaritan laws may grant limited immunity to providers responding to publicly declared disasters. Similarly, state disaster-specific laws may grant broad protections for providers assisting during a declared disaster, regardless of their licensing state, although others may require some act in addition to an official declaration (e.g., government request, agency approval).

CONCLUSION

Crisis events place significant demands on health care providers, which may result in a perception of increased legal risk, particularly as care provided becomes qualitatively different from that which is provided under normal circumstances. Resource constraints, austere environments, and unusually large numbers of patients understandably create anxiety among providers; however, fear of civil liability should not because the process by which individuals are found to be responsible for injuries to others requires consideration of what a reasonably skillful and prudent provider would do in similarly situated circumstances. Moreover, several federal and state protections are afforded to those responding to disasters. Regardless of the opportunities and challenges created by these protections, professional liability will be decided against the relevant facts of the situation. Although many would prefer to limit this uncertainty, attempts to protect health care providers from liability must be informed, deliberate, and mindful of patients and citizens who need the greatest protection when disaster strikes.

REFERENCES

Agency for Healthcare Research and Quality, U.S. Department of Health and Human Services. (2005a). *Altered standards of care in mass casualty events 1*. Retrieved from http://www.ahrq.gov/research/altstand/altstand.pdf

Agency for Healthcare Research and Quality, U.S. Department of Health and Human Services. (2005b). *Altered standards of care in mass casualty events 3*. Retrieved from http://www.ahrq.gov/research/altstand/altstand.pdf

Agency for Healthcare Research and Quality, U.S. Department of Health and Human Services. (2005c). *Altered standards of c3are in mass casualty events 23–25*. Retrieved from http://www.ahrq.gov/research/altstand/altstand.pdf

Alexander, G. C., & Wynia, M. K. (2003). Ready and willing? Physicians' sense of preparedness for bioterrorism. *Health Affairs*, 22, 189–197.

American Bar Association. (2011). *Report to the House of Delegates resolution 125, 5*. Retrieved from http://www.americanbar.org/content/dam/aba/directories/policy/2011_am_125.authcheckdam.pdf

Annas, G. (2002). Bioterrorism, public health, and civil liberties. *New England Journal of Medicine*, 346, 1337–1342.

Annas, G. (2003). Blinded by bioterrorism: Public health and liberty in the 21st century. *Health Matrix*, 13, 33–70.

Annas, G. (2010). Standards of care—in sickness and in health and in emergencies. *New England Journal of Medicine*, 362, 2126–2131.

Annas, G., & Miller, F. (1994). The empire of death: How culture and economics affect informed consent in the U.S., the U.K., and Japan. *American Journal of Law and Medicine*, 20, 357–394.

Section 1135 of the Social Security Act, 42 U.S.C. § 1320b-5 (2010).

Barnett, D. J., Balicer, R. D., Blodgett, D. W., Everly, G. S., Jr., Omer, S. B., Parker, C. L., & Links, J. M. (2005). Applying risk perception theory to public health workforce preparedness training. *Journal of Public Health Management and Practice*, 11, 33–37.

Cal. Gov't Code § 8659 (West, 2010).

Campbell v. Kessler, 848 So.2d 369, 371 (Fl. 4th Dist. Ct. App., 2003).

Del. Code. Ann. tit. 20, § 3129 (2007).

DiMaggio, C. (2005). The willingness of U.S. emergency medical technicians to respond to terrorist incidents. *Biosecurity & Bioterrorism*, 3, 331–337.

Disaster Relief Volunteers, 745 Ill. Comp. Stat. 49/68 (2007).

Emergency Management Assistance Compact, Pub. L. No. 104-321, 110 Stat. 3877 (1996). Retrieved from http://frwebgate.access.gpo.gov/cgi-bin/getdoc.cgi?dbname=104_cong_public_laws&docid=f:publ321.104.pdf

Fink, S. (2009, August 25). The deadly choices at Memorial. *New York Times*. Retrieved from http://www.nytimes.com/2009/08/30/magazine/30doctorshtml?_r=1&pagewanted=all

Florida Good Samaritan Act, Fla. Stat. § 768.13 (2011).

Florida Volunteer Protection Act, Fla. Stat. § 768.1355 (2011).

Georgetown University and Johns Hopkins University, Center for Law and the Public's Health at Georgetown University and Johns Hopkins University. (2001a). The Model State Emergency Health Powers Act 33.

Georgetown University and Johns Hopkins University, Center for Law and the Public's Health at Georgetown University and Johns Hopkins University. (2001b). The Model State Emergency Health Powers Act 37–38.

Gostin, L. O., Hanfling, D., Hodge, J. G., Jr., Courtney, B., Hick, J. L., & Peterson, C. A. (2010). Standards of care—in sickness and in health and in emergencies [Letter to the editor]. *The New England Journal of Medicine, 363*(14), 1378–1379.

Haw. Rev. Stat. § 128-18 (2002).

Health Insurance Portability and Accountability Act, Pub. L. No. 104-191, 110 Stat. 1936 (1996).

Hodge, J. G., Jr. (2006). Law and the public's health. *Public Health Reports, 121*, 205–208. Retrieved from http://www.publichealthreports.org/issuecontents.cfm?Volume=121&Issue=2

Hodge, J. G., Jr., & Gostin, L. O. (2002a). *The model state emergency health powers act—a brief commentary 3*. Retrieved from http://www.public healthlaw.net/MSEHPA/Center%20MSEHPA%20 Commentary.pdf

Hodge, J. G., Jr., & Gostin, L. O. (2002b). *The model state emergency health powers act—a brief commentary 9*. Retrieved from http://www.publichealthlaw.net/MSEHPA/Center%20 MSEHPA%20 Commentary.pdf

Hodge, J. G., Jr., & Gostin, L. O. (2002c). *The model state emergency health powers act—a brief commentary 10*. Retrieved from http://www.public healthlaw.net/MSEHPA/Center%20MSEHPA%20 Commentary.pdf

Hoffman, S. (2008). Responders' responsibility: Liability and immunity in public health emergencies. *Georgetown Law Journal, 96*, 1913–1969.

Idaho Code Ann. § 5-330 (2011).

Ind. Code § 34-30-4-2 (2005).

Ind. Code § 34-30-13.5-1 (2006).

Institute of Medicine. (1990). *Clinical practice guidelines: Directions for a new program 8*. Washington, DC: National Academies Press. Retrieved from http://www.nap.edu/openbook.php?record_ id=1626&page=R1

Institute of Medicine. (2009a). *Guidance for establishing crisis standards of care for use in disaster situations: A letter report 1*. Washington, DC: National Academies Press. Retrieved from http://www.nap.edu/openbook.php? record_ id=12749&page=R1

Institute of Medicine. (2009b). *Guidance for establishing crisis standards of care for use in disaster situations: A letter report 10*. Washington, DC: National Academies Press. Retrieved from http://www.nap.edu/openbook.php? record_id=12749&page=R1

Institute of Medicine. (2009c). *Guidance for establishing crisis standards of care for use in disaster situations: A letter report 18*. Washington, DC: National Academies Press. Retrieved from http://www.nap.edu/openbook.php? record_id=12749&page=R1

Institute of Medicine. (2009d). *Guidance for establishing crisis standards of care for use in disaster situations: A letter report 20*. Washington, DC: National Academies Press. Retrieved from http://www.nap.edu/openbook.php? record_id=12749&page=R1

Institute of Medicine. (2009e). *Guidance for establishing crisis standards of care for use in disaster situations: A letter report 28*. Washington, DC: National Academies Press. Retrieved from http://www.nap.edu/openbook.php? record_id=12749&page=R1

Institute of Medicine. (2009f). *Guidance for establishing crisis standards of care for use in disaster situations: A letter report 40*. Washington, DC: National Academies Press. Retrieved from http://www.nap.edu/openbook.php? record_id=12749&page=R1

Institute of Medicine. (2009g). *Guidance for establishing crisis standards of care for use in disaster situations: A letter report 47*. Washington, DC: National Academies Press. Retrieved from http://www.nap.edu/openbook.php? record_id=12749&page=R1

Institute of Medicine. (2009h). *Guidance for establishing crisis standards of care for use in disaster situations: A letter report 49–50*. Washington, DC: National Academies Press. Retrieved from http://www.nap.edu/openbook.php? record_id=12749&page=R1

Institute of Medicine. (2009i). *Guidance for establishing crisis standards of care for use in disaster situations: A letter report 75*. Washington, DC: National Academies Press. Retrieved from http://www.nap.edu/openbook.php? record_id=12749&page=R1

Institute of Medicine. (2009j). *Guidance for establishing crisis standards of care for use in disaster situations: A letter report 89–90*. Washington, DC: National Academies Press. Retrieved from http://www.nap.edu/openbook.php? record_id=12749&page=R1

Institute of Medicine. (2012a). *Crisis standards of care: A systems framework for catastrophic disaster response 14–15*. Washington, DC: National Academies Press. Retrieved from http://www.iom.edu/Reports/2012/Crisis-Standards-of-Care-A-Systems-Framework-for-Catastrophic-Disaster-Response.aspx

Institute of Medicine. (2012b). *Crisis standards of care: A systems framework for catastrophic disaster response 59*. Washington, DC: National Academies Press. Retrieved from http://www.iom.edu/Reports/2012/Crisis-Standards-of-Care-A-Systems-Framework-for-Catastrophic-Disaster-Response.aspx

Institute of Medicine. (2012c). *Crisis standards of care: A systems framework for catastrophic disaster response 64*. Washington, DC: National Academies Press. Retrieved from http://www.iom.edu/Reports/2012/Crisis-Standards-of-Care-A-Systems-Framework-for-Catastrophic-Disaster-Response.aspx

Institute of Medicine. (2012d). *Crisis standards of care: A systems framework for catastrophic disaster response 69*. Washington, DC: National Academies Press. Retrieved from http://www.iom.edu/Reports/2012/Crisis-Standards-of-Care-A-Systems-Framework-for-Catastrophic-Disaster-Response.aspx

Institute of Medicine. (2012e). *Crisis standards of care: A systems framework for catastrophic disaster response 70*. Washington, DC: National Academies Press. Retrieved from http://www.iom.edu/Reports/2012/Crisis-Standards-of-Care-A-Systems-Framework-for-Catastrophic-Disaster-Response.aspx

Iserson, K. V., Heine, C. E., Larkin, G. L., Moskop, J. C., Baruch, J., & Aswegan, A. L. (2008). Fight or flight: The ethics of emergency physician disaster response. *Annals of Emergency Medicine, 51*, 345–353.

Lindsay, B. R. (2008). *The emergency management assistance compact (EMAC): An overview* (CRS Report RL 34585).

Miss. Code Ann. § 73-25-37 (2007).

Mo. Rev. Stat. § 44.045 (2007).

Mont. Code Ann. § 10-3-111 (2009).

N.H. Rev. Stat. Ann. § 21-P:41 (2011).

Nonprofit Risk Management Center. (2009). *State liability laws for charitable organizations and volunteers*. Retrieved from http://nonprofitrisk.org/ downloads/state-liability.pdf

Prosser, W. L., Dobbs, D. B., Keeton, W. P., & Keeton, R. E. (1984). *Prosser and Keeton on torts*. St. Paul, MN: West.

Public Readiness and Emergency Preparedness Act, Pub. L. No. 109-148, 119 Stat. 2818 (2005) (codified at 42 U.S.C. 247d-6d).

Qureshi, K., Gershon, R. R., Sherman, M. F., Straub, T., Gebbie, E., McCollum, M., . . . Morse, S. S. (2005). Healthcare workers' ability and willingness to report to duty during catastrophic disasters. *Journal of Urban Health, 82*(3), 378–388.

Ray, J. (2009). Office of the General Counsel, Department of Health and Human Services. *Federal public health emergency: Implications for state and local preparedness and response*. Retrieved from http://www2a.cdc.gov/phlp/webinar_04_29_2009.asp

Rowe v. Sisters of Pallottine Missionary Soc'y, 211 W. Va. 16, 560 S.E.2d 491 (2001).

Tennessee Good Samaritan Act, Tenn. Code Ann. § 63-6-218 (1999).

Uniform Emergency Volunteer Health Practitioners Act, § 11 (2007).

Uniform Law Commission. (2006). *Emergency volunteer health practitioners summary*. Retrieved from http://uniformlaws.org/ActSummary.aspx?title =Emergency Volunteer Health Practitioners

University of Louisville School of Medicine, Institute for Bioethics, Health Policy and Law. (2003). *Quarantine and isolation: Lessons learned from SARS: A report for the center of disease control and prevention*. Retrieved from http://www.iaclea.org/members/pdfs/SARS%20REPORT.Rothstein.pdf

Volunteer Protection Act of 1997, 42 U.S.C. §§ 14501-14505 (2006).

Volunteer Protection Act. Ariz. Rev. Stat. Ann. § 12-982 (1997).

Weinberger v. Boyer, 956 N.E.2d 1095, 1111 (Ind. Ct. App. 2011) transfer denied, 963 N.E.2d 1122 (Ind. 2012).

CHAPTER 5

Psychological Impact of Disasters on Communities

Sharon A. R. Stanley, Susan Bulecza, and Sameer Vali Gopalani

ABSTRACT

Disaster mental health is defined as "community and individual mental and behavioral health preparedness and response as well as other psychosocial and cultural factors" (Hoffman et al., 2005, p. S141). The research included in this review was published between 2000 and 2011, capturing a snapshot of the last decade of relevant research on the psychological impact of disaster. The conceptual framework used to examine the research involves a population-based approach based on primary, secondary, and tertiary prevention levels. Aspects of conducting mental health research, to include evidence-based approaches and disaster mental health outcome measurements postdisaster, are also included. The authors conclude the review by presenting implications and future recommendations for nursing practice and research related to the psychological impact of disasters on communities.

INTRODUCTION

Disaster mental health is defined as "community and individual mental and behavioral health preparedness and response as well as other psychosocial and cultural factors" (Hoffman et al., 2005, p. S141). Disaster mental health is a comparatively new science in the field of disaster response. Hurricane Katrina in 2005 appears to be the decade's hallmark event that solidified disaster mental health's ongoing inclusion into response and research efforts. Research into psychological impact of trauma can be traced to the early 20th century with World War I veterans. World War II research outcomes provided services to the affected service members that were most often grounded in psychoanalytic approaches and focused on preexisting psychiatric conditions (Morris, 2011). It took until the 1970s for a second generation of research, this time focused on natural disasters, to make its appearance. Morris (2011) theorizes that it was the community mental health movement in the 1960s that drove this expansion, along with ongoing research from World War II. Mental health advocates gained ground with arguments for community-based prevention and care versus the traditional model of institutional care. The Community Mental Health Act of 1963 resulted in a broader view of orienting mental health services toward populations in general and those with less debilitating psychological problems.

Pilot mental health programs to address three devastating floods in 1972 paved the way for national disaster mental health relief policy. The Disaster Relief Act of 1974 authorized the U.S. National Institutes of Mental Health (NIMH) to supply counseling services to victims of disasters and provided training to disaster workers in professional counseling (Morris, 2011). Research into the efficiency and effectiveness of those services followed as a natural progression. Subsequent attempts, however, to define, develop, assess, plan, implement, and evaluate disaster mental health services has not been an easy 40-year path.

LITERATURE REVIEW METHODOLOGY
Search Criteria and Review Process

An extensive literature review was conducted in numerous research databases to include the Cochrane Database of Systematic Reviews, PubMed, CINAHL, PsycInfo, Google Scholar, and many others including the grey literature. An example demonstrating the search strategy is outlined in the following discussion. In the PubMed database, compiled by the U.S. National Library of Medicine, a literature search using Boolean operators was performed with the MeSH topic *natural disaster* and MeSH terms *classification, economics, history, legislation and jurisprudence, methods, nursing, prevention and control, psychology, statistics and numerical data*. These terms were added to the search builder along with the following terms: *mental health* and *psychological issues*. It was essential to use all the terms mentioned previously to include a comprehensive search of every possible article addressing the various issues. Results from the search with different key terms are provided in Table 5.1.

TABLE 5.1

Search Terminology Used in the Research Databases and Relevant Results

Search Terms	Cochrane Database of Systematic Reviews	PubMed	Google Scholar	CINAHL	PsycINFO
Disaster mental health	OR: 1[a] CT: 10 MS: 1 EE: 1	1281 (R: 158)	77,300	55	831
Disaster mental health and psychological issues	OR: 4 CT: 10 TA: 1 CG: 1	42 (R: 9)	21,600	4	291
Disaster mental health and nursing	CT: 2 CR: 7	92 (R: 19)	18,000	89	95
Disaster psychosocial issues and nursing	CT: 2 CR: 7	12 (R: 3)	16,400	0	16
Psychological first aid	CR: 12 CT: 37	189 (R: 30)	407,000	13	219
Psychological first aid and nursing	CR: 7 CT: 3	44 (R: 3)	28,200	1	18
Disaster psychological first aid and nursing	0	13 (R: 1)	11,200	0	5
Psychosocial disaster and nursing	CT: 1	40 (R: 9)	5,670	0	19
Triage and mental health and disaster	CR: 1	45 (R: 5)	6,410	1	17
Resiliency (Psychological Resilience) and mental health and disaster	CR: 1	11 (R: 3)	16,300	2	41
Resistance and mental health and disaster	CR: 3	7 (R: 1)	25,700	2	17
Debriefing and mental health and disaster	CR: 2 OR: 2 TA: 1 CG: 1	17 (R: 4)	8,490	6	91

Note. OR = other reviews; CT = clinical trials; MS = method studies; EE = economic evaluations; CG = Cochrane groups; CR = Cochrane reviews; TA = technology assessment; R = review article.
[a] Inter-Agency Standing Committee. (2008). *Mental health and psychosocial support in emergency settings: Checklist for field use.* Geneva, Switzerland: IASC. Retrieved from http://www.who.int/mental_health/emergencies/IASC_guidelines.pdf

Inclusion and Exclusion Criteria

The articles that were included within this review were all published between 2000 and 2011, capturing a snapshot of the last decade of relevant research on the psychological impact of disaster. All published literature was in the English language and included articles from across the globe, including those from the non–English-speaking nations. For purposes of this review, peer-reviewed journal articles were included and unpublished manuscripts, dissertations, and conference papers were excluded. Most literature was available from the four research databases highlighted previously. A few articles, however, emerged from the selected articles reference listings and a few other relevant databases. Most certainly, there are studies that we did not cover. We do believe, however, that the included articles are a representative sample of the last decade's research given the search methodologies used.

RESEARCH OVERVIEW

Conducting Disaster Mental Health Research

Sampling, Design, and Methodology Challenges

Researchers face multiple challenges when designing and implementing disaster mental health studies. One of the first challenges involves is defining the population of interest in the middle of chaos. Understandably, researchers want to assess all of those affected by an incident to confidently generalize study results, but who are those individuals and groups? Galea, Maxwell, and Norris (2008) explore some of these challenges by asking the following questions: Are all the persons in the affected area "affected"? Is it only those with property damage? If there is property damage, how much damage will include them in the sampling frame? What about those with physical injury? What about minor injuries? and What about life threat or perceived life threat? In addition, the sampling frame must be rapidly established to produce consistent implementation. Neria, Nandi, and Galea (2008) identify the need for substantial progress in all areas of disaster mental health measurement, follow-up time frames, and sampling procedures to ensure reliable estimates of postdisaster psychopathology and study comparisons (e.g., by population, by time frame, or by type of disaster).

The next challenge is *finding* persons after defining the population of interest. There are numerous reasons why this is so: breakdown in typical communication mechanisms, evacuation, and individuals who are otherwise preoccupied by reestablishing links with family and significant others, reengaging employment, and rebuilding permanent shelter who are not willing to participate in studies (especially in the immediate and short-term postevent period).

Disasters are too unpredictable to plan for research with few exceptions, forcing the research field into postincident studies (only) for the most part (Kessler, Keane, Ursano, Mokdad, & Zaslavsky, 2008). This unpredictability, of course, means having to rely on postincident-only design. Cross-sectional designs can optimize study design, but most published studies do not take advantage of this linkage (Galea et al., 2008).

How long is long enough for a study to determine the psychological impact of disaster and would these impacts be short-term, long-term, or somewhere in-between? What about the individual's preexisting mental health status? These questions are especially germane when researchers are trying to determine incidence and prevalence of postincident mental health conditions like posttraumatic stress disorder (PTSD). Long-term studies remain extremely difficult to conduct in the United States without electronic medical records. In the Netherlands, Dorn, Yzermans, Spreeuwenberg, Schilder, and van der Zee (2008) were able to follow a cohort of adult trauma survivors for 4 years after a devastating community fire, with full access to prefire mental health baselines. Den Ouden et al. (2007) used electronic medical records from survivors of the same disaster to study predisposing factors in individual use of mental health services. After the 2004 tsunami, a group of more than 3,400 Swedish survivors vacationing in Southeast Asia were assessed for mental health impact 3 years after the event by tracking their return airport registrations (Johannesson, Lundin, Fröjd, Hultman, & Michel, 2011).

Recognizing the complexity involved in disaster mental health research, the U.S. Substance Abuse and Mental Health Services Administration (SAMHSA) formed a task force in 2004 and developed a model study design and interview protocol for use in postdisaster mental health needs assessment surveys (Kessler, Keane, et al., 2008). The SAMHSA protocol was piloted and revised in conjunction with Hurricane Katrina in 2005. Also, the U.S. NIMH has established a center to implement postdisaster mental health needs, assessment surveys, and integrated study measures and designs.

Conceptual Frameworks

Davydov, Stewart, Ritchie, and Chaudieu (2010) call for better concept definition, and community-based models to help establish disaster mental health research. One such framework is cited by Grigg (2009; see Figure 5.1).

This population-based model defines support for psychological impact from disaster where (starting at the bottom of the pyramid)

1. The foundation for population well-being rests in the reestablishment of security, governance, and services that include mental health services.
2. A smaller aggregate is assisted to maintain mental health and psychosocial support well-being via key family and community support access.

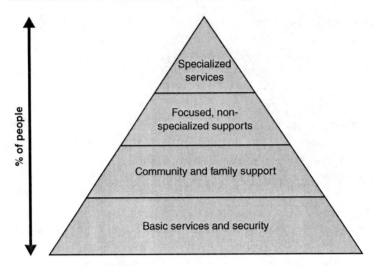

FIGURE 5.1 Intervention pyramid for mental health and psychosocial support in emergencies. Adapted from Inter-Agency Standing Committee. (2008). *Mental health and psychosocial support: Checklist for field use*. Geneva, Switzerland: Author. Retrieved from http://www.who.int/mental_health/emergencies/IASC_guidelines.pdf.

3. Support to a yet smaller segment of the population focuses on individual, family, or group interventions by trained, supervised workers (e.g., Psychological First Aid [PFA]).
4. A small percentage of the population experiencing significant problems in daily functioning and who will require psychological and psychiatric support receive services from professionally trained providers.

Given a lack of a consistent conceptual framework approach for disaster mental health, Yamashita (2011) maintains that many studies investigating relationships between disaster exposure and mental health impact over the past several decades have examined invalid combinations of psychosocial factors, producing inconsistent results. He advocates using the field of stress studies and its conceptual frameworks to rethink and redirect future mental health research.

Key Research by Nurses and Others

Nurse led or nursing implication–specific disaster mental health research is not a strong area of publication for nurse scholars. Nurse research was found in our literature review, however. Publications fell into categories of nurses as disaster workers and psychological impact (Broussard & Myers, 2010; Broussard, Myers, & Meaux, 2008; Walsh, 2009), school settings (Broussard & Myers, 2010; Broussard et al., 2008; Woolsey & Bracy, 2010), and emergency settings in nondisaster environments (Clarke, Brown, Hughes, & Motluk, 2006; Kim, Plumb, Gredig, Rankin, & Taylor, 2008).

The absolute necessity of nurse involvement in community-based approaches for population-based mental health postdisaster is clearly supported by the literature. Disaster mental health research has established that psychological casualties after a disaster outnumber physical casualties. This outcome is of special concern given the usual shortage of mental health professionals in the postdisaster environment. Nurses, as the largest group of health professional providers, are identified by Everly, Barnett, Sperry, and Links (2010) as particularly well-suited to assume a leadership role in mental health service expansion beyond mental health clinicians. Numerous publications address the essential primary prevention and early screening nature of population-based nursing practice when working with communities affected by disaster (Broussard & Myers, 2010; Hughes, Grigg, Fritsch, & Calder, 2007; Murray, 2006; Walsh, 2009; Wynaden et al., 2003).

Norris et al. (2002) and Norris, Friedman, and Watson (2002) published a two-part landmark study—"60,000 Disaster Victims Speak"—based on two decades of disaster mental health research (i.e., 1981–2001). It is a meta-analysis of research involving more than 60,000 individuals and 160 study samples. The studies were coded by sample type, disaster type, disaster location, observed outcomes, and severity of impairment postincident. Norris, Friedman, and Watson (2002) recommend specific early intervention following disasters based on the risk factors and adverse outcome, clearly identifying the sociocultural environment of the individual and groups involved as necessary to understanding and meeting psychosocial needs in the community postdisaster.

Norris (2005) went on to update that review, increasing the sample from 160 to 225 using more than 132 incidents between 1981 and 2004. In addition, Fran Norris has authored a large body of work in disaster mental health field, and numerous of her publications are referenced in this chapter (e.g., Jones, Allen, Norris, & Miller, 2009; Norris & Alegria, 2005; Norris, Hamblen, & Rosen, 2009; Norris, Stevens, Pfefferbaum, Wyche, & Pfefferbaum, 2008; Rosen, Greene, Young, & Norris, 2010).

Another group of authors have established an evidence-informed model to generate an outcome-driven paradigm for disaster mental health services to address psychological impact. The model, *The Johns Hopkins Perspectives Model of Disaster Mental Health*, involves intervention elements related to resistance and recovery (Kaminsky, McCabe, Langlieb, & Everly, 2007). The group believes that their intervention model is unlike previous work in that it is designed to achieve focus on clinically meaningful outcome measurements such as clinician-rated depression symptoms; other disease-specific measures relating to the underlying condition of PTSD; and postdisaster mental health service use, something that they have identified as missing (Everly et al., 2010; Everly, Beaton, Pfefferbaum, & Parker, 2008; Everly, Phillips, Kane, & Feldman, 2006; Hoffman et al., 2005; Nucifora, Langlieb, Siegal, Everly, & Kaminsky, 2007; Perrin, McCabe, Everly, & Links, 2009).

GUIDING CONCEPTS FOR DISASTER MENTAL HEALTH

Research into the psychological impact of disasters on communities over the last decade demonstrates an increasing trend in population-based approaches. Also, research reveals an understanding that mental health professionals/licensed practitioners will initially be in short supply, and most likely not be on site in the early response phase of disaster. There is evidence-based data that community members themselves can make a measurable difference in the early stages of a disaster incident, given advanced preparation and training.

Recent research underscores the need for a tiered community approach, where psychological disruption is viewed as normal in immediate aftermath of disaster, with a concurrent belief that community mental health wellness will return in time for most (Figure 5.1). Most of those affected recover relatively quickly based on the personal and community resistance and resilience, appropriate population-based interventions, and community assistance that rebuilds and stabilizes predisaster existence into a new normal.

Parallels to the disaster cycle of preparedness, response, recovery, mitigation, risk reduction, and prevention can help to understand the distinction among resistance, resilience, and recovery. Recovery, indeed, must be considered separate from resilience (Nucifora et al., 2007; Weissbecker, Sephton, Martin, & Simpson, 2008). Although resistance may be thought of aligning with the preparedness and prevention phases of disaster and resilience with the response phase, recovery aligns with the disaster cycle phases of recovery, mitigation, and risk reduction, with successful acclimation to the new normal postdisaster.

The recent research into disaster mental health downplays psychotrauma approaches early on, leveraging primary prevention (e.g., community resilience education) and secondary prevention (e.g., use of early population-based mental health triage tools) strategies (Everly et al., 2010; Kaminsky et al., 2007; Nucifora et al., 2007; Paton, Smith, & Violanti, 2000). Early identification of those that cannot be helped with population-based intervention, of course, remains a critical factor in disaster mental health. Also, those that will need mental health intervention (tertiary prevention) must receive it as soon as possible to prevent ongoing issues and complications related to disaster impact on psychological well-being. Davidson and McFarlane (2006) assert that disasters invite a public health approach to mental health, stating that this approach better serves both the needs of the affected community and the individual. Resistance, resilience, and recovery concepts are better understood in a population-based effort.

Population-Based Wellness versus Individually Focused Disease

Norris et al. (2008) believe that the word *resilience* is a metaphor for effective and adaptive community function postdisaster. Community resilience, then, is manifested in population wellness, defined as "high and non-disparate levels of mental and behavioral health, functioning, and quality of life" (Norris et al., 2008, p. 127). A population-based approach to disaster mental health involves protecting lives, reducing injuries, minimizing damage to public utilities, and connecting community members to necessary services and others. Norris et al. (2008) and Perrin et al. (2009) maintain that wellness levels in the community can be monitored with postdisaster needs assessments and surveillance initiatives to more accurately guide resource allocation.

Ghodse and Galea (2006) divide their post–Asian tsunami study population into three categories of survivors to better understand mental health consequences in an environment of unprecedented response: (a) Class I—survivors with mild psychological distress that will resolve in days to weeks; (b) Class II—survivors with moderate/severe distress that resolves with time or mild chronic distress; and (c) Class III—survivors with mental disorders—mild, moderate, or severe (i.e., those who will need recovery level interventions; Figure 5.2).

In determining mental health policy in the aftermath of disasters, Weiss, Saraceno, Saxena, and Van Ommeren (2003) call for clinical and social interventions that address a wide range of psychosocial impact and mental health problems rather than a sole preoccupation with PTSD (i.e., individual illness). Research related to a community exposed to three wildfires in a 1-year period showed a strong buffering role for communal coping (Afifi, Felix, & Afifi, 2011). Specifically, targeting community information and intervention through PSAs, news programs, and disaster programs with the affected population resulted in buffering the effects of uncertainty and their impact on recovery for evacuees in the study population. Davidson and McFarlane (2006) come to the conclusion that a public health approach to disaster events, with the intent to mitigate the effects of disaster before serious and lasting psychopathology occurs (i.e., primary and secondary prevention in public health), is an absolute necessity. Even those who focus on individual approaches (e.g., psychiatrists not used to dealing with disaster or population-based interventions) must ensure a community-based approach early on (López-Ibor, 2006).

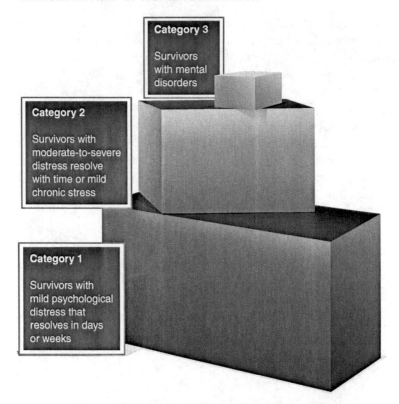

FIGURE 5.2 Population-based categories of survivors. Staging for use of mental health professional providers should be most associated with Categories 2 and 3 as opposed to Category 1 services provided by individuals with mental health training (e.g., Psychological First Aid [PFA] or nonmental health professionals). Adapted from Ghodse, H., & Galea, S. (2006). Tsunami: Understanding mental health consequences and the unprecedented response. *International Review of Psychiatry, 18*(3), 289–297.

Resistance and Resilience

Nucifora et al. (2007, p. S34) define resistance as "the ability of an individual, a group, an organization, or even an entire population to withstand manifestations of clinical distress, impairment, or dysfunction associated with critical incidents, terrorism, and even mass disasters." They compare resistance to a form of psychological immunity, equivalent to vaccination. Davydov et al. (2010) also compare this mental health protection to somatic multilevel protection and immunity models. Resistance, as defined previously, parallels the concept of human hardiness (Bonanno, 2004). Resistance building, then, compels groups and communities to take proactive steps to prepare for the reality of unfortunate events.

"Enhancing resistance . . . of the target population [ostensibly any community or aggregate] may achieve this goal" (Nucifora et al., 2007, p. 34). The authors argue that this primary prevention element of disaster mental health has been conspicuous in its absence, citing four potential interventions for both resistance and resilience: (a) realistic preparation provision, (b) promoting group cohesion and social support, (c) fostering positive cognitions, and (d) building self-efficacy and hardiness.

Resilience has been defined as the ability of an individual, a group, an organization, or population to rapidly and effectively rebound from psychological and/or behavioral disturbances postdisaster incident (Kaminsky et al., 2007). Norris et al. (2008) define community resilience as a process linking a network of adaptive capacities (resources with dynamic attributes) to adaptation after a disturbance or adversity. Four primary sets of adaptive capacities provide a strategy for disaster readiness: (a) economic development, (b) social capital, (c) information and communication, and (d) community competence. In her work, she defines community resilience as both a theory and an intervention strategy (Norris et al., 2008).

Studies focused on predictors of psychological resilience in communities focus on factors that promote or deter resilience. These factors affect the psychological impact of disaster and determine mental health intervention approaches postincident. Bonanno, Galea, Bucciarelli, and Vlahov (2007) examined patterns of association between resilience and various sociocontextual factors in the New York City area after September 11, 2001, finding that the resilience prevalence could be uniquely predicted by study participant gender, age, race/ethnicity, education, level of trauma exposure, income change, social support, frequency of chronic disease, and recent and past stressors. Other research supports findings that preincident status of both the individual and the community plays a major role in "bounce back" ability (Broussard & Myers, 2010; Den Ouden et al., 2007; Fox, White, Rooney, & Cahill, 2010; Harville et al., 2011; Horan et al., 2007; Johannesson et al., 2011; Rhodes et al., 2010; Roberts, Mitchell, Witman, & Taffaro, 2010; Ronan et al., 2008).

Another interesting finding in the research literature involves the application of appropriate social developmental phases when addressing resistance and resilience predisaster and postdisaster incidents. For example, Weissbecker et al. (2008) discuss protective factors and their role in buffering children against mental health consequences of disasters with the use of cross-cultural perspectives. Masten and Obradovic (2008) propose that decades of human development research can help prepare societies for major disaster when it is integrated with human research on resilience.

Recovery

Kaminsky et al. (2007, p. 5) define recovery as the ability ". . . to literally recover the ability to adaptively function, both psychologically and behaviorally, in the wake of a significant clinical distress, impairment, or dysfunction subsequent to critical incidents, terrorism, and even mass disasters." Bonanno (2004) calls for the distinction of recovery and resilience concepts.

Studies focused on disaster trauma impact tend to concentrate on PTSD, estimating population prevalence for PTSD diagnostic criteria and individual need for professional intervention in the recovery phase. The most frequently used PTSD prevalence outcome in current postdisaster research is 30%–40%, although the actual percentage of those affected and needing individualized and/ or group intervention, however, remains in question. PTSD prevalence rate estimates vary widely (40.0%–44.6%) based on the study's sample size, the disaster type, and the research methods employed to include assessment tools (Davidson & McFarlane, 2006; Neria et al., 2008). Adding to the complexity of identifying the need of recovery interventions is the comorbidity of other postdisaster psychopathology in addition to PTSD such as depression and anxiety disorders (Davidson & McFarlane, 2006; Meewisse, Olff, Kleber, Kitchiner, & Gersons, 2011; Norris et al., 2002; Weissbecker et al., 2008).

To assist in recovery, current research recommends addressing three fundamental concepts in psychotherapy (Kaminsky et al., 2007):

1. Establish a sense of control—Individuals learn to master and own their experiences, establishing a sense of safety and control to include approaching memories of the experience.
2. Decondition fear—Individuals learn to decondition the fear and anxiety related to the traumatic memories themselves, to include an understanding of the past and the role he or she played without self-blame for failure to prevent the trauma.
3. Reestablish integrity and control—Individuals find a feeling of personal integrity and control by "making sense" of his or her life to include the provision of future hope.

PSYCHOLOGICAL IMPACT

The key works by Norris and colleagues (2008), discussed previously, have provided a strong foundation for understanding how diversely a population can be impacted by a disaster as well as how the different types of disasters influence the psychological outcomes of affected populations. Variability of impact is correlated with the degree of individual exposure to the disaster event as well as type of event. Norris, Friedman, and Watson (2002) identified psychological outcomes that could be classified into six general categories—(a) specific psychological problems, (b) nonspecific distress, (c) health problems and concerns, (d) chronic problems in living, (e) psychosocial resource loss, and (f) problems specific to youth. In addition, their review found populations experiencing mass violence-type disasters (e.g., Oklahoma City bombing) were more likely to have severe to very severe psychological impacts compared to natural or technological disasters.

An area in which there is sparse information about mental health consequences is biological events either naturally occurring such as severe acute respiratory syndrome (SARS) or an intentional terrorist act like the anthrax letters. Perrin et al. (2009) state that

> although people may be facing the same fears and unknown health risk during any given epidemic, there are considerable individual differences in the extent of anxiety and coping strategies used. Furthermore, the anxiety level and coping strategies of individuals can change over the life-course of the epidemic. (p. 224)

Depending on the type of event, biological events can also result in stigmatization, marginalization, and/or unnecessary restriction of affected groups, which increase the risk of adverse mental health consequences. In addition, biological events can generate behavioral and psychological actions such as paranoia and health care service surge that can be disruptive to community stability (Perrin et al., 2009).

Severity of exposure has been measured at the individual and community level, and generally focuses on accumulation of stressors as measures of severity. Although there was significant measurement variability in studies, there were greater and more lasting negative consequences to mental health for individuals with injury, threat to life stressors, and extreme personal loss stressors, especially when coupled with high community destruction (Norris et al., 2002). The authors also found gender, age, ethnicity, socioeconomic status, family factors, secondary stressors, predisaster functioning, and psychosocial resources were factors in increasing risk of adverse consequences or to be protective. An important caveat is the interactive relationship of these factors is complex and depending on the event may modify, confound, or mediate one or more of others (Norris et al., 2002).

Mental Health Consequences

Time is a significant variable in development of mental health consequences. Studies have found that most affected individuals will experience a short-term stress reaction to the disaster because of individual and community disruption but recover in a short period after the disaster (Ghodse & Galea, 2006; Meewisse et al., 2011; Norris, 2005). The most prevalent mental health disorders occurring after disasters are PTSD, depression, and generalized anxiety disorder (Meewisse et al., 2011; Norris et al., 2002).

Posttraumatic Stress Disorder

PTSD prevalence has been found generally to be 30%–40% of directly impacted disaster victims. Type of disaster does influence these percentages with the lowest prevalence in natural disasters and the highest in man-made disasters (Neria et al., 2008). Degree of physical injury, immediate risk of life, severity of property destruction and fatality frequency has been documented in the disaster literature as consistent PTSD predictors. Development of PTSD is thought to be an abnormal resolution of acute stress response and is considered as a relevant diagnosis greater than 4 weeks postdisaster exposure. Rhoads, Pearman, and Rick (2007) suggest individuals in disasters go through distinct phases before being diagnosed with PTSD.

PTSD symptoms that resolve within 3 months are considered acute PTSD and symptoms that continue for more than 3 months is considered chronic PTSD. Although very rare following disasters, delayed onset PTSD, symptoms develop at least 6 months after exposure, can occur (Foa, Stein, & McFarlane, 2006). Several long-term follow-up studies have validated that there is significant decline in PTSD rates after initial diagnosis (Johannesson et al., 2011; Meewisse et al., 2011; Van der Velden et al., 2006). In addition, studies have identified factors that increase risk for PTSD development (Foa et al., 2006) and factors that decrease risk (Rhoads et al., 2007). However, it is still problematic to determine which risk factors or a combination of risk factors are accurate predictors of potential PTSD development.

There is also a high degree of comorbidity associated with PTSD. Major depression is the most common comorbid condition with generalized anxiety disorder, the second most frequent comorbid condition (Norris et al., 2006). Meewisse et al. (2011) found that survivors with PTSD alone had significantly faster recoveries than those with PTSD and one or more comorbid conditions.

Depression and Anxiety

Assessment of depression following disasters is not as prevalent (Meewisse et al., 2011). Persons with a history of depression prior to a disaster are at risk for developing PTSD. Depression combined with PTSD has a synergistic effect resulting in more severe symptoms and decreased functioning as well as delayed remission of symptoms (Foa et al., 2006).

Generalized anxiety disorder more often is the primary diagnosis with PTSD developing afterward when it is the comorbid condition (Foa et al., 2006).

Sparse data is available about anxiety prevalence following disasters independent of its comorbid condition with PTSD (Davidson & McFarlane, 2006; Meewisse et al., 2011; Van der Velden et al., 2006).

Other Mental Health Consequences
There is a range of other adverse conditions that can arise following a disaster as survivors attempt to adjust to their "new normal" and begin to rebuild their lives. Often, those with psychological distress will manifest a range of somatic symptoms unrelated to any physical injuries sustained in the disaster (Foa et al., 2006; Norris et al., 2002; Polusny et al., 2008).

Prior to seeking assistance from health care providers, survivors may attempt to manage their distress through self-medication with alcohol and drugs. This is especially common among survivors with PTSD and data suggests this relationship is more a result of the PTSD than increased stress from the disaster alone (Foa et al., 2006). In addition to self-medication efforts, survivors experiencing mental health distress may increase use of health care services either for psychological or physical symptoms (Den Ouden et al., 2007; Dorn et al., 2008; Olteanu et al., 2011; Van der Velden et al., 2006).

Population-Based Considerations
A disaster creates potential risk for all exposed individuals. However, there are some individuals who are at greater risk for adverse mental health outcomes because of certain characteristics, degree of exposure or proximity to the incident, occupation, and/or living environment.

Catastrophically Affected Populations
Hurricane Katrina and the 2004 Asian tsunami survivors were exposed to extreme community devastation, experienced threat to life, considerable death and injuries involving family and friends, as well as significant failure of the response system. Thus, the event severity and high degree of traumatic stress experienced by survivors is comparable to survivors of a mass violence disaster, thereby increasing the probability of PTSD and other adverse mental health conditions that can remain at higher levels over time (Johannesson et al., 2011; Kessler, Galea, Jones, & Parker, 2006; Kim et al., 2008; Lee, Shen, & Tran, 2008).

Ethnic Minorities
As stated previously, it is imperative to use a community approach to mental health care following disasters to ensure that minority populations are assessed and receive needed services. Culture and ethnicity influence "the need for help, the availability of help, comfort in seeking help, and the appropriateness of that help" (Norris & Alegria, 2005, p. 132). In the systematic review by Neria and colleagues (2008), several studies that differentiated ethnicity found a higher

prevalence of PTSD in the ethnic populations compared to the White population. However, the evidence base for how to effectively reach these populations is thus far limited (Harville, Xiong, Pridjian, Elkind-Hirsch, & Buekens, 2009; Kessler et al., 2006; Lee et al., 2008; Olteanu et al., 2011; Rhodes et al., 2010).

In addition, it is important to identify criteria that foster resilience in minority populations. The literature review by Lee et al. (2008) summarizes several studies of African American Hurricane Katrina survivors that found talking, staying informed, praying and spirituality helped reduce psychological stress and foster resilience.

Children, Adolescents, and Families

Children are especially at risk for adverse short- and long-term mental health outcomes during disasters, primarily because their physical, mental, and social states are still developing. Even though children as young as 5 years old may have the cognitive ability to understand a disaster's effects, they do not have the psychological maturity to mitigate the disaster stressors such as loss of pets, loss of personal belongings, and evacuation. As a result, they can develop chronic psychological and physiological stress reactions (Weissbecker et al., 2008). Several diverse studies have focused on the mental health effects in children following disasters (Dorn et al., 2008; Goenjian et al., 2005; Kar, 2009; Madrid, Grant, Reilly, & Redlener, 2006; McDermott, Lee, Judd, & Gibbon, 2005; Olteanu et al., 2011; Roberts et al., 2010; Woolsey & Bracy, 2010). Adverse responses in children following a disaster generally fall into two categories—short term and long term. Figure 5.3 provides a model of these impacts of disasters on children's health.

As with adults, similar patterns of overall decline in PTSD and other psychological symptoms occur over time regardless if interventions are provided (Dogan-Ates, 2010; Dorn et al., 2008; Goenjian et al., 2005). Similarly, research suggests that degree of exposure is a mitigating factor for recovery (Goenjian et al., 2005; Roberts et al., 2010).

Stage of development plays a significant role in symptom manifestation in children. In preschoolers, it is not uncommon for them to reenact disaster events in their play as a way to express their feelings (Dogan-Ates, 2010). School-age children may exhibit a range of somatic, cognitive, behavioral, and social problems along with more symptoms indicative of psychological distress. Adolescents, although somewhat more resilient because of greater ability to manage the physical and psychological impact of disaster, are at increased risk of adverse mental health effects from loss of community, friends, possessions, and/or evacuation (Crane & Clements, 2005; Harden et al., 2006).

Although it is important to understand the needs of children during disasters, it is equally important to understand the effects in the context of the family.

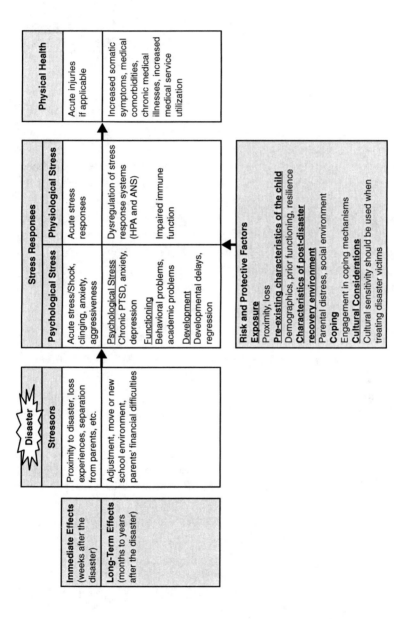

FIGURE 5.3 Impact of disasters on children's health. PTSD = posttraumatic stress disorder; HPA = hypothalamic-pituitary-adrenal system; ANS = autonomic nervous system. Adapted with permission from Weissbecker, I., Sephton, S. E., Martin, M. B., & Simpson, D. M. (2008). Psychological and physiological correlates of stress in children exposed to disaster: Current research and recommendations for intervention. *Children, Youth and Environments, 18*(1), 30–70.

Several disaster studies have addressed both children and parents following disasters (Abramson, Stehling-Ariza, Garfield, & Redlener, 2008; Harville et al., 2009; Harville et al., 2011; Rhodes et al., 2010). Likewise, studies by Harville et al. (2011) and Harville et al. (2009) suggest that there is no increased risk of adverse mental health outcomes for postpartum women above that of the general population with equal exposure. Also, research has shown that low-income families are at increased risk to develop serious mental health consequences following disasters (Abramson et al., 2008; Rhodes et al., 2010).

Older Adults

There are several factors that increase the vulnerability of older adults—less likely to evacuate, increased distress because of disrupted routine, greater risk for physical injury, and less economic resources to repair, replace possessions/housing and residing in a nursing home (Brown, 2007; Brown et al., 2010). However, research has also shown that older adults are somewhat more resilient than younger adults, and demonstrate less psychological and emotional dysfunction (Brown, 2007; Cherniack, 2008). This is not meant to infer that older adults are psychologically unaffected. Delay in recovery, sustained environmental disruption and stress, limited financial resources, and relocation are all factors that can increase psychological distress for older adults (Brown, 2007).

Persons With Preexisting Mental Health Disorders

Individuals with preexisting mental health disorders are particularly vulnerable during disasters because of type of mental health condition, disruption in ongoing health care, medication access, routine/support, and living environment (Horan et al., 2007). Likewise, individuals with mental health disorders living in custodial care settings are at additional risk because of staffing disruptions, evacuation, isolation from family, and limited ability to comprehend current situations (Grigg, 2009; Hughes, 2010).

Responder Workforce

The definition of *first responder* is very broad and includes public safety, health care and public health, local/state/federal government, volunteers, and military. Although many first responders' everyday job is responding to some type of emergency event, a disaster changes the dynamic of their actions, frequently presenting high stress austere conditions with large numbers of adversely affected individuals including their own families and friends. As result, they may be at increased risk of physical and mental health consequences (Benedek, Fullerton, & Ursano, 2007). Biological events disproportionately affect health care providers because of the increased demand for health services. For example, studies following the 2003 SARS epidemic found varying degrees of adverse mental health conditions (Benedek et al., 2007; Lung, Lu, Chang, & Shu, 2009). Both studies found factors such as stigmatization and rejection by the workers' communities, professional isolation, and increased somatic symptoms enhanced distress.

Several studies have shown risk factors for first responders developing mental health consequences are not unlike those found in the affected population. However, Walsh (2009) and Benedek et al. (2007) in comprehensive literature reviews suggest that there are several unique factors that seem to increase mental health risk for first responders: proximity to an event, emotional distancing, exposure to dead bodies and remains, nontraditional roles, and previous limited disaster experience. That said, in the landmark meta-analysis of disaster mental studies by Norris and colleagues, responder mental health postdisaster appears to be surprisingly resilient (Norris, Friedman, & Watson, 2002; Norris et al., 2002). Self-care remains paramount for the disaster workforce, of course, and training related to this workforce is addressed later in this chapter.

ASSESSMENT METHODS AND TOOLS

The previous research design section of this chapter presents the overall methodological components of study design and considerations. This section will specifically focus on assessment methods and tools. Mental health assessments following disaster can be challenging for both the affected population and health care providers (Connor, Foa, & Davidson, 2006). Affected individuals may be hesitant because of fear or safety concerns, survivor guilt, or shame. Health care providers' own current disaster experience or previous traumatic exposure, lack of comfort with the topic, or inexperience with psychological assessments may inhibit their assessment capability. In addition, cultural issues are an overarching influence affecting individuals' willingness to participate and health care providers' ability to conduct effective assessments (Connor et al., 2006).

There are several methods, subjective and objective, that have been used to assess the psychological effects of disasters on populations. However, many of these methods have focused on the impact of the disaster on the affected populations and subsequent health outcomes without significant consideration for preexisting factors that may have influenced those outcomes (Yamashita, 2011). Resistance and resilience capabilities, as discussed previously, along with predisposing risk factors are important factors that need consideration when conducting psychological assessments of disaster-affected populations. Yamashita (2011) states inclusion of these factors are valuable in "(a) assessing changes (ameliorating and worsening, respectively) in the psychological conditions of stressors and (b) explaining why only some people develop stress-related psychiatric disorders following disaster" (p. 1). However, ability to validate psychosocial factor effect and subjectivity of assessments present challenges in assessment standardization, study replication, and generalization of findings. In studies where these psychosocial factors have been included, only one or two have been included and there is great variability and modification across studies in the types of measures used and their psychometric validity (Yamashita, 2011). The author has identified three factors as ones that are frequently used in disaster mental health assessments as measures of resilience or risk factors but are problematic for the reasons summarized:

1. Social support—questionable internal and external validity, variable assessment approaches.
2. Resource loss and coping self-efficacy—inappropriate combinations of related factors in assessments, lack of concurrent examination, and redundancy.
3. Chronic stress—limited use because of lack of psychometric validation in different types of disasters (e.g., some identified assessment measures have proven useful in hurricane disasters), adaptations differ from operational definitions.

As a way to enhance measure reliability, Yamashita (2011) recommends that researchers should consider the use of assessment measures that have been well tested and validated in general stress–illness studies. In choosing appropriate assessment measures, ones should be selected with psychometric properties validated by a range of stress–illness relationships and/or under more than one disaster setting. In addition, assessment measures should be combined appropriately based on sound theoretical rationale (Yamashita, 2011). Used in this way, subjective assessment measures can accurately identify specific stressful relationships between the disaster and affected population.

Frequently, these assessment measures are combined into tools. These tools typically fall into two categories—screening and diagnostic. Screening tools are used to identify persons at risk for potential adverse mental health outcomes, and who need further in-depth assessment for specific disorders (Connor et al., 2006). These tools often use a rating-scale format, can be self- or interviewer administered and can be completed quickly. Connor et al. (2006) suggest that the SPAN tool is a reliable PTSD screening tool that has well established psychometric reliability and broad use. A four-item scale—the SPAN—is named for its top four items: startle, physiological arousal, anger, and numbness. Likewise, Balaban (2006) conducted a systematic review of screening tools appropriate for use with children and adolescents following disasters to identify risk of PTSD, depression, anxiety, and behavioral disorders. The review provides tool psychometric reliability data, administration time, age usage, and degree of use in disasters.

Diagnostic assessment tools are used to ascertain presence of psychiatric disorder. Many of these tools require trained personnel to administer as well as take longer to complete. The Diagnostic Interview Schedule (DIS) and Composite International Diagnostic Interview (CIDI) are examples of interviewer-administered diagnostic tools (Connor et al., 2006). Several self-administered psychometrically validated diagnostic tools are also available. Two examples that have been very useful for diagnosing PTSD are the Posttraumatic Diagnostic Scale (PDS) and the Davidson Trauma Scale (DTS; Connor et al., 2006).

In addition to providing insight into individual and community resiliency, assessments are critical drivers for determining appropriate interventions, timing of interventions, and overall mental health service need. Assessments help differentiate those individuals who are experiencing normal reactions and need only short-term support from those that may need intensive longer term support (Macy et al., 2004). Similarly, assessment data is used to determine service need and intensity (Norris et al., 2009; Rosen et al., 2010; Siegel, Wanderling, & Laska, 2004). Altogether, screening and diagnostic assessments are integral to an effective disaster mental health response.

MENTAL HEALTH INTERVENTION AND SERVICE USE

The public health system has a crucial role and responsibility in promoting and preserving resistance and resilience in communities, before and after disaster incidents. When targeted interventions and effective/efficient resource use are aligned with the incident phase, true asset staging for disaster preparedness, response, and recovery can be achieved. There is a more flexible availability of professional mental health providers, better use of other health professionals and other pretrained community responders and volunteers, and a multifaceted resource support net. Readiness for disaster and emergencies is currently a major goal for communities, with much national, state, and local funding devoted to messaging and resource planning over the last decade. The identification of available community resources in disaster is a part of public health function, to include the identification of mental health agencies and their respective roles, responsibilities, and potential resources in disaster.

Early in the response phase, there is a requirement for a rapid needs assessment, a public health assessment that is vital to understanding community mental and behavioral health needs and identifying needed services (Beaton et al., 2009). Hobfoll et al. (2007) advocate for population-based interventions that (a) promote a sense of safety, (b) promote calming, (c) promote a sense of self and collective efficacy, (d) promote connectedness, and (e) promote hope. These five essential immediate and midterm mass trauma intervention recommendations are the outcome of scores of intervention research recommendations in the last decade. The interventions also clearly fit within a public health model of primary and secondary prevention, that is, preventing negative outcomes from the psychological impact of disaster on community health before they occur and addressing disaster mental health issues as soon as possible to prevent further complications and return the individual/community to predisaster baseline.

When addressing recovery or tertiary prevention services, the role of public health services are to "reduce the impact of secondary stressors, identify unmet needs, reestablish normalcy, evaluate the event's effects on the community, and evaluate the effects of interventions provided" (Beaton et al., 2009, p. E7). The timely availability of professional mental health providers along with readily accessible disaster mental health systems remains an area to address in the United States. Internationally, the disaster management framework mainly deals with housing, food, emergency supplies, without much direct linkage to long-term mental health needs of the survivors (Satapathy & Subhasis, 2009). This is, in part, because of the unavailability of mental health providers in many developing countries and their continued emphasis on health services as opposed to mental health services.

This section on disaster mental health intervention and service use builds on the chapter's previous findings to include who (population-based aggregates), what (interventions based on public health prevention levels), and when (disaster incident phase and subsequent resource staging). Figure 5.4 displays these areas using a 3D graphic for visual assistance.

Primary Prevention Interventions and Services

Even though traumatic stress and PTSD dominated disaster mental health research prior to the last decade, Reyes and Elhai (2004, p. 401) emphasize that "disaster psychology is not synonymous with traumatology." They contend that such an emphasis on trauma can divert attention from other problems found in the larger population, creating a mismatch between needs and services. Their solution is for more effective and efficient psychosocial interventions, focusing on community resources in the postdisaster environment, using community-based psychology (Reyes & Elhai, 2004). This involves the use of disaster mental health professionals as consultants and bolstering the capacity of community leaders and local healers versus an inundation of outside providers. Although primary prevention is initially targeted for the entire community, the group that it best serves comprised Category 1 survivors in Figure 5.4, with the interventions offered as early as possible and optimally even before the disaster strikes for maximum community resistance strengthening.

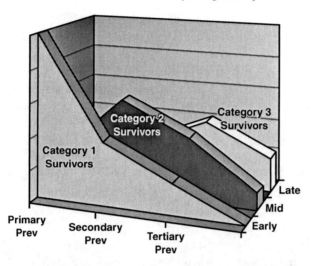

FIGURE 5.4 Intervention schematic created by authors based on who (survivor categories), what (prevention levels), and when (early, mid, or late incident). The graphic depicts the need for preplanning limited disaster mental health resources across population need and time factors postdisaster. Adapted from Ghodse, H., & Galea, S. (2006). Tsunami: Understanding mental health consequences and the unprecedented response. *International Review of Psychiatry*, *18*(3), 289–297.

In primary prevention, there is a crucial need to expand and operational-ize available human resources to enhance the psychological resiliency of affected populations (Everly et al., 2010). The use of PFA is emerging as a preferred early response and primary prevention intervention. PFA is recommended by name in the Federal guidelines of the National Response Framework and is capable of supporting community resiliency, reducing acute distress following disas-ter, and encouraging short- and long-term adaptive functioning (Allen et al., 2010; Uhernik & Husson, 2009). Although disaster mental health professionals are well-equipped to deliver PFA, this population-based early intervention can also be used by others in the community for primary and secondary prevention efforts with little additional training (Reyes & Elhai, 2004). PFA is an extension of caring which focuses on the immediate biopsychosocial needs of a client and five principles of crisis intervention: safety, calming, connectedness, self-efficacy, and hope (Everly et al., 2010; Hobfoll et al., 2007).

In PFA, the *crisis intervention* principle does not mean "critical incident stress debriefing or CISD." In CISD, based on a late 1970s military model and employed freely into the 1990s, a psychotherapy-like cathartic approach is fre-quently used on asymptomatic and symptomatic individuals alike in an effort to reduce symptoms of PTSD and other mental trauma (Uhernik & Husson, 2009). In fact, the research investigation and literature from the last decade provides mixed reviews on the effectiveness and even the safety of using CISD as an intervention (Choe, 2005; Macy et al., 2004; Reyes & Elhai, 2004; Ruzek et al., 2007; Te Brake et al., 2009; Uhernik & Husson, 2009; Vernberg et al., 2008). Instead, the crisis intervention of PFA focuses on palliating emotional distress, connecting the survivor to available community resources, and helping to structure a short-term plan for recovery (Reyes & Elhai, 2004).

PFA is versatile in application as a methodology as well as with different target audiences, with research studies demonstrating success in group use, use with children and adolescents, and older adults (Brown et al., 2009; Everly et al., 2006; Pairojkul, Siripul, Prateepchaikul, Kusol, & Puytrakul, 2010; Plummer, Cain, Fisher, & Bankston, 2009; Ruzek et al., 2007).

Another primary prevention intervention found in the research literature includes psychoeducation. This intervention's purpose is to reduce the confusion and perceived sense of lost efficacy after disaster. It includes providing messages to address expectable reactions and resource information. The education is intended to encourage empathy, social support, and help-seeking (Reyes & Elhai, 2004). Other primary prevention interventions include information gathering, practical assistance, connection with social supports, and stress inoculation, which may or may not be offered as a part of PFA efforts (Nucifora et al., 2007; Vernberg et al., 2008).

Secondary Prevention Interventions and Services

Secondary prevention in the disaster incident involves ongoing response and early recovery phases. PFA can be used as a secondary prevention intervention in disaster mental health services. For example, a PFA intervention post-Katrina with a group of school-age children (ages 5–12 years) found slight mean improvements in reduction of stress symptoms (Plummer et al., 2009). In Figure 5.4, Category 2 survivor interventions are often best addressed in the midrange time period (i.e., up to 6–8 weeks postincident). It is at this time these survivors will have passed from primary prevention intervention effort, starting to display identifiable behaviors and symptoms that can be linked to the disaster incident. Research shows that disaster survivors may be less reluctant to use mental health services than the general population (i.e., there may be less associated stigma given a disaster incident), making secondary prevention service outreach an important intervention option (Elhai et al., 2006; Goenjian et al., 2005; Polusny et al., 2008; Van der Velden et al., 2006). Provision of timely mental health services is recommended in various community settings to include schools (Goenjian et al., 2005).

Cognitive behavioral therapy (CBT) is a technique that uses behavioral and verbal techniques to identify and correct problematic thinking patterns that are at the root of dysfunctional behavior (Nuccifora et al., 2007). Like PFA, CBT crosses prevention categories: secondary and tertiary prevention categories. In the area of secondary prevention intervention, if CBT is applied early in response to assessed dysfunctional behavior, it can actually assist the individual or group in quickly returning to baseline function. Te Brake et al. (2009) developed guidelines on early psychosocial interventions (to include CBT) which are implemented within the first 6 weeks after a major incident to provide early assessment and intervention for survivors experiencing mental health symptoms. Guidelines recommend that CBT can be used as an early preventive psychosocial intervention (i.e., secondary prevention) as well as in curative psychosocial interventions (i.e., tertiary prevention).

Walser et al. (2004) summarizes a grouping of CBT interventions that are relevant for early to midrange response in disaster mental health and include emergency stage intervention, motivation enhancement, reduction of physiological arousal, increase in adaptive coping, and facilitation of emotional processing. CBT involves systematic training of coping skills and elements to include careful specification of the desired, behaviors, use of self-monitoring, and social reinforcement of coping efforts (Walser et al., 2004). The authors found it especially important to restructure negative trauma-related beliefs. Also included in secondary prevention interventions are ongoing psychological triage, continued practical assistance, and connection with social support (Vernberg et al., 2008).

Tertiary Prevention Interventions and Services
In later phases (Figure 5.4) of the disaster incident, ongoing mental health recovery work begins for communities as well as for a select group of individuals— Category 3 survivors. By this time, these individuals will, on assessment, display abnormal findings in terms of mental health diagnostics. Previous individual mental health diagnoses that are unrelated to the disaster incident can complicate the situation (Milligan & McGuinness, 2009). Tertiary prevention interventions focus on the treatment realm versus simple intervention. They also become less population or aggregate based and more individually focused.

CBT and medication are included in therapeutic approaches for PTSD (Rhoads et al., 2007). Psychotherapy involving CBT assists clients in modifying or replacing debilitating patterns of thinking and acting with health patterns. Even a limited number of therapy sessions can help the individual experiencing disaster-related mental illness (Rhoads et al., 2007). Walser et al. (2004) indicate that CBT has been proven as the most consistently effective psychotherapy treatment and it appears in the literature with significance in intervention success (Jones et al., 2009; Weissbecker et al., 2008).

Other psychological therapies in the treatment of PTSD include exposure therapy and cognitive restructuring (Rhoads et al., 2007). Exposure therapy exposes individuals to simulated or imagined trauma, with interventions directed at trying to attain a sense of control over the situation (Walser et al., 2004). Cognitive restructuring is often combined with CBT to assist individuals in realizing the unhealthy thinking can produce negative thoughts resulting in behavioral or physical issues. Also used in tertiary prevention would be the screening and assessment of PTSD symptoms, previously covered in the assessment section of this chapter.

WORKFORCE TRAINING

How do the community responders and disaster workforce prepare for disaster? Previous study findings in this chapter underscore the need for an initial approach that is community based and nontrauma focused as well as inclusion of the community itself in terms of resistance and resilience to meet disaster incident outcomes. Interestingly, in the largest review of research studies (60,000 affected individuals and, ultimately, 225 studies), rescue and recovery worker study samples did not show routine adverse impact from their disaster work (Norris, 2005; Norris, Friedman, & Watson, 2002; Norris et al., 2002). This may change as traditional definitions of response workforce continue to be broadened in future disaster incidents to include the use of individuals not steeped in disaster self-care and without easy access to organized workforce health protection interventions.

Reyes and Elhai (2004) emphasize that even for professional mental health providers, disaster mental health response is not business as usual. They warn that there are many professional expectations, which nondisaster-based mental health clinicians hold that do not translate into disaster chaos and field clinician work at the disaster site. Their research indicates that mental health clinicians must be aware of special disaster expectations and work through these expectations in advance of the disaster to include differently defined community-based risk groups, concepts of incident command and clinician fit, and an inability to form the usual therapist–client relationship (Reyes & Elhai, 2004). Paton et al. (2000) emphasize that a traditional medical model of mental health delivery is not appropriate in disaster mental health, but that participation in such response for mental health professionals can be a growth experience, building resilience, and skill strength in the individual clinician.

It is increasingly apparent that other health professionals must have disaster mental health content to prepare for and provide primary and secondary prevention interventions within the affected communities (Broussard et al., 2008;

Clarke et al., 2006; Everly et al., 2008; Guscott, Guscott, Malingambi, & Parker, 2007; Hoffman et al., 2005; Walsh, 2009). This planned support anticipates the low availability of mental health professionals in the early phases of the disaster incident. It also fits with the concept of resource asset staging, using disaster mental health clinicians for oversight of population-based interventions in early through midrange disaster response phases and for treatment provision in mid through late phases (Figure 5.3).

Clarke et al. (2006) determined that psychological triage effectiveness in a group of emergency department nurses conducting generic patient intake was significantly increased with minimal training and clinical oversight by mental health professionals. This concept could easily transfer into the disaster mental health world and is already used in organizations such as the American Red Cross and Medical Reserve Corps. There must also be understanding that although certain health care workers may not be "at the scene," they are still very much a part of the disaster aftermath by virtue of their usual health provider positions (e.g., school nurses; Broussard et al., 2008; Guscott et al., 2007). Walsh (2009) proposes a data reduction model to build prior formal education and continuing education training in disaster mental health content into various health professions curricula (i.e., nonmental health clinicians).

During the past decade, work has advanced in determining education and training content for disaster mental health as well as related competencies. The Centers for Disease Control and Prevention (CDC) and the Association of Schools of Public Health (ASPH) established the Centers for Public Health Preparedness (CPHP) for public health workforce training in 2000. CDC and ASPH then went on to establish a content-specific group within the CPHP devoted to Mental Health and Psychosocial Preparedness (Hoffman et al., 2005). After conducting a review of existing disaster mental health education, the group found 28 CPHP-funded training products in the psychosocial and mental health preparedness area. The group transitioned into the Mental Health Collaborative group in 2006, going on to develop five core competencies in disaster mental health (Everly et al., 2008). The group emphasizes that the competencies are population focused and disaster phased with temporal acuity, distinct from traditional mental health treatment. That is, these competencies are for public health workers in general; not for the mental health clinician per se. The five competencies include (Everly et al., 2008, p. 541)

1. An ability to define and/or describe key concepts related to disaster mental health/psychosocial/behavioral health preparedness and response;
2. A defined set of communication skills;
3. Assessment skills including referral recognition abilities;

4. Development of an action plan to meet needs; and
5. An ability to care for self and other response workers (i.e., force health protection).

SUMMARY OF IMPLICATIONS FOR NURSING

Although the reader has been introduced to nursing implications throughout this chapter, this section summarizes the major points for nursing involvement in disaster mental health response. Research over the last decade in disaster mental health is not a strong publication area for nursing. Even so, it is obvious that nurses are collaborators in such research and that their presence, whether they practice as primary mental health clinicians or in other specialty areas, remains very much needed in a disaster mental health response.

With disaster mental health research findings indicating that psychological casualties far outnumbering physical casualties, combined with the expected shortage of mental health professionals, it is imperative that all nurses are familiarized with the ability to enhance the psychological resiliency of disaster survivors (Everly et al., 2010). The way that makes the most sense in light of this decade's research studies and subsequent product availability is formal training in PFA. The core elements of PFA involve what all nurses receive in their entry level education in human psychosocial care: reflective listening, need assessment, basic triage through nursing diagnosis, implementation of appropriate interventions, and evaluation involving implementation effectiveness and/or referral and linkages for ongoing care. It is for this reason that the training of nurses, the largest health care provider cohort in the United States, is touted as key to a community's disaster mental health response (Everly et al., 2010).

Disaster mental health needs remain an area that requires more skill building among nurses, yet the stress and grief that present as postdisaster psychological symptoms are considered normal reactions to abnormal situations from which most people recover (Corrarino, 2008). It is important that nurses initiate and/or participate in action-based care planning for disaster phases, all prevention levels, and survivor disaster mental health needs (to include vulnerable groups) at both the population-based (community) and individual levels. This care plan implementation is never carried out in isolation but requires a team approach involving other providers, community leaders, and most importantly, the clients involved.

Lastly, nurses must not forget about their own mental health needs as a care provider in disaster response. Nurses in the community may themselves be impacted, both personally and through the health care system where they are working. For this reason, nurses must be trained to gain awareness and mediate in the psychosocial impact of disaster on survivors, to include themselves (Everly et al., 2010; Hughes et al., 2007).

RECOMMENDATIONS FOR FUTURE RESEARCH AND CONCLUSION

"It is imperative that the future investigations of loss and trauma include more detailed study of the full range of possible outcomes; simply put, dysfunction cannot be fully understood without a deeper understanding of *health* [italics added] and resilience" (Bonanno, 2004, p.26).

"Nursing is the protection, promotion, and optimization of *health* [italics added] and abilities, prevention of illness and injury, alleviation of suffering through the diagnosis and treatment of human response, and advocacy in the care of individuals, families, communities, and populations" (American Nurses Association, 2010, p.1).

When focusing on research on the psychological impact of disaster, Galea et al. (2008) recommends that research design must assure population representative samples, assess multiple factors and their potential levels of influence, build in longitudinal components, and use mixed methods (e.g., quantitative and qualitative). Disaster mental health providers will most certainly continue to provide treatment to those affected across all phases of the disaster cycle. Many stressors underlying psychological impact that appears in the long term, however, are amenable to psychosocial interventions that must be quickly and efficiently delivered in the short term and midterm to survivors (Davidson & McFarlane, 2006). Identification of groups within a society that are at increased risk must also occur, before and during the incident, to address community vulnerabilities as well as use their strengths in capacity building for resistance and resilience (Davidson & McFarlane, 2006; Neria et al., 2008).

It should be apparent to the reader that nurses have a major role to play in disaster mental *health* preparedness, response, and recovery. Nurses in all areas, to include advanced practice nurses in primary and mental health care, should understand public health prevention levels, the disaster cycle, and how disaster impacts the psychological status of individuals, families, and vulnerable groups within the population. Although nurses have a critical role to play across all phases of the disaster, early to late, it is extremely critical that all nurses are prepared and engaged in intervention provision in the 6-week period postdisaster, the time when primary and secondary prevention activities must occur (e.g., PFA and health education).

It is also imperative that nurses remain contributors in the body of literature on disaster mental health research. Because there is room for growth in this area, the priorities for research by nursing research organizations (e.g., the National Institute of Nursing Research [NINR]) and education centers should assist in supporting the agenda for a more visible disaster mental health integration into nursing practice. Also, nurses practicing in the field of mental health need to effectively tell the story of the psychological impact disaster could have on the communities that they serve, working evidence-based solutions with other team members throughout the health care system to mediate that impact.

There is no question that disasters will continue to happen in all forms and to all sectors of populations. The largest question for nursing practice is whether we are "all in."

REFERENCES

Abramson, D., Stehling-Ariza, T., Garfield, R., & Redlener, I. (2008). Prevalence and predictors of mental health distress post-Katrina: Findings from the Gulf Coast Child and Family Health Study. *Disaster Medicine and Public Health Preparedness*, 2(2), 77–86.

Afifi, W. A., Felix, E. D., & Afifi, T. D. (2011). The impact of uncertainty and communal coping on mental health following natural disasters. *Anxiety, Stress & Coping*, 1–19.

Allen, B., Brymer, M. J., Steinberg, A. M., Vernberg, E. M., Jacobs, A., Speier, A. H., & Pynoos, R. S. (2010). Perceptions of psychological first aid among providers responding to Hurricanes Gustav and Ike. *Journal of Traumatic Stress*, 23(4), 509–513.

American Nurses Association. (2010). *Nursing: Scope and standards of practice* (2nd ed.). Silver Spring, MD: Author.

Balaban, V. (2006). Psychological assessment of children in disasters and emergencies. *Disasters*, 30(2), 178–198.

Beaton, R. D., Murphy, S. A., Houston, J. B., Reyes, G., Bramwell, S., McDaniel, M., . . . Pfefferbaum, B. (2009). The role of public health in mental and behavioral health in children and families following disasters. *Journal of Public Health Management Practice*, 15(6), 1–11.

Benedek, D. M., Fullerton, C., & Ursano, R. J. (2007). First responders: Mental health consequences of natural and human-made disasters for public health and public safety workers. *Annual Review of Public Health*, 28, 55–68.

Bonanno, G. A. (2004). Loss, trauma and human resilience: Have we underestimated the human ability to thrive after extremely adverse events? *American Psychologist*, 59(1), 20–28.

Bonanno, G. A., Galea, S., Bucciarelli, A., & Vlahov, D. (2007). What predicts psychological resilience after disaster? The role of demographics, resources, and life stress. *Journal of Consulting and Clinical Psychology*, 75(5), 671–682.

Broussard, L., & Myers, R. (2010). School nurse resilience: Experiences after multiple natural disasters. *The Journal of School Nursing*, 26(3), 203–211.

Broussard, L., Myers, R., & Meaux, J. (2008). The impact of hurricanes Katrina and Rita on Louisiana school nurses. *The Journal of School Nursing*, 24(2), 78–82.

Brown, L. M., Bruce, M. L., Hyer, K., Mills, W. L., Vongxaiburana, E., & Polivka-West, L. (2009). A pilot study evaluating the feasibility of psychological first aid for nursing home residents. *Clinical Gerontology*, 32(3), 293–308.

Brown, L. M., Hyer, K., Schinka, J. A., Mando, A., Frazier, D., & Polivka-West, L. (2010). Use of mental health services by nursing home residents after hurricanes. *Psychiatric Services*, *61*(1), 74–77.

Brown, L. S. (2007). Issues in mental health care for older adults after disasters. *Generations*, *31*(4), 21–26.

Cherniack, E. P. (2008). The impact of natural disasters on the elderly. *American Journal of Disaster Medicine*, *3*(3), 133–139.

Choe, I. (2005). The debate over psychological debriefing for PTSD. *The New School Psychology Bulletin*, *3*(2), 71–82.

Clarke, D. E., Brown, A. M., Hughes, L., & Motluk, L. (2006). Education to improve the triage of mental health patients in general hospital emergency departments. *Accident and Emergency Nursing*, *14*(4), 210–218.

Connor, K. M., Foa, E. B., & Davidson, J. R. (2006). Practical assessment and evaluation of mental health problems following a mass disaster. *Journal of Clinical Psychiatry*, *67*(Suppl. 2), 26–33.

Corrarino, J. E. (2008). Disaster-related mental health needs of women and children. *The American Journal of Maternal/Child Nursing*, *33*(4), 242–248.

Crane, P. A., & Clements, P. T. (2005). Psychological response to disasters: Focus on adolescents. *Journal of Psychosocial Nursing*, *43*(8), 31–38.

Davidson, J. R., & McFarlane, A. C. (2006). The extent and impact of mental health problems after disaster. *Journal of Clinical Psychiatry*, *67*(Suppl. 2), 9–14.

Davydov, D. M., Stewart, R., Ritchie, K., & Chaudieu, I. (2010). Resilience and mental health. *Clinical Psychology Review*, *30*(5), 479–495.

Den Ouden, D.-J., van der Velden, P. G., Grievink, L., Morren, M., Dirkzwager, A. J., & Yzermans, C. J. (2007). Use of mental health services among disaster survivors: Predisposing factors. *BMC Public Health*, *7*, 173.

Dogan-Ates, A. (2010). Developmental differences in children's and adolescents' post-disaster reactions. *Issues in Mental Health Nursing*, *31*(7), 470–476.

Dorn, T., Yzermans, J. C., Spreeuwenberg, P. M., Schilder, A., & van der Zee, J. (2008). A cohort study of the long-term impact of a fire disaster on the physical and mental health of adolescents. *Journal of Traumatic Stress*, *21*(2), 239–242.

Elhai, J. D., Jacobs, G. A., Kashdan, T. B., DeJong, G. L., Meyer, D. L., & Frueh, B. C. (2006). Mental health service use among American Red Cross disaster workers responding to the September 11, 2001 U.S. terrorist attacks. *Psychiatry Research*, *143*(1), 29–34.

Everly, G. S., Jr., Barnett, D. J., Sperry, N. L., & Links, J. M. (2010). The use of psychological first aid (PFA) training among nurses to enhance population resiliency. *International Journal of Emergency Mental Health*, *12*(1), 21–31.

Everly, G. S., Jr., Beaton, R. D., Pfefferbaum, B., & Parker, C. L. (2008). On academics: Training for disaster response personnel: The development of proposed core competencies in disaster mental health. *Public Health Reports*, *123*(4), 539–542.

Everly, G. S., Jr., Phillips, S. B., Kane, D., & Feldman, D. (2006). Introduction to and overview of group psychological first aid. *Brief Treatment and Crisis Intervention*, *6*(2), 130–136.

Foa, E. B., Stein, D. J., & McFarlane, A. C. (2006). Symptomatology and psychopathology of mental health problems after disaster. *Journal of Clinical Psychiatry*, *67*(Suppl. 2), 15–25.

Fox, M. H., White, G. W., Rooney, C., & Cahill, A. (2010). The psychosocial impact of Hurricane Katrina on persons with disabilities and independent living center staff living on the American Gulf Coast. *Rehabilitation Psychology*, *55*(3), 231–240.

Galea, S., Maxwell, A. R., & Norris, F. (2008). Sampling and design challenges in studying the mental health consequences of disasters. *International Journal of Methods in Psychiatric Research*, *17*(Suppl. 2), S21–S28.

Ghodse, H., & Galea, S. (2006). Tsunami: Understanding mental health consequences and the unprecedented response. *International Review of Psychiatry, 18*(3), 289–297.

Goenjian, A. K., Walling, D., Steinberg, A. M., Karayan, I., Najarian, L. M., & Pynoos, R. (2005). A prospective study of posttraumatic stress and depressive reactions among treated and untreated adolescents 5 years after a catastrophic disaster. *The American Journal of Psychiatry, 162*(12), 2302–2308.

Grigg, M. (2009). Psychosocial issues in emergencies: Implications for nursing. *Southeast Asian Journal of Tropical Medicine and Public Health, 40*(Suppl. 1), 79–87.

Guscott, W. M., Guscott, A. J., Malingambi, G., & Parker, R. (2007). The Bali bombings and the evolving mental health response to disaster in Australia: Lessons from Darwin. *Journal of Psychiatric and Mental Health Nursing, 14*(3), 239–242.

Hardin, S. B., Weinrich, S., Weinrich, M., Garrison, C., Addy, C., & Hardin, T. L. (2002). Effects of a long-term psychosocial nursing intervention on adolescents exposed to catastrophic stress. *Issues in Mental Health Nursing, 23*(6), 537–551.

Harville, E. W., Xiong, X., Pridjian, G, Elkind-Hirsch, K., & Buekens, P. (2009). Postpartum mental health after Hurricane Katrina: A cohort study. *BMC Pregnancy and Childbirth, 8*, 9–21.

Harville, E. W., Xiong, X., Smith, B. W., Pridjian, G., Elkind-Hirsch, K., & Buekens, P. (2011). Combined effects of Hurricane Katrina and Hurricane Gustav on the mental health of mothers of small children. *Journal of Psychiatric and Mental Health Nursing, 18*(4), 288–296.

Hobfoll, S. E., Watson, P., Bell, C. C., Bryant, R. A., Brymer, M. J., Friedman, M. J., & Ursano, R. J. (2007). Five essential elements of immediate and mid-term mass trauma intervention: Empirical evidence. *Psychiatry, 70*(4), 283–315.

Hoffman, Y., Everly, G. S., Jr., Werner, D., Livet, M., Madrid, P. A., Pfefferbaum, B., & Beaton, R. (2005). Identification and evaluation of mental health and psychosocial preparedness resources from the Centers for Public Health Preparedness. *Journal of Public Health Management and Practice*, S138–S142.

Horan, W. P., Ventura, J., Mintz, J., Kopelowicz, A., Wirshing, D., Christian-Herman, J., . . . Liberman, R. P. (2007). Stress and coping responses to a natural disaster in people with schizophrenia. *Psychiatry Research, 151*(1–2), 77–86.

Hughes, F. A. (2010). H1N1 pandemic planning in a mental health residential facility. *Journal of Psychological Nursing, 48*(3), 37–41.

Hughes, F., Grigg, M., Fritsch, K., & Calder, S. (2007). Psychosocial response in emergency situations— the nurse's role. *International Nursing Review, 54*(1), 19–27.

Inter-Agency Standing Committee. (2008). *Mental health and psychosocial support: Checklist for field use.* Geneva, Switzerland: Author. Retrieved from http://www.who.int/mental_health/emergencies/IASC_guidelines.pdf

Johannesson, K. B., Lundin, T., Fröjd, T., Hultman, C. M., & Michel, P. O. (2011). Tsunami-exposed tourist survivors: Signs of recovery in a 3-year perspective. *The Journal of Nervous and Mental Disease, 199*(3), 162–169.

Jones, K., Allen, M., Norris, F. H., & Miller, C. (2009). Piloting a new model of crisis counseling: Specialized crisis counseling services in Mississippi after Hurricane Katrina. *Administration and Policy in Mental Health, 36*(3), 195–205.

Kaminsky, M., McCabe, O. L., Langlieb, A. M., & Everly, G. S., Jr. (2007). An evidence-informed model of human resistance, resilience, and recovery: The Johns Hopkins' outcome-driven paradigm for disaster mental health services. *Brief Treatment and Crisis Intervention, 7*(1), 1–11.

Kar, N. (2009). Psychological impact of disasters on children: Review of assessment and interventions. *World Journal of Pediatrics, 5*(1), 5–11.

Kessler, R. C., Galea, S., Gruber, M. J., Sampson, N. A., Ursano, R. J., & Wessely, S. (2008). Trends in mental illness and suicidality after Hurricane Katrina. *International Journal of Methods in Psychiatric Research, 13*(4), 374–384.

Kessler, R. C., Galea, S., Jones, R. T., & Parker, H. A. (2006). Mental illness and suicidality after Hurricane Katrina. *Bulletin of the World Health Organization, 84*(12), 930–939.

Kessler, R. C., Keane, T. M., Ursano, R. J., Mokdad, A. & Zaslavsky, A. M. (2008) Sample and design considerations in post-disaster mental health needs assessment tracking surveys. *International Journal of Methods in Psychiatric Research, 17*(Suppl 2), S6–S20.

Kim, S. C., Plumb, R., Gredig, Q. N., Rankin, L., & Taylor, B. (2008). Medium-term post-Katrina health sequelae among New Orleans residents: Predictors of poor mental and physical health. *Journal of Clinical Nursing, 17*(17), 2335–2342.

Lee, O. E.-K., Shen, C., & Tran, T. V. (2008). Coping with Hurricane Katrina: Psychological distress and resilience among African American evacuees. *Journal of Black Psychology, 35*(5), 5–23.

López-Ibor, J. J. (2006). Disasters and mental health: New challenges for the psychiatric profession. *The World Journal of Biological Psychiatry, 7*(3), 171–182.

Lung, F. W., Lu, Y. C., Chang, Y. Y., & Shu, B. C. (2009). Mental symptoms in different health professionals during the SARS attack: A follow-up study. *The Psychiatric Quarterly, 80*(2), 107–116.

Macy, R. D., Behar, L., Paulson, R., Delman, J., Schmid, L., & Smith, S.F. (2004). Community-based, acute posttraumatic stress management: A description and evaluation of a psychosocial-intervention continuum. *Harvard Review of Psychiatry, 12*(4), 217–228.

Madrid, P. A., Grant, R., Reilly, M. J., & Redlener, N. B. (2006). Challenges in meeting immediate emotional needs: Short-term impact of a major disaster on children's mental health: Building resiliency in the aftermath of Hurricane Katrina. *Pediatrics, 117*(5, Pt. 3), S448–S453.

Masten, A. S., & Obradovic, J. (2008). Disaster preparation and recovery: Lessons from research on resilience in human development. *Ecology and Society, 13*(1), 1–16.

McDermott, B. M., Lee, E. M., Judd, M., & Gibbon, P. (2005). Posttraumatic stress disorder and general psychopathology in children and adolescents following a wildfire disaster. *The Canadian Journal of Psychiatry, 50*(3), 137–143.

Meewisse, M. L., Olff, M., Kleber, R., Kitchiner, N. J., & Gersons, B. P. (2011). The course of mental health disorders after a disaster: Predictors and comorbidity. *Journal of Traumatic Stress, 24*(4), 405–413.

Milligan, G., & McGuinness, T. M. (2009). Mental health needs in a post-disaster environment. *Journal of Psychological Nursing, 47*(9), 23–30.

Morris, A. J. (2011). Psychic aftershocks: Crisis counseling and disaster relief policy. *History of Psychology, 14*(3), 264–286.

Murray, J. S. (2006). Addressing the psychosocial needs of children following disasters. *Journal for Specialists in Pediatric Nursing, 11*(2), 133–137.

Neria, Y., Nandi, A., & Galea, S. (2008). Post-traumatic stress disorder following disasters: A systematic review. *Psychological Medicine, 38*(4), 467–480.

Norris, F. H. (2005). *Range, magnitude, and duration of the effects of disasters on mental health: Review update 2005.* Retrieved from http:www.redmh.org/research/general/REDMH_effects.pdf

Norris, F. H., & Alegria, M. (2005). Mental health care for ethnic minority individuals and communities in the aftermath of disasters and mass violence. *CNS Spectrums, 10*(2), 132–140.

Norris, F. H., Friedman, M. J., & Watson, P. J. (2002). 60,000 disaster victims speak: Part II. Summary and implications of the disaster mental health research. *Psychiatry, 65*(3), 240–260.

Norris, F. H., Friedman, M. J., Watson, P. J., Byrne, C. M., Diaz, E., & Kaniasty, K. (2002). 60,000 disaster victims speak: Part I. An empirical review of the empirical literature, 1981–2001. *Psychiatry, 65*(3), 207–239.

Norris, F. H., Hamblen, J. L., & Rosen, C. S. (2009). Service characteristics and counseling outcomes: Lessons from a cross-site evaluation of crisis counseling after Hurricanes Katrina, Rita and Wilma. *Administration and Policy in Mental Health and Mental Health Services Research, 36*(3), 176–185.

Norris, F. H, Stevens, S. P., Pfefferbaum, B., Wyche, K. F., & Pfefferbaum, R. L. (2008). Community resilience as a metaphor, theory, set of capacities, and strategy for disaster readiness. *American Journal of Community Psychology, 41*(1–2), 127–150.

Nucifora, F., Jr., Langlieb, A. M., Siegal, E., Everly, G. S., Jr., & Kaminsky, M. (2007). Building resistance, resilience, and recovery in the wake of school and workplace violence. *Disaster Medicine and Public Health Preparedness, 1*(Suppl. 1), S33–S37.

Olteanu, A., Arnberger, R., Grant, R., Davis, C., Abramson, D., & Asola, J. (2011). Persistence of mental health needs among children affected by Hurricane Katrina in New Orleans. *Prehospital and Disaster Medicine, 26*(1), 3–6.

Pairojkul, S., Siripul, P., Prateepchaikul, L., Kusol, K., & Puytrakul, T. (2010). Psychosocial first aid: Support for the child survivors of the Asian tsunami. *Journal of Developmental & Behavioral Pediatrics, 1*(9), 723–727.

Paton, D., Smith, L., & Violanti, J. (2000). Disaster response: Risk, vulnerability and resilience. *Disaster Prevention and Management, 9*(3), 173–180.

Perrin, P. C, McCabe, O. L., Everly, G. S., Jr., & Links, J. M. (2009). Preparing for an influenza pandemic: Mental health considerations. *Prehospital and Disaster Medicine, 24*(3), 223–230.

Plummer, C. A., Cain, D. S., Fisher, R. M., & Bankston, T. Q. (2009). Practice challenges in using psychological first aid in a group format with children: A pilot study. *Brief Treatment and Crisis Intervention, 8*(4), 313–326.

Polusny, M. A., Ries, B. J., Schultz, J. R., Calhoun, P., Clemensen, L., & Johnsen, I. R. (2008). PTSD symptom clusters associated with physical health and health care utilization in rural primary care patients exposed to natural disaster. *Journal of Traumatic Stress, 21*(1), 75–82.

Reyes, G., & Elhai, J. D. (2004). Psychosocial interventions in the early phases of disasters. *Psychotherapy: Theory, Research, Practice, Training, 41*(4), 399–411.

Rhoads, J., Pearman, T., & Rick, S. (2007). Clinical presentation and therapeutic interventions for posttraumatic stress disorder post-Katrina. *Archives of Psychiatric Nursing, 21*(5), 249–256.

Rhodes, J., Chan, C., Paxson, C., Rouse, C. E., Waters, M., & Fussell, E. (2010). The impact of hurricane Katrina on the mental and physical health of low-income parents in New Orleans. *American Journal of Orthopsychiatry, 80*(2), 237–247.

Roberts, Y. H., Mitchell, M. J., Witman, M., & Taffaro, C. (2010). Mental health symptoms in youth affected by hurricane Katrina. *Professional Psychology: Research and Practice, 41*(1), 10–18.

Ronan, K. R., Crellin, K., Johnston, D. M., Finnis, K., Paton, D., & Becker, J. (2008). Promoting child and family resilience to disasters: Effects, interventions, and prevention effectiveness. *Children, Youth and Environments, 18*(1), 332–352.

Rosen, C. S., Greene, C. J., Young, H. E., & Norris, F. H. (2010). Tailoring disaster mental health services to diverse needs: An analysis of 36 crisis counseling projects. *Health and Social Work, 35*(3), 211–220.

Ruzek, J. I., Brymer, M. J., Jacobs, A. K., Layne, C. M., Vernberg, E. M., & Watson, P. J. (2007). Psychological first aid. *Journal of Mental Health Counseling, 29*(1), 17–49.

Satapathy, S., & Subhasis, B. (2009). Disaster Psychosocial and Mental Health Support in South & South-East Asian Countries: A synthesis. *Journal of South Asia Disaster Studies, 2*(1), 21–45.

Siegel, C., Wanderling, J., & Laska, E. (2004). Coping with disasters: Estimation of additional capacity of the mental health sector to meet extended service demands. *The Journal of Mental Health Policy and Economics, 7*(1), 29–35.

Te Brake, H., Dückers, M., De Vries, M., Van Duin, D., Rooze, M., & Spreeuwenberg, C. (2009). Early psychosocial interventions after disasters, terrorism, and other shocking events: Guideline development. *Nursing and Health Sciences, 11*(4), 336–343.

Uhernik, J. A., & Husson, M. A. (2009). Psychological first aid: An evidence informed approach for acute disaster behavioral response. In G. R. Walz, J. C. Bleuer, & R. K. Yeps (Eds.),

Compelling counseling interventions: VISTAS 2009 (pp. 271–280). Arlington, VA: American Counseling Association. Retrieved from http://counselingoutfitters.com/vistas/vistas09/Article_24_UhernikHusson.pdf

Van der Velden, P. G., Grievink, L., Kleber, R. J., Drogendijk, A. N., Roskam, A. J., Marcelissen, F., . . . Gersons, B. P. (2006). Post-disaster mental health problems and the utilization of mental health services: A four-year longitudinal comparative study. *Administration and Policy in Mental Health and Mental Health Services Research, 33*(3), 279–288.

Vernberg, E. M., Steinberg, A. M., Jacobs, A. K., Brymer, M. J., Watson, P. J., Osofsky, J. D., . . . Ruzek, J. I. (2008). Innovations in disaster mental health: Psychological first aid. *Professional Psychology: Research and Practice, 39*(4), 381–388.

Walser, R. D., Ruzek, J. I., Naugle, A. E., Padesky, C., Ronell, D. M., & Ruggiero, K. (2004). Disaster and terrorism: Cognitive-behavioral interventions. *Prehospital and Disaster Medicine, 19*(1), 54–63.

Walsh, D. S. (2009). Interventions to reduce psychosocial disturbance following humanitarian relief efforts involving natural disasters: An integrative review. *International Journal of Nursing Practice, 15*(4), 231–240.

Weiss, M. G., Saraceno, B., Saxena, S., & Van Ommeren, M. (2003). Mental health in the aftermath of disasters: Consensus and controversy. *The Journal of Nervous and Mental Disease, 191*(9), 611–615.

Weissbecker, I., Sephton, S. E., Martin, M. B., & Simpson, D. M. (2008). Psychological and physiological correlates of stress in children exposed to disaster: Current research and recommendations for intervention. *Children, Youth and Environments, 18*(1), 30–70.

Woolsey, C., & Bracy, K. (2010). Emergency response and the psychological needs of school-age children. *Traumatology, 16*(2), 1–6.

Wynaden, D., Chapman, R., McGowan, S., McDonough, S., Finn, M., & Hood, S. (2003). Emergency department mental health triage consultancy service: A qualitative evaluation. *Accident and Emergency Nursing, 11*(3), 158–165.

Yamashita, J. (2011). A holistic theoretical framework for studying disaster mental health. *Psychological Trauma: Theory, Research, Practice, and Policy, 999*(999).

CHAPTER 6

Reconsidering "Special Needs" Populations During a Disaster

Roberta Proffitt Lavin, Lisa Schemmel-Rettenmeier, and Molly Frommelt-Kuhle

ABSTRACT

Meeting the "special needs" of at-risk populations affected by disasters is of the utmost importance. In the United States, there are 54 million people who fit into the special needs category who are defined as handicapped, disabled, vulnerable, challenged, or having special needs. The paramount importance for the special needs population is maintaining human dignity throughout the disaster management cycle. Government agencies, nongovernmental organizations, and advocacy organizations have all worked together to attempt to address and ensure that the needs of all individuals are addressed throughout the disaster cycle. Each provider and emergency responder should be familiar with the Americans with Disabilities Act requirements, but this alone does not begin to address the needs of children, the elderly, or other individuals and their special needs. There are multiple theoretical frameworks that may be useful, but the most human approach may be to consider needs based on Maslow's hierarchy of needs.

© 2012 Springer Publishing Company
http://dx.doi.org/10.1891/0739-6686.30.125

INTRODUCTION

Fifty-four million people or 19% of the U.S. population have disabilities and 11 million of these individuals need personal assistance with activities of daily living (U.S. Census Bureau, 2010a). However, this only begins to define what is currently referred to as the "special needs" population during a disaster. It is generally accepted that the special needs population includes visually impaired, hearing impaired, mobility impaired, single working parents, non–English-speaking persons, people without vehicles, people with special dietary needs, people with medical conditions, people with intellectual disabilities, and people with dementia (Federal Emergency Management Agency [FEMA], 2011).

No discussion of special needs populations during a disaster can begin without first defining special needs. This may seem a straightforward task, but the stakeholders have had difficulty agreeing on a definition that does not diminish, offend, or lessen the true humanity of individuals. Each individual has needs that necessarily must be addressed during a disaster. In addressing both the definition of special needs and one's approach to reaching that definition, one's ethical and theoretical approaches are revealed. Indeed, how we approach those labeled as having special needs speaks to us as a nation, a society, and as individuals.

DEFINING SPECIAL NEEDS

All federal government agencies have adopted definitions of special needs as it relates to disasters that include populations with specific disaster-related needs requiring additional assistance or capabilities. These definitions are consistent with the National Response Framework (NRF) definition of special needs populations. The NRF defines special needs populations as

> populations whose members may have additional needs before, during, and after an incident in functional areas, including but not limited to: maintaining independence, communication, transportation, supervision, and medical care. Individuals in need of additional response assistance may include those who have disabilities; who live in institutionalized settings; who are elderly; who are children; who are from diverse cultures; who have limited English proficiency or are non-English speaking; or who are transportation disadvantaged. (Department of Homeland Security, 2008)

The U.S. Department of Health and Human Services (HHS) uses the term *at risk* instead of special needs and believes it to be fully compatible with the NRF definition while including the requirements in the Pandemic and All-Hazards Preparedness Act. At-risk populations are defined as follows:

> Before, during, and after an incident, members of at-risk populations may have additional needs in one or more of the following functional areas: communication, medical care, maintaining independence, supervision, and transportation. In addition to those individuals specifically recognized as at-risk in the Pandemic and All-Hazards Preparedness Act (i.e., children, senior citizens, and pregnant women), individuals who may need additional response assistance include those who have disabilities, live in institutional-ized settings, are from diverse cultures, have limited English proficiency or are non-English speaking, are transportation disadvantaged, have chronic medical disorders, and have pharmacological dependency. (HHS, 2011)

According to HHS (2011), the significant difference in the two definitions is its inclusion of "pregnant women, those with chronic medical disorders, and those who have pharmacological dependency."

The U.S. Department of Transportation (2009) includes in its special needs definition: people with disabilities, people with medical conditions, congregate and residential care facilities, people with no access to a vehicle, homeless popu-lations, correctional facilities, and people with service animals and household pets. The addition of the homeless population, those in correctional facilities, and those with household pets is a significant addition worthy of further consid-eration by other departments.

It is clear that there is not one standard or required definition of special needs by the U.S. government. What is not as evident in the definitions is the controversy over the use of the term special needs. The term is used so broadly that to know what is being said, one must seek the definition of the organiza-tion using the term. It would seem obvious that it would be better to say what one means rather than trying to generalize. If one means medical needs, or hearing needs, or visual needs, or transportation needs, or even accommodation for household pets, it is clearer to use those terms. For example, FEMA (2011) defined the various disability and other functional needs but then in documents still refers to special or functional needs (see Table 6.1). Moreover, it is more respectful of the individual to be specific. There should never be any doubt that words hold meaning and they impact how we treat each other. The old adage "sticks and stones may break my bones, but words will never hurt me" simply is not true. Although this chapter has used the term special needs, it is the authors' belief that the term should be abandoned for more precise language. If one means homeless or lack of transportation then that should be stated because not all conditions are equal.

TABLE 6.1
Disabilities and Other Functional Needs

Disability and Other Functional Needs	Step to Address Needs
Visually impaired	• May be reluctant to leave familiar surroundings when the request is from a stranger • Guide dog may be confused or disoriented • People who are blind or partially sighted my need to depend on others to lead them, and their dog, during a disaster
Hearing impaired	• Special arrangements to receive warnings
Mobility impaired	• Special arrangements to get to a shelter
Single working parent	• May need help to plan for disasters and emergencies
Non-English speaking	• May need assistance planning for and responding to emergencies • Community and cultural groups may be able to help keep people informed
Without vehicles	• May need to make arrangements for transportation
Special dietary needs	• Take special precautions for adequate emergency food supply
Medical conditions	• Know the location and availability of more than one facility if dependent on a dialysis machine or other life-sustaining equipment or treatment
Intellectual disabilities	• May need help responding to emergencies and getting to a shelter
Dementia	• Should be registered in the Alzheimer's Association safe return program at http://www.alz.org/safetycenter/we_can_help_safety_medicalert_safereturn.asp

Adapted from Federal Emergency Management Agency. (2011). *People with disabilities and other functional needs*. Retrieved from http://www.fema.gov/plan/prepare/specialplans.shtm

AMERICANS WITH DISABILITIES ACT

The Americans with Disabilities Act (ADA) has two main purpose: (a) to prevent discrimination "against a qualified individual on the basis of disability in regard to job application procedures, the hiring, advancement, or discharge of employees, employee compensation, job training, and other terms, conditions, and privileges of employment" and (b) to ensure that "no qualified individual with a disability shall, by reason of such disability, be excluded from participation in or be denied the benefits of services, programs, or activities of a public entity, or be subjected to discrimination by any such entity" (ADA of 1990 as amended, 2009). Although there are waivers for many rules and regulations during a disaster, recent guidance from the Department of Justice (DOJ) has made clear that the ADA still applies during a disaster and specifically applies to access to shelters (DOJ, 2009).

The ADA defines disability as "(a) a physical or mental impairment that substantially limits one or more of the major life activities of such individual; (b) a record of such an impairment; or (c) being regarded as having such an impairment (as described in paragraph 3)" (Jones, 2010, p. 2). When the ADA was passed, it did not specifically address disaster or emergency preparedness and, consequently, some believed that the protections against discrimination did not apply during a disaster. It was after the events of hurricanes Katrina and Rita that the impact of disasters on persons with disabilities was brought to public attention. In 2010, the DOJ interpreted the prohibitions against discrimination to apply during disasters. In the same year, Titles II and III of the ADA were amended to include "references to emergencies in the provisions relating to communication" (Jones, 2010, p. 2).

The combined FEMA and DOJ guidance on the inclusion of the ADA in disaster preparedness, response, and recovery has greatly enhanced the likelihood of accessibility to people with disabilities. The DOJ maintains an ADA homepage that provides guidance on complying with the ADA requirements during a disaster. The *ADA Best Practices Tool Kit for State and Local Governments* addresses the responsibility of the government to protect all residents and visitors (DOJ, 2009). FEMA published its *Guidance on Planning for Integration of Functional Needs Support Services in General Population Shelters* to provide guidance to enhance access and function support needs in shelter state and local shelter plans (FEMA, 2010). The required accommodations of the two guidance documents are summarized in Table 6.2.

Shelters and temporary housing are of particular importance during a disaster. Issues that may have a substantial impact on a person with a disability may include the following:

1. Accessible notification system and information.
2. Evacuation and especially evacuation with caregivers and service animals.
3. Accessible emergency transportation.
4. Accessible shelters and temporary housing, including access to mobility devices while in the shelter or in transit (including service animals).
5. Access to medications, refrigeration, and back-up power supplies.
6. Access to mobility and assistive technology devices.

TABLE 6.2

Americans With Disabilities Applied to Emergencies

Department of Justice	FEMA
Incorporate input from people with various types of disabilities	Children and adults with disabilities have the same right to services as the general population
Notification for people with disabilities of an emergency	Any facility that is rebuilt as a result of a disaster must comply with ADA standards for accessibility
Evacuation plans enable people with disabilities to safely evacuate	Reasonable modification to policies, practices, and procedures
Sheltering of people with disabilities by removing barriers, not separating from service animals, refrigerating medications, etc.	Have durable medical equipment
Return people with disabilities to accessible homes	Have adequate consumable medical supplies
Ensure contracts require providers to follow the guide's action steps	Have personal assistance services and other goods and services as needed

Note. FEMA = Federal Emergency Management Agency. Adapted from Jones, N. (2010). *The Americans with Disabilities Act and emergency preparedness and response.* Washington, DC: Congressional Research Service.

If the issues previously mentioned had been addressed adequately prior to Hurricane Katrina affecting the families then individuals with special needs may have been more willing to evacuate. One example offered by a case worker following Hurricane Katrina was of a family that did not evacuate their Mississippi home because their adult daughter required total care and they had difficulty finding a place that could provide the resources that were needed for her care. The entire family was lost in the storm.

A second example of how the previous steps may have a positive impact involves the barriers that people in wheelchairs may face. After a disaster, temporary shelters may have temporary outdoor showers. The showers are helpful to those with full mobility and sight, but may not be adequate for those with functional limitations. Well-meaning people will build a shower that provides privacy out of plywood and with doors. Picture a shower that is the length and height of an average piece of plywood with a plywood door that only swings one way and with no handle. A plywood ramp leads up the 3 in. or so to the shower, but there are no handrails and the ramp is only the width of the narrow door.

The ramps may be slippery when wet and because there are no handrails, people without sight may step off the edge or a wheelchair may slip off the edge or if a person gets to the door, he or she will not be able to open it. A person with limited mobility will not have a way to steady himself or herself. Once one is in the shower, other issues may exist.

OVERVIEW OF NEEDS

A quick CINAHL, PubMed, Google Scholar, and PsycINFO search will identify many articles about disaster, but few nursing articles that are research focused. The current state of disaster nursing research is dismal at best. As is the case with much of the nursing research, it is qualitative research focused on the nurse's perception, whether the education and understanding is adequate, and whether the nurse will actually respond during a disaster. The research that actually occurs during a disaster is, well, nonexistent as it relates to patient care. The paucity of research that does exist is retrospective and generally focuses on the perceptions of the nurse and their experiences (Stangeland, 2010). This leaves a gapping hole in actual evidence-based disaster nursing care because it relates to physical impairments (chronic health conditions and pregnancy), sensory impairments (visual and auditory), barriers to health care (language, transportation, socioeconomic status, homelessness, learning disabilities), and age-related concerns.

Physical Impairments

The Centers for Disease Control and Prevention (CDC; 2011) estimated that 48.6 million people in the United States do not have health insurance (see Table 6.3). Although not having insurance is problematic during the best

TABLE 6.3
Lack of Health Insurance

	Under 65	Children Under 18	Adults 18–64
Uninsured	18.2%	7.8%	22.3%
Private insurance	61.2%	53.8%	64.1%
Public health plan		39.8%	15.%
Number in millions without insurance	48.2	42.5	5.8

Adapted from Centers for Disease Control and Prevention, National Center for Health Statistics. *National Health Interview Survey, 1997–2010, Family Core component.* Retrieved from http://www.cdc.gov/nchs/nhis/released201106.htm#1

of times, it is even worse during a disaster as is generally linked to not having a medical home. The medical home is, "the infrastructure capable of rendering that care effectively, i.e., the point of "first contact" for new problems while retaining the essential properties of comprehensiveness, continuity and coordination, and capable of empowering patients for self-care" (DeSalvo & Kertesz, 2007, p. 1378). Desalvo and Kertesz (2007) identified the lack of resiliency of the health care safety net following a disaster that must be corrected and suggested that one way to improve the resiliency is to implement a web-based medical home.

In 2010, the CDC estimated that 7 out of every 10 deaths in the United States were caused by chronic disease. Of those with chronic health conditions, 25% have a limitation in one or more activities of daily living (see Table 6.4). It is clearly indicated in Table 6.4 that as a person ages, the limitations increase in incidence. This is significant during a disaster because it indicates the percentage of individuals that are likely to need accommodation in a sheltering situation and the types of nursing care that will be needed following a disaster. In surveys of

TABLE 6.4
Limitations of Activities of Daily Living

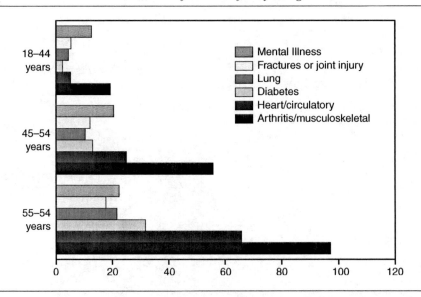

Note. Activity limitation among adults caused by chronic conditions, 2004–2005. Adapted from Centers for Disease Control and Prevention, National Center for Health Statistics. (2007). *Health, United States, 2007.* Hyattsville, MD: Author.

persons living in trailer parks in Louisiana and Mississippi following Hurricane Katrina, 50% of respondents reported one or more chronic illnesses (Larrance, Anastario, & Lawry, 2007). Moreover, it was reported that for 40% of those surveyed, the nearest health facility was greater than a 20-minute drive and 31% reported that the nearest pharmacy was greater than a 20-minute drive.

Following a disaster, the incidence of major depression, suicide, substance abuse, and gastrointestinal and cardiovascular symptoms generally increase (Larrance et al., 2007). The incidence of chronic illness is exacerbated by the requirement for evacuations with little or no notice. If an individual is not prepared with an adequate supply of medications and necessary equipment, that person may find himself or herself in a medical special needs shelter in need of care. Following Hurricane Gustav in 2008, hypertension (67%) was defined as the most common among the chronic illnesses, with anxiety/depression (24%), diabetes mellitus (36%), and severe arthritis (30.5%; Missildine et al., 2009). Although there was some variation in the chronic illnesses based on geographical area impacted, average age of the population, along with race and gender differences, the list of the most common chronic illness generally stayed the same with some variation in rank order.

Pregnancy and childbirth, a time of great joy for most, is a special problem during a disaster. Pregnancy requires special planning not only for the mother and infant but also for any additional children that will need care and supervision during and following the delivery. It is essential to maintain all basic and essential care for a pregnant woman and to reduce her stress to the extent possible. Studies have shown that prenatal stress can cause adverse effects including "preterm birth, smaller birth weight, and smaller head circumference" (Hobel, Goldstein, & Barrett, 2008). Recent research has shown that exposure to stress from a disaster, such as an earthquake, resulted in significant decline in gestational age and a significant increase in preterm labor (Torche & Kleinhaus, 2012). It has been speculated that the changes are caused by maternal behavioral changes, increased stress, impaired sleep, and decreased appetite (Dancause et al., 2011). Therefore, in the aftermath of a disaster, it is critical to ensure adequate sleep and nutrition for pregnant women and to attempt to identify and mediate early signs of stress.

Each year, there are approximately 4,058,000 live births in the United States alone and an additional 1,995,840 pregnancy losses. Of these pregnancies, an estimated 47% were unplanned (American Pregnancy Association, n.d.). It is widely accepted that the rate of unplanned pregnancies increases during a disaster, because of stress-reducing behavior or lack of family planning. During a disaster, it is essential to take the time to remember the importance of discussing family planning with all clients of reproductive age.

Sensory Impairments

According to the World Health Organization (WHO; 2011), visual function is divided into four categories by the International Classification of Diseases-10: normal vision, moderate visual impairment, severe visual impairment, and blindness. Uncorrected refractive errors, cataracts, and glaucoma are the major causes of impaired visual function with 285 million people worldwide impacted. Of those with visual impairment, 39 million are blind (WHO, 2011). In the United States, it is estimated that 21.5 million reported "either 'have trouble' seeing, even when wearing glasses or contact lenses, or that they are blind or unable to see at all" (American Foundation for the Blind, 2012, para.3).

The WHO 2012 describes hearing loss as either partial or complete in one or both ears. Worldwide, there are approximately 275 million people with moderate-to-profound hearing loss (WHO, 2012). In the United States, it is estimated that 9–22 of every 1,000 people in the United States are functionally deaf or has a severe hearing impairment (Mitchell, 2005).

For those with diminished visual or hearing function, FEMA (2012) recommends additional steps that should be taken:

1. May be extremely reluctant to leave familiar surroundings when the request for evacuation comes from a stranger.
2. A guide dog could become confused or disoriented in a disaster. People who are blind or partially sighted may have to depend on others to lead them, as well as their dog, to safety during a disaster.
3. May need to make special arrangements to receive warnings.

Nurses and other health care providers should also keep the diminished visual or hearing function steps recommended by FEMA in mind as they interact with individuals in a disaster situation.

Barriers to Care

Among the major barriers to health care during a disaster are language, transportation, socioeconomic status, homelessness, and learning disabilities. Those with financial means and transportation are generally able to self-evacuate or make arrangements during a disaster, but those that are poor, homeless, or without transportation have a more difficult time evacuating and accessing care.

Homelessness is generally defined as

(1) an individual or family who lacks a fixed, regular, and adequate nighttime residence; (2) an individual or family with a primary nighttime residence that is a public or private place not designed for or ordinarily used as a regular sleeping accommodation for human beings, including a car, park, abandoned building, bus or train station, airport,

or camping ground; (3) an individual or family living in a supervised publicly or privately operated shelter designated to provide temporary living arrangements (including hotels and motels paid for by Federal, State, or local government programs for low-income individuals or by charitable organizations, congregate shelters, and transitional housing); (4) an individual who resided in a shelter or place not meant for human habitation and who is exiting an institution where he or she temporarily resided; (5) an individual or family who—(A) will imminently lose their housing, including housing they own, rent, or live in without paying rent, are sharing with others, and rooms in hotels or motels not paid for by Federal, State, or local government programs for low-income individuals or by charitable organizations, as evidenced by—(i) a court order resulting from an eviction action that notifies the individual or family that they must leave within 14 days; (ii) the individual or family having a primary nighttime residence that is a room in a hotel or motel and where they lack the resources necessary to reside there for more than 14 days; or (iii) credible evidence indicating that the owner or renter of the housing will not allow the individual or family to stay for more than 14 days, and any oral statement from an individual or family seeking homeless assistance that is found to be credible shall be considered credible evidence for purposes of this clause; (B) has no subsequent residence identified; and (C) lacks the resources or support networks needed to obtain other permanent housing; and (6) unaccompanied youth and homeless families with children and youth defined as homeless under other Federal statutes who—(A) have experienced a long term period without living independently in permanent housing, (B) have experienced persistent instability as measured by frequent moves over such period, and (C) can be expected to continue in such status for an extended period of time because of chronic disabilities, chronic physical health or mental health conditions, substance addiction, histories of domestic violence or childhood abuse, the presence of a child or youth with a disability, or multiple barriers to employment. (b) Domestic violence and other dangerous or life-threatening conditions. Notwithstanding any other provision of this section, the Secretary shall consider to be homeless any individual or family who is fleeing, or is attempting to flee, domestic violence, dating violence, sexual assault, stalking, or other dangerous or life-threatening conditions in the individual's or family's current housing situation, including where the health and safety of children are jeopardized, and who have no other residence and lack the resources or support networks to obtain other permanent housing. (U.S. Congress, n.d.)

Nurses must develop an attitude of cultural relativism. It is important to understand what the population being served considers being sick and how they care for themselves. To impose one's own values on such a vulnerable population is impractical and arrogant. Health care must be adapted to fit the unique needs of the homeless, but to do that, health care professionals first must understand what those needs are. Knowing the most frequently expressed self-care deficit facilitates understanding the needs of the homeless population. Some suggestions for providing appropriate care include locating clinics in areas where the homeless congregate, providing transportation to and from medical appointments, and even going out to the shelters where the homeless live to provide basic screening service. Just because a disaster shelter is established to provide shelter, food, and medical care does not mean the homeless will come to it.

Nurses must realize that their care does not end with the physical person. Housing is essential to a person's health. Although a person may be homeless prior to a disaster, it is never appropriate to return the person to homelessness. Inadequate housing is the most common self-care deficit experienced by the homeless person. Nurses often believe that housing is a problem for social workers, yet frequently, there is no funding for social workers or they are too few in number to care for the homeless population after a disaster. If there were a disaster case management program, it would be a good starting point. Furthermore, if a trusting relationship is developed between the individual being served and the nurse, then the nurse is better positioned to offer advice and help. Lack of housing is not only a deterrent to care, but oppressive living conditions put the homeless person at greater risk of disease and injury. To escape oppressive living conditions, a person must either secure a job or community aid.

Age-Related Conditions
Children and elders both require special precautions during and after a disaster. Both are considered vulnerable populations. However, there is relatively consistent evidence that elders are impacted more during a disaster than other segments of the population. Consequently, there is more available literature and disaster research related to elders.

In the United States, 24% of the population is younger than 18 years and 13% is older than 65 years (U.S. Census Bureau, 2010a). Children younger than 15 years are 13%–46% of the population worldwide, whereas elders older than 65 years ranged 2%–23% of the population worldwide (Population Reference Bureau, 2010). Not all elders are vulnerable and in need of assistance. However, the elderly are disproportionately impacted by disaster. During the hurricanes Katrina and Rita elderly persons accounted for 71% of the deaths and this consistently the case with heat waves (Aldrich & Benson, 2008). The high death rate is related to the estimates of more than 80% of those older than 65 years have one or more chronic health conditions (Aldrich & Benson, 2008). When assisting the elderly, it is important to assess for the ability to carry out activities of daily living and the availability of a support network. It is also important to remember that in many cases, the elderly have a great deal of life experience and may be of assistance to others. It should never be assumed that age equals an inability to function independently.

Children are approximately 25% of the population and, therefore, are deserving of a great deal of attention in disaster planning and response. It has become common to hear, "children are not little adults." That statement is never truer than in a disaster. Children must be considered throughout the disaster cycle and it is inappropriate to lump them with special needs populations. They become lost in the bureaucracy as they do during the disaster. For example, if one assumed that a child cannot self-evacuate, requires law enforcement or social services to assume custody of them in the absence of a parent or guardian, and should be segregated from the general population for their safety, then one might think it makes sense to lump groups together that meet these same criteria. The problem with this process is that it would result in children being placed in the same evacuation and holding area as the sex offenders. Least one thinks this is an unrealistic possibility; it was at one point the actual plan before the actual consequences of the plan were realized.

The National Commission on Children and Disaster did a comprehensive review of the needs of children during a disaster. Their findings are available at http://cybercemetery.unt.edu/archive/nccd/20110427002908/http:/www .childrenanddisasters.acf.hhs.gov/index.html and fully address the medical and human services needs of children throughout the disaster cycle. It is generally agreed that children should be provided with a safe environment that provides space for recreation, they should return to normal daily activities as soon as possible, that there must be the availability of child care, and medical caches should include medications and supplies specific for infants and children.

The considerations of the needs of individuals with functional limitations are addressed in Table 6.5. However, it is not a comprehensive list.

THEORETICAL APPROACH

There are two distinct theoretical approaches that should be considered in designing and implementing the provision of services to people during a disaster. The first is from an ethical and moral perspective and addresses the approach to allocation of resources. The second is an approach to frame the prioritization of services. Both must be addressed, and both are of equal importance.

TABLE 6.5

Considerations in Meeting the Needs of Individuals

Chronic Illnesses

- Medication issues—adequate supply, inability to pay, inability to remember names or dosages of medications, difficult to store
- Medical records—lost in the disaster, not available electronically
- Increased anxiety—may result in worsening of condition
- Power—loss of electrical power may impact some devices or the ability to maintain sanitation and climate control
- Access to care—access to dialysis, physical therapy, psychotherapy, and other medical treatments may be limited

Pregnancy

- Water—1 to 3 gallons of water per day
- Food—access to nutritional food
- Pregnancy testing—many pregnancies are unplanned and women may not be aware they are pregnant. Many women use contraceptives and may not have them. Information on pregnancy prevention and natural family planning should be available
- Health care—all pregnant women should receive health care and prenatal vitamins
- Transfer—it may be necessary to arrange transfer to an area for safe delivery
- Supplies—general supplies, supplies for mothers (sanitary pads), infant formula, blankets, suction bulb, clothing, diapers
- Breastfeeding—available space for mothers to feed
- Care of children—plan for care of other children during a delivery
- Increased anxiety—from injury and separation from family and especially children

Sensory Impairments

- Service animals—may become disoriented during a disaster, should remain with the owner, should not be treated as a pet by providers
- Assistive devices— should remain with the individual
- Leading the blind—may need to depend on others for assistance, but proper etiquette should be followed
- Warnings—need special arrangements to receive warnings and to relay information for the deaf and the blind such as announcements in large print and vocal
- Large print—label emergency supplies with large print or Braille

Barriers to Care

- Language—work through community organizations and target small ethnic communities when possible, make translation services available, find responder that are multilingual when possible
- Transportation—may need help with transportation for evacuation

TABLE 6.5
Considerations in Meeting the Needs of Individuals (Continued)

Barriers to Care

- Intellectual disabilities—may need assistance getting to shelter and applying for assistance
- Homeless—may not be trusting, may suffer from mental illness, may need help with transportation, will need help finding long-term housing after the disaster

Age-Related Conditions

Frail elders
- Relationships—public health and agencies on aging should partner in advance to identify and assist elders
- Disabilities—apply appropriate recommendations based on the recommendations for sensory impairments and chronic illnesses
- Nutrition—work to facilitate food deliver to elders
- Case management—may need assistance with online applications and have concerns about losing their current benefits and/or not understand the sequence of delivery for benefits

Children
- Safety—ensure that there is a safe environment with adult supervision (only persons with an appropriate background check)
- Nutrition—provide food that is palatable to children and include infant formula
- Recreation—age-appropriate recreational activities should be provided to reduce stress
- Media exposure—limit exposure to the media because the constant reliving of the disaster may increase anxiety in children
- Reaction to disaster—children react to a disaster based on their developmental level. Preschoolers may feel helpless and elementary school children may have some understanding of what has happened
- Medical supplies—plan for appropriate medication and supplies for children, keeping in mind that children will be 25% of the population

Allocation of Resources

Nursing has not used utility to the extent that it has been used in medicine and health policy, but it has received wide use in nursing to address quality of life issues. This may be because of the confusion surrounding the term *utility*. Utility is "a number for comparing gambles such that the gamble with the highest expected utility should be preferred by the patient" (Sox, Blatt, Higgins, & Marton, 1988, p. 169). This definition is meant to correspond with the von Neumann and Morgenstern model but does not clarify the meaning of utility.

A standard dictionary (*Webster's New Word Dictionary of the American Language*, 1970) defines utility as

> (1) the quality or property of being useful; usefulness; (2) the greatest happiness of the greatest number (3) something useful; (4) a) something useful to the public, esp. the service of electric power, gas, water, telephone, etc. b) a company providing such a service . . . (5) [E]con. The power to satisfy the needs or wants of humanity . . . [and] (6) able to play several positions on a baseball team (utility infielder). (p. 1565)

Most of these definitions are useful and directly associated with utility. The concept of utility is most closely linked to happiness, satisfying the needs of humanity, and usefulness. In addition, utility has served as a measure to study nursing practice models, access cost-effectiveness of clinical nurse specialists, guide health care decision making regarding the allocation of resources, and identify patient preferences (Anthony, Brennan, O'Brien, & Suwannaroop, 2004; van der Hout, Tijhuis, Hazes, Breedveld, & Vliet Vlieland, 2003).

Interestingly, utility has been rejected by some nurses for ethical decision making because it is too connected to the scientific method, too time consuming, and too rigid in its separation of moral thought from reality (Crowden, 1994). Regardless of this fact, utility clearly influenced the American Nurses Association's (ANA) *Code of Ethics* (ANA, 2010). Despite reservations of some, utilitarianism has been the predominate approach to allocation of care and the basis of much nursing ethics, including the work by the HHS for the allocation of scarce resources after a nuclear detonation and work by the ANA on adapting standards of care during a disaster (ANA, 2008; Knebel et al., 2011).

Theory of Justice

The theory of justice may be a better approach for addressing the needs of all people with special conditions during a disaster. The theory is built on the same basic premise as utilitarianism with the exception that inequality is accepted as long as it benefits the worst off. Rawls (1971) adds the concept of primary goods to utility. A *primary good* is something a rational person wants such as respect and liberty. Interestingly, health is not considered a primary good because it is not something one can distribute (Olsen, 1977). Rights are used to distinguish states in which the utility consequences are equal (Dasgupta, 1993). Rawls holds that if preferences are based on a veil of ignorance, individuals will always choose to maximize their primary goods because they will not know if they may someday be the person who is worst off. This is the same principle as "Do unto others as you would have them do unto you." This approach is based on lexical order of two principles:

1. Each person is to have an equal right to the most extensive total system of equal basic liberties compatible with a similar system of liberty for all.
2. Social and economic equalities are to be arranged so that they are both: (a) to the greatest benefit of the least advantaged, consistent with the just savings principle, and (b) attached to offices and positions open to all under conditions of fair equality of opportunity (Rawls, 1971, p. 302).

If actions should benefit the least advantaged, the result is the least advantaged not being made worse off.

Applying the concept of utility and a Rawlsian approach can result in various consequences based on the theoretical approach. The best way to understand this is through an example. Wealthy people have better access to health care even in times of emergency or disaster than do the poor who are generally less educated. Should a society spend more money to make sure the less educated have the same access to health care in a disaster as the most skilled, even though doing so will decrease the utility of the wealthy and potentially cost the life of a genius? The consequences will depend on this approach. A utilitarian would only be concerned about maximizing the total utility, whereas a Rawlsian would be more concerned about increasing the utility of the least advantaged.

PRIORITIZING RESOURCES

If it is assumed that the allocation of resources must take into consideration the needs of the least advantaged then there must be additional assumptions about the prioritization of the needs of the least advantaged. The most basic way to prioritize all needs is through the use of Maslow's hierarchy of needs (Figure 6.1). Maslow's hierarchy of needs considers that one of the most important determinants in providing health care is the needs of the client. This is true whether the needs are physical, psychological, or spiritual.

Maslow arranged human needs in a hierarchical pyramid that at its base has the physiological needs of oxygen, food, elimination, temperature control, sex, movement, rest, and comfort, which always take priority. Within the context of disaster response and recovery, this would necessarily include access to the following:

1. Life-saving measure for those that are injured.
2. Safe air in a radiation of biological event.
3. Clean food and water that is appropriate to one's needs, including infant formula and foods appropriate to children or those with special dietary requirements.

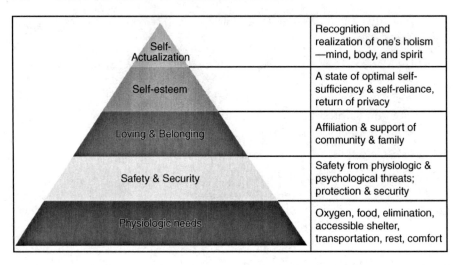

FIGURE 6.1 Prioritization of needs for disaster survivors based on Maslow's Hierarchy of Needs.

4. Protection from the elements—safe from excessive heat, cold, or weather conditions.
5. Freedom of movement, which requires shelter that is accessible to those with assistive devices.
6. Comfort from the events that have occurred including provision of spiritual care and recreation for children.
7. Provision of psychological and spiritual care that is sensitive to an individual's needs and beliefs. This is a time when those with no prior spiritual affiliation may need as much support as those who have a strong foundation. Clergy and lay leaders must seek out and identify those who are not part of their communities, but may be in distress.

The next two tiers address psychological needs of safety and security needs and love and belongingness. The safety and security needs will likely be among the highest priorities to be addressed in the hours to days following a disaster when the response addresses saving lives and protecting property. The love and belongingness needs will get greater attention as the response moves into recovery and the faith-based organizations mobilize within communities. The needs may include the following:

1. Ensuring that children are reunited with parents or guardians and protected from exploitation.
2. Ensuring that service animals and assistive devices remain with the owner.

3. Providing safe environments that are accessible to all people and provide areas for those with specific needs and areas where families may remain together.
4. Provision of emergency and life-sustaining medical care that takes into consideration all people.

The last two tiers are the higher level needs of self-esteem and self-actualization. These are the needs that everyone strives for to feel self-value. It is the return to self-reliance and autonomy that may be lost as a result of a disaster. This may take weeks, months, or years to regain; is part of the recovery process; and can be facilitated within disaster case management. Specific areas of consideration may include the following:

1. Identifying appropriate housing.
2. Enrolling children in schools—new ones if necessary.
3. Gaining employment.
4. Applying for disaster assistance.
5. Replacing damaged or destroyed assistive devices.
6. Reuniting with one's faith community.

The highest priority will always be life-threatening situations and maintaining the client's safety following a disaster. However, the provider must always be planning for the future and recognize the unique needs of all individuals. The old approach that relies on doing the greatest good for the greatest number of people may appear to be the best option in the short run, but does not recognize that those who are fully functional individuals without special needs may be better able to care for themselves and have fewer long-lasting impacts than those with special needs. Thus, doing the "greatest good for the greatest number" may mean doing significant harm to those with greater needs and ignoring that more should be done for those with the least resources and the greatest needs.

RECOMMENDATIONS

There is an unending list of recommendations that could be provided and have been provided by advocacy groups and most recently in the *National Commission on Children and Disasters 2010 Report to the President and Congress* (National Commission on Children and Disasters, 2010). However, to exhaust the list of recommendations, one would have to basically list every flaw of every plan, which is not practical. Therefore, four broad and overarching recommendations are offered.

1. *Special Needs Terminology*. Reconsider the use of the terms special needs and at risk in planning, response, and recovery documents and instead take the time to say what one actually means. Needs are needs. When some

needs are designated as "special" it gives the opportunity, from the utilitarian perspective, to dismiss the need as not meeting the requirement for doing the greatest good for the greatest number of people and potentially ignores the needs of some. To say that a need for a service animal is different than a need for corrective lenses implies that one need is lesser or greater than the other. More clearly stated the needs are to be able to navigate and communicate adequately.

2. *Disaster Case Management.* A nationwide network of disaster case management providers—that specifically takes into consideration the needs of all people—would address the unique needs of individuals. Priority should be given to those that are at the greatest risk of harm if their needs are not addressed. Those best able to accomplish this task are the faith-based organizations in the local communities who know the needs of those in their communities, are familiar with the available resources, and work in the community daily. They must be augmented by a state or federal level system until they are to be up and running as they will be in the impacted area and are likely to have been affected by the disaster.

3. *Ethical Approach to Allocation of Resources.* A new ethical approach should be considered to prioritize the allocation of resources during a disaster. Giving priority to those with the least among us may ensure that there are adequate resources for all.

4. *Conflicting Terminology in Law, Regulations, and Policies.* As with any areas of laws, regulations, and policies there are conflicts over the years. This results in confusion for the planners and implementers. A careful review of the definitions of special needs and at risk should be undertaken to revise terminology so that it consistent across federal, state, and local governments. It should be consistent in all documents so that there is little to no doubt what is being conveyed. Until this is done, there will remain confusion for those who must implement the policies, grants, cooperative agreements, and contracts issued by the various levels of government.

5. *Specific Recommendations for Nurses.* Nurses are frequently requested to assist in the disaster cycle including preparedness, response, and recovery. Nursing competencies should be assessed to determine the qualities and competencies of an effective nurse in the field. Specifically, the research should assess practice during the response process to address gaps in the current retrospective research. In addition, clinical practice standards based on the type of response and the population are currently based on consensus. Research is needed to determine the best use of registered nurses and advanced practice nurses along with the changes in practice standards including expansion of scope of practice during a disaster.

RESOURCES

- ADA home page available at http://www.ada.gov/
- Administration for Children and Families, Office of Human Services Emergency Preparedness and Response provides support to Special Needs Populations and works on disaster case management. Available at http://www.acf.hhs.gov/ohsepr/snp/snp.html
- American Foundation for the Blind provides information and resources related to the blind. Available at http://www.afb.org/section.aspx?SectionID=15
- Center for Special Needs Populations at The Ohio State University provides interdisciplinary support and is available at https://www.csnp.ohio-state.edu/
- Children and Disasters Website offers various tools for addressing the needs of children during a disaster. Available at http://www2.aap.org/disasters/index.cfm
- Civil rights. Federal laws prohibit discrimination against individuals based on race, color, national origin, disability, or age in programs and activities that receive federal financial assistance including emergency preparedness and response programs. Available at http://www.hhs.gov/ocr/civilrights/resources/specialtopics/emergencypre/index.html
- Disability.gov. Search for disaster resources by state or national. This is probably the best starting point for searching for available resources and information. Available at https://www.disability.gov/emergency_preparedness
- Disability preparedness proposes a paradigm shift and is available at http://www.disabilitypreparedness.gov/paradigm.htm
- FEMA has many resources for addressing special needs at http://www.fema.gov/index.shtm
- Pregnancy care. Available at http://emergency.cdc.gov/disasters/pregnant disasterhcp.asp
- Section 689 Reference Guide. Accommodating individuals with disabilities in the provision of disaster mass care, housing, and human services. Available at http://www.fema.gov/oer/reference/index.shtm
- University of Southern Mississippi Institute of Disability Studies. Resources to help those who have children with disabilities at your child care center, or have questions regarding the law, strategies for implementation of inclusion, adapting the curriculum, or developmentally appropriate activities. Available at http://www.usm.edu/ids/prepare/

REFERENCES

Aldrich, N., & Benson, W. (2008). Disaster preparedness and the chronic disease needs of vulnerable older adults. *Preventing Chronic Disease, 5*(1), A27.

American Foundation for the Blind. (2012). *Snapshots*. Retrieved from http://www.afb.org/section.aspx?SectionID-15

American Nurses Association. (2010). *Code of ethics with interpretive statements.* Silver Spring, MD: Author.

American Nurses Association. (2008). *Adapting standards of care under extreme conditions: Guidance for professionals during disasters, pandemics, and other extreme emergencies.* Silver Spring: Author.

American Pregnancy Association. (n.d.). *Statistics: Pregnancy.* Retrieved from American Pregnancy Association Promotion Pregnancy Wellness Website: http://www.americanpregnancy.org/main/statistics.html

Americans with Disabilities Act of 1990 as Amended. (2009). Retrieved from http://www.ada.gov/pubs/adastatute08.htm#12131

Anthony, M., Brennan, P., O'Brien, R., & Suwannaroop, N. (2004). Measures of nursing practice models using multiattribute utility theory: Relationship to patient and organizational outcomes. *Quality Management in Health Care, 13*(1), 40–52.

Centers for Disease Control and Prevention. (2010). *Chronic disease prevention and health promotion.* Retrieved from http://www.cdc.gov/chronicdisease/overview/index.htm

Centers for Disease Control and Prevention. (2011). *Early release of selected estimates based on data from 2010 National Health Interview Survey.* Retrieved from http://www.cdc.gov/nchs/released201106.htm#1

Crowden, A. (1994). On the moral nature of nursing practice. *Journal of Advanced Nursing, 20,* 1104–1110.

Dancause, K., Laplante, D., Oremus, C., Fraser, S., Brunet, A., & King, S. (2011). Disaster-related prenatal maternal stress influences birth outcomes: Project ice storm. *Early Human Development, 87,* 813–820.

Dasgupta, P. (1993). *An inquiry into well-being and destitution.* New York, NY: Oxford University Press.

Department of Homeland Security. (2008). *Glossary/Acronyms.* Retrieved from http://www.fema.gov/emergency/nrf/glossary.htm#5

Department of Justice. (2009). *ADA best practices tool kit for state and local governments.* Retrieved from http://www.ada.gov/pcatoolkit/chap7shelterprog.htm

DeSalvo, K., & Kertesz, S. (2007). Creating a more resilient safety net for persons with chronic disease: Beyond the "medical home." *Journal of General Internal Medicine, 22*(9), 1377–1379.

Federal Emergency Management Agency. (2010). *FEMA.* Retrieved from Guidance on Planning for Integration of Functional Needs Support Services in General Population Shelters Website: http://www.fema.gov/pdf/about/odic/fnss_guidance.pdf

Federal Emergency Management Agency. (2011). *People with disabilities and other access and functional needs.* Retrieved from http://www.fema.gov/plan/prepare/specialplans.shtm#resources

Federal Emergency Management Agency. (2012). *People with disabilities and other access and functional needs.* Retrieved from http://www.fema.gov/plan/prepare/specialplans.shtm

Hobel, C. J., Goldstein, A., & Barrett, E. S. (2008). Psychosocial stress and pregnancy outcome. *Clinical Obstetrics and Gynecology, 51*(2), 333–348.

Jones, N. (2010). *The Americans with Disabilities Act and emergency preparedness and response.* Washington, DC: Congressional Research Service.

Knebel, A., Coleman, N., Cliffer, K., Murrain-Hill, P., McNally, R., Oancea, V., . . . Yeskey, K. (2011). Allocation of scarce resources after a nuclear detonation: Setting the context. *Disaster Medicine and Public Health Preparedness, 5*(Suppl.), S20–S31.

Larrance, R., Anastario, M., & Lawry, L. (2007). Health status among internally displaced persons in Louisiana and Mississippi travel trailer parks. *Annals of Emergency Medicine, 49*(5), 590–601.

Missildine, K., Varnell, G., Williams, J., Grover, K., Ballard, N., & Stanley-Hermanns, M. (2009). Comfort in the eye of the storm: A survey of evacuees with special medical needs. *Journal of Emergency Nursing, 35*(6), 515–520.

Mitchell, R. (2005). *Gallaudet Research Institute*. Retrieved from Gallaudet University Website: http://www.research.gallaudet.edu/Demographics/deaf-US.php

National Commission on Children and Disasters. (2010). *2010 Report to the President and Congress* (AHRQ Publication No. 10-M037). Rockville, MD: Agency for Healthcare Research and Quality.

Olsen, J. (1997). Theories of justice and their implications for priority setting in health care. *J. Health Econ, 16* (6), 625-639.

Population Reference Bureau. (2010). *2010 World population data sheet*. Washington, DC: United States Agency for International Development.

Rawls, J. (1971). *The theory of Justice*. Cambridge, MA: Belknap Press of Harvard University Press.

Sox, H., Blatt, M., Higgins, M., & Marton, K. (1988). *Medical decision making*. Boston, MA: Butterworth-Heinermann.

Stangeland, P. (2010). Disaster nursing: A retrospective review. *Critical Care Nursing Clinics of North America, 22*(4), 421–436.

Torche, F., & Kleinhaus, K. (2012). Prenatal stress, gestational age and secondary sex ratio: The sex-specific effects of exposure to a natural disaster in early pregnancy. *Human Reproduction, 27*(2), 558–567.

U.S. Census Bureau. (2010a, May 26). *Newsroom: Profile America facts for features*. Retrieved from http://www.census.gov/newsroom/releases/archives/facts_for_features_special_edition/cb10-ff13.html

U.S. Census Bureau. (2010b). *State and county quick facts*. Retrieved from http://quickfacts.census.gov/qfd/states/00000.html

U.S. Congress. (n.d.). *42 USC § 11302—general definition of homeless individual*. Retrieved from http://www.law.cornell.edu/uscode/text/42/11302#FN-1

U.S. Department of Health and Human Services. (2011). *Office of the Assistant Secretary for Preparedness and Response*. Retrieved from http://www.phe.gov/Preparedness/planning/abc/Documents/at-risk-individuals.pdf

U.S. Department of Transportation. (2009, May 19). *Evacuating populations with special needs*. Retrieved from http://ops.fhwa.dot.gov/publications/fhwahop09022/sn1_overview.htm

Van der Hout, W., Tijhuis, G., Hazes, J., Breedveld, F., & Vliet Vlieland, T. (2003). Cost effectiveness and cost utility analysis of multidisciplinary care in patients with rheumatoid arthritis: A randomised comparison of clinical nurse specialist care, inpatient team care, and day patient team care. *Annals of the Rheumatic Diseases, 62*(4), 308–315.

Webster's New Word Dictionary of the American Language (2nd ed.). (1970). New York, NY: World.

World Health Organization. (2011). *Visual impairment and blindness*. Retrieved from http://www.who.int/mediacentre/factsheets/fs282/en/

World Health Organization. (2012). *Deafness and hearing impairment*. Retrieved from http://www.who.int/mediacentre/factsheets/fs300/en/index.htm

CHAPTER 7

The Role of Technology and Informatics in Disaster Planning and Response

Elizabeth Weiner and Lynn A. Slepski

ABSTRACT

It is clear that technology and informatics are becoming increasingly important in disasters and humanitarian response. Technology is a critical tool to recording, analyzing, and predicting trends in data that could not be achieved prior to its implementation. Informatics is the translation of this data into information, knowledge, and wisdom. Combining technology and informatics applications with response efforts has resulted in various enhanced biosurveillance efforts, advanced communications, and information management during disasters. Although these efforts have been well described in the literature, research on the impact of technology and informatics during these efforts has been limited. As a result, this chapter will provide an overview of these technology and informatics solutions and present suggestions for further research in an era when disaster and humanitarian response efforts continue to increase as well. A literature search was performed using PubMed search tools with the National Library of Medicine Medical Subject Headings (MeSH) terms of "disasters," "disaster planning," "disaster medicine," "technology," "informatics," and "research." Search limitations were set for 5 years and in English. Because of the limited number of research articles in this field, the MeSH term research was deleted.

© 2012 Springer Publishing Company
http://dx.doi.org/10.1891/0739-6686.30.149

NURSING INFORMATICS RESEARCH ISSUES IN DISASTER AND HUMANITARIAN RESPONSE

The World Health Organization (WHO) convened the First Consultation on Nursing and Midwifery Contributions in Emergencies in Geneva during November 22–24, 2006 (WHO, 2007). Weiner (2011) described the research issues for nursing and midwifery contributions that were discussed during this event. Although many factors were considered as impacting nursing research in this area (such as the more recent development of emergency nursing as a specialty, the uncoordinated efforts for competency development, the difficulties with field research, the lack of policy development, the lack of funding for nursing research in emergency planning and response, and the need for more multi-disciplinary research), there were also technology and informatics-related factors.

Standardized terminology is one of the basic foundations to the science of informatics. Although classic definitions have been provided by WHO, various terms have continued to be used to describe the same thing (e.g., disasters and emergencies). Emergency nursing also means a specialty in the emergency department of hospitals rather than the more global use of the term of providing nursing care during emergency situations. The term "terrorism" has grown in popularity, and "bioterrorism" has sometimes taken on more importance in funding than other forms of disasters. This confusion about existing terminology makes finding relevant literature a more difficult task, thus hampering the ability to draw conclusions about the support of the data to contribute to the knowledge of the discipline.

Knowledge synthesis tools have become more important to health care practitioners as we strive to understand the data and its impact on our knowledge. Clinical decision support tools such as Zynx Health (http://www.zynxhealth.com/) or UpToDate (http://www.uptodate.com) are based on clinical knowledge-based systems primarily organized around acute and chronic health care conditions. Clinicians typically practice during disaster situations where there are scarce resources, and extreme fluctuations in symptoms of disease states caused by the increased stress of situations. As a result, clinicians must be able to extrapolate from these databases to make clinical decisions that are customized to their patients and situations. Even during nondisaster situations, most published evaluations of the impact of clinical decision support on health care quality have been published in large academic medical centers having adequate resources (Berner, 2009).

Access to data and information resources is a necessary prerequisite to its integration into nursing practice, education, or research. In today's time, access requires technology literacy as well as the technology itself. Furthermore, network access to the Internet or to other databases housed in the "cloud" is essential. Cloud computing refers to the storage and service of data delivery while accessing servers via the network. In other words, software applications and data are not self-contained on a hard drive of the user's computer, but rather via servers in a remote location. Recent networking advances into mobile broadband (using 3G and 4G technologies) have only increased methods of data access. Compounding the situation is the need for power to drive the technology to obtain the access. During disaster and humanitarian aid situations, there are many times that technology itself is not available. If available, there may not be power to drive the technology or network, thereby making access impossible. The distribution of information resources that have been predetermined to be helpful to organizations during and following events should be disseminated throughout the organization prior to the event and available in nonelectronic formats. Cell phone communications have become ubiquitous yet towers may be down after an event, making this form of communication impossible. If cell phone towers remain intact, the increase in cell phone traffic may cause blockages in the system rendering their use impossible as well. Victims of Hurricane Katrina found that sending text messages worked because the messages were held on a server and relayed later when traffic was decreased (Shklovski, Burke, Kiesler, & Kraut, 2010).

Meaningful access requires a user interface that directs clinicians to the appropriate data being sought. How these databases are organized presents challenges to those specializing in informatics. Many specialists in informatics have not yet understood that they, too, can make a contribution during emergency relief efforts. Organizing available resources into a searchable database can be as important as providing hands-on care.

Data repositories are another important area of contribution. Researchers must be able to access databases that contain information about funding sources. Many times, these are specific to the country, thus do not always support international research. Furthermore, interdisciplinary research needs also should be included in these funding databases to encourage teamwork in research as well as planning and response efforts.

Perhaps one of the most comprehensive disaster information repositories is the Disaster Information Management Research Center sponsored by the National Library of Medicine (NLM; 2011). This site contains not only disaster health links on topic that range from animals to types of disasters such as tornadoes, but this site also includes links to categories of response such as biological and chemical warfare agents. In addition, the site includes "A–Z Disasters and Health" as well as a series of links that take you to current information posted by the Centers for Disease Control and Prevention (CDC), and specific content related to the environmental health concerns related to natural disasters. In the section Disaster and Emergency Response Tools from NLM, there are links to chemical hazards emergency medical management, radiation emergency management, and the Wireless Information System for Emergency Responders (WISER)—a system designed to help responders identify hazardous materials and respond to emergencies involving more than 400 chemicals as well as radiologic agents. Bundling responder information into a "one-stop shop" allows responders to review and bookmark the site in advance or even download the application on to their mobile device.

Perhaps no other resource repository is as important to response efforts in the United States as the Strategic National Stockpile (SNS). Run by the CDC, the SNS has large quantities of pharmaceuticals and medical supplies to protect the American public if there is a public health emergency severe enough to cause local authorities to deplete their own resources (CDC, 2012a). State and local jurisdictions must prepare in advance of the need for the SNS to know how to request, receive, coordinate, transport, and transfer SNS assets.

Another example of how informatics aided in the emergency response effort was during Hurricane Katrina. KatrinaHealth was an online service that was established to help individuals affected by the hurricane work with their health professionals to gain access to their own electronic prescription medication records (Markle Foundation, 2006). This data repository was made possible by the collaboration of federal, state, and local governments working with a national foundation, several private businesses, and national organizations of health professionals.

HEALTH INFORMATION EXCHANGE EFFORTS

Health information exchange (HIE) is critical to victims of disasters or other humanitarian crises events. Many times, the medical record is destroyed during an event, or if victims are forced to relocate to another area, there may be no possibility for access to their health information. Further contributing to this information dearth is the fact that stressful situations do not promote accurate recall of health information by victims involved. Technology can be used to store and control access to health care information but requires that the data and information are in electronic format.

In the United States, the Health Information Technology for Economic and Clinical Health (HITECH) Act provided the health care community with a transformational opportunity to support the adoption and use of electronic health records (EHRs; Blumental & Tavenner, 2010). The Act authorizes incentive payments (up to $27 billion over 10 years) through Medicare and Medicaid to clinicians and hospitals to achieve "meaningful use" of EHRs promoting improvements in care delivery. Payment is tied specifically to achievement of health care processes and outcomes operationalized by objectives and measures. Ninety-five percent of hospitals participating in the January 2011 American Hospital Association survey reported that they plan to pursue the meaningful use requirements (Hsiao, Hing, Socey, & Cai, 2011).

There are three graduated stages for implementing meaningful use and certification of EHR software. Stage I focuses on capturing data in a coded format, Stage II expands the exchange of information, and Stage III focuses on clinical decision support for high priority conditions, patient self-management, and access to comprehensive data. Clearly, all three stages will support improved health care to victims of disasters or humanitarian displacement. Health care providers must first collect data in an electronic format before they can attempt to share or exchange information, but this sort of access is well worth the time and effort spent negotiating appropriate privacy and security safeguards.

The exchange of information across the many entities that deliver care is necessary for coordinated, accountable, patient-centered care during times of nondisaster and is even more critical during disaster situations when victims are displaced. In a recent report released by the Bipartisan Policy Center (BPC), barriers to interoperability include (a) lack of a business case for HIE, (b) lack of an infrastructure to support HIE, (c) lack of agreement on and adoption of many of the standards required for interoperability and exchange, and (d) lack of agreement on a path forward (BPC, 2012). Furthermore, recommendations are made by the Task Force to accelerate HIE culminating in the support of bidirectional exchange of health information. HIE may further benefit the health care of refugees and other dislocated individuals by opening up clinical data exchange query functions to providers in other areas via a rapid credentialing process that would permit authorization and access (Shapiro, Mostashari, Hripcsak, Soulakis, & Kuperman, 2011).

Shapiro et al. (2011) note that when mass casualty events occur, hospitals are often overwhelmed with requests for information regarding loved ones who have gone missing or are feared dead. Currently, no such system exists for disseminating this information across health systems, but the authors describe how a patient locator function could be fulfilled through a record locator service architecture designed to receive ongoing admission-discharge-transfer messages from clinical registration systems. The authors further describe that varying architectures could be designed to support public health use including (a) centralized repositories (such as the Veterans Affairs EHR), (b) hybrid peer-to-peer file-sharing models, and (c) patient-controlled health records. They conclude that HIE can improve the efficiency and quality of public health reporting, facilitate public health investigation, improve emergency response, and enable public health to communicate information to the clinical community (Shapiro et al., 2011).

INFORMATICS DISASTER PLANNING TOOLS

Accurate public health data about air, water, sanitation, utilities, and all health care facilities (including shelters and other surge capacity facilities) are imperative for effective disaster planning and response efforts. It is also important to track such data on a predisaster and post-disaster basis. This information will allow for the assessment of the disaster impact and will aid in planning where emergency services are needed, determining the level of health providers required and where community infrastructure improvements are needed (Harrison, Harrison, & Smith, 2008).

It is important for health care facilities to be able to expand their typical bed structure beyond normal service levels to accommodate the additional surge of victims and families requiring treatment. Adding additional beds and services to an already established facility brings its own set of data and information challenges because the typical information systems are designed around room and bed designations. The Agency for Healthcare Research and Quality released a report that explored the feasibility of a national real-time, hospital bed tracking system named the National Hospital Available Beds for Emergencies and Disasters System. The system includes a geographical information system (GIS), established communications protocols, a database, and standardized hospital bed definitions (Clancy, 2007).

Clancy (2007) further describes the Emergency Preparedness Resource Inventory, a web-based tool that can be used to assess the regional supply of critical resources, prepare for incident response, identify deficiencies in services, and support resource decisions that need to be made in a timely fashion. The Inventory also includes a catalog of emergency equipment and medicines, their location and amount, and where to obtain additional supplies.

Harrison et al. (2008) also discuss the use of predictive modeling software that helps in disaster relief planning. The Bioterrorism and Epidemic Outbreak Response Model predicts the staff needed to respond to a major disease outbreak or bioterrorism attack. Use of this tool allows planners to realistically plan for mass vaccination and antibiotic distribution. Predictive modeling software for the health care industry, however, has not kept pace with the growth of its use in the nuclear disaster industry (Hallbert, 2010).

Bayram and Zuabi (2012) did attempt to model the principal parameters necessary to quantitatively benchmark the prehospital medical response in trauma-related mass casualty events. They found that it is difficult to quantitatively benchmark trauma-related prehospital response for mass casualty events because simultaneous occurrences of multiple prehospital activities take place. They used two determinants—the Injury to Patient Contact Interval (IPCI) and Injury to Hospital Interval (IHI). These measurements were compared to maximum time allowed (MTA) in the literature. The authors defined MTA as the maximum time from the occurrence of injury until transfer of care to the hospital and used MTA as the conceptual framework. Although the authors applied the model to a hypothetical example, they concluded that prospective studies of this model are needed to validate its applicability and formalize the collection of additional data.

THE INFLUENCE OF INFORMATICS ON PUBLIC HEALTH EMERGENCIES

The responsibility for the health of the public is an overwhelming task made easier with the inclusion of technology transforming trends into meaningful information and knowledge. Consider these recent events where informatics and technology solutions have played a role in managing a health emergency.

Severe Acute Respiratory Syndrome

Eysenbach (2003) described an early use of informatics and population health technology applications to detect, diagnose, and track new cases of severe acute respiratory syndrome (SARS)—an atypical pneumonia that started in Asia and rapidly spread to several continents. At the request of WHO, scientists from nine countries used e-mail and a secure web portal in real time to gather and exchange electronic information globally, as partners in a multi-site study, to identify and characterize the causative agent. Information exchanged included study results, viral genetic sequence maps, and even postmortem tissue and electron-microscope pictures. Hospitals in affected cities and the CDC quickly established webpages and listserves to provide local physicians with constantly changing case definitions and treatment recommendations.

Pandemic Influenza

The U. S. government sponsored and directed years of planning and preparations in both the public and private sector for a worst-case catastrophic pandemic influenza starting most likely in an underdeveloped portion of the world. However, in late April of 2009, the CDC began noting reported cases of an H1N1 swine-original influenza A respiratory infection in California. Using an event-defined case definition and standard state reporting mechanisms, CDC soon learned that case counts dramatically underestimated the actual prevalence of disease because most infected were not hospitalized and did not die. As a result, planning thresholds to escalate and de-escalate disease transmission activities were not crossed. Instead, scientists and political leaders looked to other measures to track the effects and project impacts of the disease. The Department of Education examined student and teacher absences and school closures as proxies to the level of community disease activity. Purchase of over-the-counter medications, like fever reducers, was tracked in more than 29,000 retail grocery, mass merchandise, and pharmacy locations through the National Retail Data Monitoring System. To encourage people with minor flu-like illness to treat themselves, CDC published updated self-treatment guidance and established nurse advice call lines. When H1N1 vaccine became available, they launched a flu vaccine locator site that used zip codes to direct the public to clinics with vaccine supplies.

Fukushima Daiichi

In March of 2011, the world watched as the Japan nuclear emergency evolved from the initial 9.0 earthquake and the subsequent tsunami to a full-blown nuclear accident. The accident triggered significant public relocation and abandonment of food crops and animal products after radiation contamination in Japan, as well as widespread nuclear monitoring as far away as Europe and the United States. Informatics and technology solutions helped forecast and inform the trajectory, duration and magnitude of the incident, and helped decision makers to take actions quickly to dampen the ongoing negative social, economic, environmental, and health impacts. Social media helped keep Japanese citizens informed with up-to-date recommendations for evacuation or sheltering-in-place.

Pertussis

More recently in 2012, some of the earliest signals of a blossoming pertussis outbreak in Washington State occurred when health officials noticed increased numbers of Twitter and Facebook inquiries from parents seeking methods to manage children with severe, persistent coughing spells. On further examination, officials learned that the number of reported cases of pertussis was skyrocketing to more than a six-fold increase from the previous year (640 cases vs. 94), leading to the declaration of an epidemic by that State's Secretary of Health on April 3, 2012 (Washington State Department of Health, 2012) and prompting health officials to recommend pertussis vaccine for children and adults.

These examples highlight why the need to rapidly detect and characterize a potential event that could affect the health of humans, animals, or plants is enormously important. Currently, critical pieces of data that could raise the alarm reside in multiple and disparate data systems within local, state, or federal governments and the private sector. No single entity is charged to collect, integrate, analyze, and report these data even though it is well known that rapid detection and early warning can save lives and improve incident outcomes. Rapid information sharing facilitates timely decision making, regardless whether a health incident is a naturally occurring phenomenon or accidental or deliberate in nature.

BIOSURVEILLANCE

Homeland Security Presidential Directive (HSPD) 21 defines the term *biosurveillance* as

> the process of active data gathering with appropriate analysis and interpretation of biosphere data that might be related to disease activity and threats to human or animal health—whether infectious, toxic, metabolic, or otherwise, and regardless of intentional or natural origin—in order to achieve early warning of health threats, early detection of health events, and overall situational awareness. (White House, 2007, p.1, para.2)

A catastrophic health event such as a terrorist attack with a weapon of mass destruction (WMD), a naturally occurring pandemic, or a catastrophic meteorological or geological event could cause tens or hundreds of thousands of casualties or more; and as a result, will further weaken our global economy, damage public morale and confidence, and threaten our national security. It is therefore critical that we establish ways to detect the earliest indicators of an event and facilitate the earliest possible warning and projection of impact. How could informatics and technology solutions be used to help identify an incident and inform decision making and time sensitive actions needed at all levels to manage a health emergency?

Since enactment in 2007, the International Health Regulations (WHO, 2005) require that the 194 signature countries work together to prevent, detect, and respond to public health risks that could threaten the world. Member countries must report certain types of disease outbreaks and improve their capacities and capabilities for both public health surveillance and timely response. As a result, there have been great improvements in global surveillance intended to confirm conditions, and rapidly identify the emergence of new patterns or trends, while assessing their significance.

The Global Public Health Intelligence Network, a part of the WHO's Global Outbreak Alert and Response Network, and Project ARGUS are two examples of biosurveillance systems that can provide early detection and warning of unusual events that may threaten human, plant, and animal health globally (Eysenbach, 2003; Thomas, Nelson, Jahn, Niu, & Hartley, 2011). Both systems continually examine open source news articles and the Internet with preset search terms for more than 30 communicable diseases. They also look for information about natural disasters and drug-resistant disease causing agents. Use of "open source" reporting often is much timelier than government statements or reports. These systems serve as "tipping points" identifying end users of events where actions may be considered; however, the systems themselves do nothing more than identify a novel event. Although these approaches may be helpful in countries where there is unfettered news reporting and access to the Internet, neither offers much assistance when media or Internet access is controlled by the government or the report is in a foreign language.

A research group in the Clinical Informatics Lab at McGill University (Canada) is developing and evaluating automated public health surveillance methods using health care utilization data. By using already available data such as appointing, billing, and laboratory test requests and results, they hope to detect deviations from normal usage indicating an evolving incident (McGill, 2012).

The CDC has had its community level and cloud-based surveillance system deployed since 2003. BioSense combines current health data from multiple sources such as health departments, hospital emergency rooms, and pharmacies to quickly detect and respond to health events by providing public health situational awareness (CDC, 2012b).

Boston Children's Hospital has been developing HealthMap as a disease outbreak monitoring and real-time public health surveillance tool since 2006 (Mayor, 2008). The free system scans for and categorizes online reports of infectious diseases using sources such as news outlets, government agencies, international organizations, and social media using an automated process. It integrates information from the news aggregators with eye witness reports from multiple forms including an "Outbreak Near Me" application for mobile devices, and official reports; it then trends reports using count measures. Spikes in the volume or geography of reports are flagged for further investigation. The system integrates disparate data flows to achieve a more comprehensive surveillance picture. Especially in the beginning of an incident, tools like HealthMap can capture early signals more quickly than traditional surveillance mechanisms.

COMMUNICATION AND INFORMATION MANAGEMENT DURING RESPONSE

Being able to track patients and supplies during times of disasters is also critical. The use of geographical information systems (GIS) technology has expanded this ability into real-time reporting that is important to the incident response team management. Jokela et al. (2012) examined the feasibility of a prototype system that used commercially available, low-cost components including Radio Frequency Identification (RFID) and mobile phone technology during two simulated mass-casualty incidents. One of the incidents was in Finland, involving a passenger ship accident resulting in multiple drowning and hypothermia patients. The other incident was at a major airport in Sweden using an aircraft crash scenario. Triage documentation was completed using both an RFID-based system and a traditional method using paper triage tags. Situational awareness was measured by comparing the availability of current information at different points in the care chain using both systems. Results indicated that when using the RFID system, information regarding the numbers and triage classification of the casualties was available approximately 1 hour earlier using the RFID system as compared to the data using the typical paper triage tags. The tested RFID system was quick, stable, and easy to use, and proved to work even in harsh field conditions. The only negative feedback received was that it was not simple to use. Researchers concluded, however, that further development should take place, particularly during nonsimulated incidents.

Legemaate, Burkle, and Bierens (2012) also used simulation exercise situations in which to determine the applicability of certain instruments for disaster research. The researchers noted the difficulty in being able to fully evaluate the quality of the performance of a health care system during a disaster. They chose to investigate whether disaster exercises could be used as a proxy environment to evaluate potential research instruments designed to study the application of medical care management resources during a disaster. In their study, they assessed the following three areas during a ministerial-level exercise in the Netherlands: (a) command and control (through an incident management system questionnaire), (b) patient flow and distribution (through registration of data at various points in the exercise), and (c) hospital coping capacity (through timed registration reports from participating trauma centers). Results indicated that the incident management questionnaire could be used but would benefit from some minor modifications. Patient flow and distribution, however, could not be studied because of inconsistencies among data, and lack of data from various collection points. While coping capacity was able to be measured, the data provided little information regarding bottlenecks in surge capacity.

DISASTER MOBILE HEALTH TECHNOLOGY

Mobile health (mHealth) technology has the potential to play an important role in providing much needed alerts and updates, tracking and patient flow data, patient care data, facility management data, and data collected at the point of care (typically out in the field). It is feasible for mHealth platforms to create a common operational framework that improves disaster response by standardizing data acquisition, organizing information storage, and facilitating medical communication. This is particularly important during patient handoffs between volunteer providers. In addition, mHealth technology serves as the basis for the provision of a broad stream of services, depending on the remaining infrastructure following an event. Smartphones allow for phone calls and text messaging, as well as connections to several social media applications that are popular for communicating with one's peers in today's society.

The Advanced Health and Disaster Aid Network (AID-N) was a test bed designed to improve communications and provide access to pertinent information for the user community during emergencies (Johns Hopkins University Applied Physics Laboratory, 2007). Although not all aspects of the network were mobile, the intent was to develop a next generation electronic triage system to improve the effectiveness of victim care during large-scale disasters. The system included (a) electronic triage tags, (b) wearable vital sign sensors, (c) robust ad hoc mesh networking software suitable for small embedded computers with limited memory and computational power, (d) base station laptops with scalable algorithms to manage large number of patients, (e) pervasive tracking software to locate patients at all stages of the disaster response process, (f) handheld Smartphones to provide a lightweight supplement to base stations for first responders and health care personnel, and (g) a web portal for the different organizational groups involved in the response effort to be fully aware of the situation in real time. Augmenting the data collection at the scene was an information dissemination system that interfaced with three deployed systems. Results indicated that paramedics could triage and assess patients more frequently and emergency personnel could view patient and disaster scene information in real time, which improved understanding and decision making during the situation.

Callaway et al. (2012) described a unique application of mHealth following the 2010 earthquake in Haiti. Using Apple's iPhone as the hardware, researchers used a novel electronic patient medical record and tracking system by modifying the commercially available iChart version 1.39. The iChart application was not specifically developed for the disaster situation but had other attributes that served to enhance its selection as the tool of choice. For example, iChart functions with or without Internet connectivity. In this situation, 75% of the users in this disaster relief effort already had iPhones. There was bidirectional information flow between providers and the database. Testing began with the deployment of the iChart electronic medical record on Day 7 post-earthquake.

Modifications were made daily following morning and evening structured meetings. Improvements included the customization of "encounter notes" and modifications to typical data fields in the existing program to fit more naturally with field locations. Prior to using the iChart mHealth system, there had been no patient log for operations, and no longitudinal patient record. The iChart application resulted in an adequate ability to triage patients as they arrived or were transferred into the treatment facility. The application also improved provider handoffs and continuity of care at the single facility that was included in testing. There were noted limitations, however, such as the limited ability to generate aggregate data for logistics, operations, and staffing requirements. There was also a limited ability to generate summary data in real time for analysis and reporting.

Researchers concluded that disaster mobile health technology is feasible in a resource-poor, chaotic setting that is most often the setting following incidents.

Haiti was also the site of another implementation of portable technology—handheld ultrasound. Shorter and Macias (2012) served in the response effort as part of the New Mexico Disaster Medical Assistance Team (NM DMAT-1). During their deployment, a portable handheld ultrasound machine was tested for usefulness in aiding with patient care decisions. Ultrasound was used for evaluation of hypotension, torso trauma, pregnancy, nontraumatic abdominal pain, deep venous thrombosis and pulmonary embolism, and dyspnea–chest pain, as well as assisting with procedures. Qualitative data were reviewed to identify whether ultrasound influenced management decisions, and results were categorized in terms of percent of scans that influenced management. Fifty-one ultrasound scans on 50 patients were performed, and ultrasound influenced decisions on patient care in 70% of scans. The authors concluded that the use of a handheld portable ultrasound machine was effective for patient management decisions in resource-poor settings, and decreased the need to triage selected patients to higher levels of care. Ultrasound was also useful for guidance during procedures, and had the additional advantage in being able to diagnose parasitic diseases.

INFORMATICS AND INCIDENT MANAGEMENT

One of the few research studies reported on the impact of IT on emergency preparedness and planning was a survey of U.S. state government departments of emergency management during July and August 2008 (Reddick, 2011). According to the survey responses (27 of 50 states), IT has impacted all four functions of emergency management (mitigation, preparedness, response, and recovery). The largest impact, however, has been on the recovery phase. Furthermore, the survey measured the impact of IT on emergency planning in the following areas: (a) providing accurate knowledge of the threat and likely human response through a hazard assessment and vulnerability analysis, (b) helping to decide on the appropriate actions necessary to the situation, (c) emphasizing response flexibility so that those involved in operations can adjust to changing disaster demands, (d) addressing interorganizational coordination and collaboration among responding groups, (e) integrating plans for each individual community into a comprehensive approach for multihazard management, (f) helping with plans that have a training component, (g) testing of the proposed response operations, (h) providing a continuous process for planning in response to the threat environment, (i) planning in the face of conflict and resistance, and (j) helping with management of the plan by implementing what was discussed in the planning stage. Only four of the 10 areas had a positive impact (were statistically significant when performing Fisher's exact test): (a) helping with plans that have a training component, (b) testing of the proposed response operations, (c) planning in the face of conflict and resistance, and (d) helping with management of the plan by implementing what was discussed in the planning stage (Reddick, 2011).

Weiner and Slepski (2011) also list functions for technology and informatics contributions to incident management. Functions are data for the incident command center, communications, patient tracking, provider safety, ambulance tracking, and patient data acquisition and monitoring. Furthermore, the authors provide examples of possible technologies coupled with the informatics processing that empowers each set of technology. In a similar vein, Reddick (2011) examined the effectiveness of IT in emergency management and found the Internet to be very effective (66.7%), followed by GIS technology (58.0%), and wireless networks (45.8%). Direct and remote sensing, emergency management decision support systems, and hazard analysis modeling were viewed as the least effective of the technologies examined.

PERSONAL AND ORGANIZATIONAL AGILITY FOR DISASTER MANAGEMENT

Table-top exercises and full scale on-site drills have often been used to practice response efforts. Whether these are local, regional, or national in scope, they offer an excellent opportunity to evaluate response efforts and revise plans as needed for future events.

Informatics and technology have recently played an increased role in these "practice" events. High-fidelity simulators have set the stage for faculty to program any number of events that can be the center of a simulation designed for the typical skills lab settings. There are many single case study descriptions evaluating the use of simulation for disaster management, but it is not within the scope of this chapter to summarize the results. Typical of this sort of evaluation is the one completed with emergency medicine residents by Franc, Nichols, and Dong (2012). These researchers found no statistically significant difference in pretest and posttest knowledge scores following an 8-hour simulation session. The emergency medicine residents did report the simulation to be a valuable component of their medical training and increased their confidence in personal and departmental disaster management capabilities.

Briggs (2008) described the Idaho State innovation that used the virtual world of Second Life to set the stage for a flu pandemic. This synchronous exercise (called Play2Train) requires avatars to attend to stricken patients lying on the streets around an over-capacity virtual hospital. Roles are assigned, and a command center is put into play to continue the exercise. A similar project was developed by researchers at the University of Wisconsin, OshKosh (2009), using an airplane disaster as the focal point of the drill.

DISCUSSION

The modern movement toward HIE could go a long way to expanding information outreach to victims of disasters and humanitarian crises. Although not the primary reason for the legislation that has provided such sanctioned growth in electronic health care records, for once an unintended consequence has a possible positive effect. Other efforts to expand and upgrade communications to all populations have benefits for the disaster community as well.

As an example, radiofrequency identification (RFID) technology holds such promise with early prototypes tagging victims with treatment and other information. Longer range RFID tags and readers will make it possible to continuously track victims as they move through the system from evacuation to treatment facilities (National Research Council, Committee on Using Information Technology to Enhance Disaster Management, 2007).

Continuing increases in network bandwidth, improvements in the cost and capabilities of all aspects of computing and data processing, and continued progress toward transforming communication systems will only increase functionality during times of disaster. Interoperability and open source software methodology will allow for better high-reliability systems on which to base disaster planning and response efforts. Continued linking of geographic information to existing and future data applications and all types of databases can only increase the information needed for better decision making. Rapid progress in biochemistry, electronics, micro-mechanics, and nanotechnology can be expected to lead to cheaper, smaller, and better-performing sensors and other devices. Other advances such as self-managing and repairing networks, passive and active embedded links and relays (for enhancing communication in rubble and underground), tactile interfaces, adaptive networks, and advanced power sources have the ability to positively influence better disaster outcomes.

Improved decision support and resource tracking/allocation tools bring added intelligence to the disaster situation. For example, better available collaboration software and file sharing have benefitted the recent business world and can serve to better reduce duplication of effort during times of disaster. At the same time, distributed emergency operation centers provide resources in a less centralized manner that aids in the distribution of planning, coordination, and scheduling. Computer-assisted decision-making tools and intelligent adaptive planning provide alternatives to decisions that are typically made in a vacuum.

Biosurveillance is a key capability of obtaining and maintaining situational awareness before and during a health emergency. Early recognition and understanding of departures from human, animal, plant and environmental baselines, including detection of novel occurrences, is necessary to give early warning and save lives; however, detecting deviations from the norm is complicated because of the complexities of systems and variables and the multiple stovepipes that exist. Many efforts are underway to improve data collection, sharing, and analysis. Informatics and technology solutions such as smartphones, tablets, and other wireless devices may help to gather signals to detect potential incidents earlier, regardless of the cause, and communicate early warning and critical updates and foster electronic information exchange worldwide. Rapid detection is critical to save lives and improve incident outcomes, and the United States serves in a key role as part of a global surveillance network.

IMPLICATIONS FOR FURTHER RESEARCH

Having more data and information available during times of disaster may be an overwhelming situation if the health care provider does not know how to be decisive. Simply collecting vast amounts of data from large groups does not in itself provide the analysis necessary to determine if an incident is real or whether responses are the result of fear.

Furthermore, research involving at-risk populations has been extremely difficult to accomplish to date, primarily because there is no national-level institutional review board (IRB) that can convene early in a developing disaster to review and approve a disaster-related protocol. This may no longer be an issue as the National Biodefense Science Board (NBSB) met and forwarded a report to the Secretary of Health and Human Services on April 28, 2011. The report states ". . . scientific investigations must be an essential component of emergency preparedness and response planning, and should be initiated at the outset of an emergency that threatens public health" (NBSB, 2011, p. 15). Three specific recommendations pertain to technology and informatics: (a) establishing an Interdepartmental Center for Scientific Investigations During Disaster Response, charged with anticipating, planning, coordinating, facilitating, and evaluating scientific investigations conducted before, during, and after disasters; (b) support of rapid scientific investigation and data collection by the development of concepts, doctrine, infrastructure, and personnel; and (c) development of standard operating procedures to integrate the Public Health Emergency Research Board for review of research before, during, and after a disaster response. Having an established and dedicated IRB that can review can approve disaster-related protocols will help ensure that critical data are available to assist decision makers.

Furthermore, the report recommends that data collection and sharing approaches be standardized so that federal, state, and local response organizations and the private sector and volunteer organizations can freely share information, especially baseline health data, environmental data, identification of populations of concern, as well as registries of individual to be followed over time.

Much remains to be learned. Recent advances in technology allow for even more questions to be explored. Some examples of research questions include the following:

1. What are these critical information requirements that transect most health emergencies?
2. Can disease-related behaviors (i.e., care-seeking and absenteeism) serve as proxies for case finding?
3. What are the science and technology capabilities that will facilitate biosurveillance activities including new detection and HIE approaches?
4. Are there innovative ways to combine information and known facts early in an incident to forecast what is likely to transpire?
5. How do we create more robust, interoperable, and priority-sensitive communications needed for disaster management?
6. Is it possible to integrate voice/data/video to provide a better communication solution for our first responders?
7. How do we improve data mining capabilities so that we extract meaningful knowledge from a diverse set of information sources that inform us about never before seen data patterns?
8. How do we improve situational awareness and subsequent modeling so that we are more successful at acquiring and distributing necessary resources?
9. How can we better use the GIS field to integrate within our other IT systems for more efficient use?
10. What are some ways that portable unmanned aerial vehicles and robots might be used in disaster management?
11. How can communication be improved between and among government and nongovernmental responders?
12. Can simulations be increased in their realism to better test research tools that can be later implemented during disaster situations?

CONCLUSIONS

There remain several unmet informational needs in disaster planning and response. Regardless of the population involved, protecting the health and safety of people, animals, plants, and the environment is a top security priority for all nations. Especially in these times of financial constraints, efforts must be undertaken to leverage existing technologies and systems, enable efficiencies, and, where able, create opportunities to help each other.

The intersection of technology, informatics, and disaster planning and response provides a rich background in which researchers can explore possible solutions that would benefit all. Thinking of clinical documentation inside one (typically hospital) setting is no longer reasonable. Information sharing needs to take place across multiple settings and incorporated into population-based health to become effective. Lastly, nurses specializing in informatics now have career possibilities that also extend beyond the typical hospital environment. This chapter presents such challenges and possibilities for those willing to take on such tasks. The examples of research questions provided illustrate specific roles that nursing informatics specialists could play in contributing to the overall disaster agenda.

REFERENCES

Bayram, J., & Zuabi, S. (2012). Disaster metrics: A proposed quantitative model for benchmarking prehospital medical response in trauma-related multiple casualty events. *Prehospital and Disaster Medicine*, 27(2), 1–7. http://dx.doi.org/10.1017/S1049023X12000416

Berner, E. S. (2009). *Clinical decision support systems: State of the art* (AHRQ Publication No. 09-0069-EF. Rockville, MD: Agency for Healthcare Research and Quality). Retrieved from Agency for Healthcare Research and Quality Website: http://healthit.ahrq.gov/images/jun09cdsreview/09_0069_ef.html

Bipartisan Policy Center Task Force on Delivery System Reform and Health Information Technology. (2012). *Transforming health care: The role of health IT*. Retrieved from http://bipartisanpolicy.org/sites/default/files/Transforming%20Health%20Care.pdf

Briggs, L. L. (2008). Idaho State simulates emergency response in Second Life. *Campus Technology*. Retrieved from http://campustechnology.com/articles/2008/05/idaho-state-simulates-emergency-response-in-second-life.aspx

Callaway, D. S., Peabody, C. R., Hoffman, A., Cote, E., Moulton, S., Baec, A. A., & Nathanson, L. (2012). Disaster mobile health technology: Lessons from Haiti. *Prehospital and Disaster Medicine*, 27(2), 1–5. http://dx.doi.org/10.1017/S1049023X12000441

Centers for Disease Control and Prevention. (2012a). *Strategic National Stockpile (SNS)*. Retrieved from http://www.cdc.gov/phpr/stockpile/stockpile.htm

Centers for Disease Control and Prevention. (2012b). *BioSense*. Retrieved from http://www.cdc.gov/biosense/

Clancy, C. (2007). Emergency departments in crisis: Implications for disaster preparedness. *American Journal of Medical Quality*, 22(2), 123–126.

Eysenbach, G. (2003). SARS and population health technology. *Journal of Medical Internet Research*, 5(2), e14. http://dx.doi.org/10.2196/jmir.5.2.e14

Franc, J. M., Nichols, D., & Dong, S. L. (2012). Increasing emergency medicine residents' confidence in disaster management: Use of an emergency department simulator and an expedited curriculum. *Prehospital and Disaster Medicine*, 27(1), 31–35. http://dx.doi.org/10.1017/S1049023X11006807

Hallbert, B. (2010). *Situation awareness and decision-making in emergency mass casualty events* (Unpublished doctoral dissertation). Vanderbilt University, Nashville, TN.

Harrison, J. P., Harrison, R. A., & Smith, M. (2008). Role of information technology in disaster medical response. *The Health Care Manager, 27*(4), 307–313.

Hsiao, C., Hing, E., Socey, T. C., & Cai, G. (2011, November). *Electronic health record systems and intent to apply for meaningful use incentives among office-based physician practices: United States, 2001–2011* (NCHS Data Brief No. 79). Hyattsville, MD: National Center for Health Statistics.

Johns Hopkins University Applied Physics Laboratory. (2007). *Advanced health and disaster aid network final report.* Retrieved from http://www.jhuapl.edu/AID-N/Pub/AID-N_Final_Report_v_0_7__091807.pdf

Jokela, J., Radestad, M., Gryth, D., Nilsson, H., Ruter, A., Svensson, L., . . . Castren, M. (2012). Increased situation awareness in major incidents—radio frequency identification (RFID) technique: A promising tool. *Prehospital and Disaster Medicine, 27*(1), 81–87. http://dx.doi.org/10.1017/S1049023X12000295

Legemaate, G. A. G., Burkle, F. M., & Bierens, J. J. L. M. (2012). The evaluation of research methods during disaster exercises: Applicability for improving disaster health management. *Prehospital and Disaster Medicine, 27*(1), 18–26. http://dx.doi.org/10.1017/S1049023X11006789

Markle Foundation. (2006). *Lessons from KatrinaHealth.* Retrieved from http://www.policyarchive.org/handle/10207/bitstreams/15501.pdf

Mayor, S. (2008). Internet crawler uses unconventional information sources to track infectious disease outbreaks. *British Medical Journal, 337*(7661), 70. http://dx.doi.org/10.1136/bmj.a742

McGill University. (2012). *Clinical Informatics Lab.* Retrieved from http://132.216.183.136/index.html

National Biodefense Science Board. (2011). *Call to action: Include scientific investigations as an integral component of disaster planning and response.* Retrieved from http://www.phe.gov/Preparedness/legal/boards/nbsb/Documents/nbsbrec14.pdf

National Library of Medicine. (2011). *Disaster information management research center.* Retrieved from http://sis.nlm.nih.gov/dimrc/subjectguides.html

National Research Council, Committee on Using Information Technology to Enhance Disaster Management. (2007). *Improving disaster management: The role of IT in mitigation, preparedness, response, and recovery.* Retrieved from http://www.nap.edu/catalog/11824.html

Reddick, C. (2011). Information technology and emergency management: Preparedness and planning in US states. *Disasters, 35*(1), 45–61. http://dx.doi.org/10.1111/j.0361-3666.2010.01192.x

Shapiro, J. S., Mostashari, F., Hripcsak, G., Soulakis, N., & Kuperman, G. (2011). Using health information exchange to improve public health. *American Journal of Public Health, 101*, 616–623. http://dx.doi.org/10.2105/AJPH.2008.158980

Shklovski, I., Burke, M., Kiesler, S., & Kraut, R. (2010). Technology adoption and use in the aftermath of Hurricane Katrina in New Orleans. *American Behavioral Scientist, 53*(8), 1228–1246. http://dx.doi.org/10.1177/0002764209356252

Shorter, M., & Macias, D. J. (2012). Portable handheld ultrasound in austere environments: Use in the Haiti disaster. *Prehospital and Disaster Medicine, 27*(2), 1–6. http://dx.doi.org/10.1017/S1049023X12000611

Thomas, C. S., Nelson, N. P., Jahn, G. C., Niu, T., & Hartley, D. M. (2011). Use of media and public-domain Internet sources for detection and assessment of plant health threats. *Emerging Health Threats Journal.* Advance online publication. http://dx.doi.org/10.3402/ehtj.v4i0.7157

University of Wisconsin Oshkosh College of Nursing. (2009). *CONtact.* Retrieved from http://jaimeceglahunt.weebly.com/uploads/4/7/8/1/4781920/contact_spring09_mag_web.pdf

Washington State Department of Health. (2012). *Whooping cough cases reach epidemic levels in much of Washington.* Retrieved from http://www.doh.wa.gov/Publicat/2012_news/12-038.htm

Weiner, E. (2011). Research issues for nursing and midwifery contributions in emergencies. *Prehospital and Disaster Medicine, 26*(2), 109–113. http://dx.doi.org/10.1017/S1049023X11000124

Weiner, E., & Slepski, L. (2011). Informatics solutions for emergency planning and response. In V. K. Saba & K. A. McCormick (Eds.), *Essentials of nursing informatics* (pp. 513–524). New York, NY: McGrawHill Medical.

White House. (2007). *Homeland Security Presidential Directive 21: Public health and medical preparedness.* Retrieved from http://www.hsdl.org/?view&did=480002

World Health Organization. (2005). *International health regulations.* Retrieved from http://www.who.int/features/qa/39/en/index.html

World Health Organization. (2007). *The contribution of nursing and midwifery in emergencies: Report of a WHO consultation WHO Headquarters, Geneva, 22–24 November 2006.* Retrieved from http://www.who.int/hac/events/2006/nursing_consultation_report_sept07.pdf

CHAPTER 8

Update on Competencies and Education

Kristine M. Gebbie, Alison Hutton, and Virginia Plummer

ABSTRACT

The beginning of the 21st century has been marked by an increase in attention to the quality of emergency and disaster response, particularly the preparedness of health workers of all kinds. The increase in natural disasters, civil unrest, and dislocation of populations has seen health workers mobilized. These workers are moving, both within countries and across borders, as members of long-organized teams such as the National Disaster Medical System (NDMS), volunteers joining through a nongovernmental organization (NGO) such as a Red Cross/Red Crescent unit, or individuals self-deploying to the scene of the emergency. Postevent evaluations have consistently identified the need for those responding to be able to join in an organized response that includes taking on assigned roles, communication through established channels and minimization of the number of "SUVs" or "spontaneous unrequested volunteers." Although bystanders and self-deployed helpers (some with professional qualifications) are the first at any disastrous event, the subsequent response efforts are expected to be organized, efficient, and effective. This requires advance training of the responders.

© 2012 Springer Publishing Company
http://dx.doi.org/10.1891/0739-6686.30.169

There has been a growing awareness of the intersection between what has traditionally been understood as two separate fields: humanitarian response and disaster response. Not all humanitarian crises (large populations living in temporary quarters, often short of food and without a safe water supply) arise as a result of a specific identifiable event, and not all disastrous events lead to ongoing humanitarian crises. The overlap is perhaps clearest in the case of a large population displaced by an earthquake or tsunami. The line between the response needed in the immediacy of the disaster, and the sustained health support needed for many months by those living in a tent city is blurred, and many of the same NGOs and individuals have responded to both phases of events.

Development of the entire health workforce in the area of disaster preparedness and response has been highlighted in the U.S. national policy through the Pandemic and All-Hazards Preparedness Act (PAHPA; 2006) workforce, which requires "a national strategy for establishing an effective and prepared public health workforce, including defining the functions, capabilities, and gaps in such" (Section 304, sub-section 4, p. 3). Policy has been focused on multiple facets of preparedness, including planning processes, deployment of response supplies, intergovernmental cooperative agreements, and regular exercises of plans in addition to worker education. Within education, attention has turned to clarifying the expected competencies of health workers; methods of delivering preprofessional, continuing and just-in-time education; and efficient ways to maintain competencies over time. As the largest professional group in the health field, nurses form a major target audience for training programs being established as a result of this increased attention.

In this review of research on competencies and education, the authors made two decisions: to include research over the past decade rather than on the past year or two, and to include research on competencies and education of all health professionals as well as that focused specifically on nurses. The longer time line is needed because of the sudden expansion of interest in this area during the decade, with early research providing the basis for more current activities; and the high level of overlap in what is taught to all health professionals with that specifically designed for nurses makes the narrower view inappropriate. In preparation for this review, CINAHL and MEDLINE were both searched, using multiple terms: Competenc* AND Nurs*; Competenc* AND Public Health; Competenc* AND Med*; Competenc* AND Humanitarian; and Competenc* AND Education. From that beginning, the references cited in identified papers were added, as were reports and similar grey literature from organizations working in this field. The references included in this chapter represent the results of that search.

COMPETENCY RESEARCH

Nursing

Competencies serve as the foundation of both evidence-based practice and standards development as well as supporting learning and assessment, and their systematic application minimizes the risks related to disaster response (Yamamoto & Watanabe as cited in World Health Organization [WHO] & International Council of Nursing [ICN], 2009). Although nurses are the largest group of health professionals able to respond in disaster, on some occasions, they have been turned away from a disaster scene or they have left because of poor understanding of what was required of them (ICN, 2009). Arbon et al. (2006) found that 80% of those who volunteered to assist in the Sumatra–Andaman earthquake and tsunami did so for the first time and were inexperienced and educationally unprepared. Nurses in a disaster response may be required to practice beyond their usual scope of practice and with procedures and injuries they may rarely see outside of the disaster environment (Arbon et al., 2006; Gebbie & Qureshi, 2002). In addition, some who volunteer may be poorly prepared for the work, including difficulties in prioritizing patients and working with inadequate resources (ICN, 2009). Some who are competent are unwilling to respond because of personal fears, eldercare or child care, for example. Moreover, threats of infection dramatically impact the willingness and preparedness of nurses to respond (Smith, 2007).

One of the authors (Gebbie, 2010) has suggested that every nurse should be considered as a disaster nurse because the skills required in disaster are the same as those required on a regular shift, although the setting is different and the resources are stretched or absent. The example she describes is the operating room nurse who may not have the large backup team of the range of equipment but is able to assist so that the surgery is done. Each nurse maintains (or should maintain) some practice or specialty competencies on a regular basis, consolidating and updating them in the workplace. This cannot be done for any dedicated disaster competency, which may be practiced annually at best and experienced rarely, if ever. There is some evidence that nursing in the military health services may assure a higher level of preparedness or competency in practice than for those in civilian hospitals. These findings were based on interviews with 10 perioperative and emergency nurses who volunteered to join rescue teams during the Wenchuan magnitude 7.9 earthquake of 2008 in northwestern Sichuan province of China (Robinson, 2010).

Nurses not only are able to respond to emergencies but also do have a right to the needed preparation for effective response (Wisniewski, 2004). Those most likely to be responsible for planning, response and/or recovery in a local disaster should be able to achieve and assess a useful level of competence.

The inability of professionals to respond during an emergency has also been raised as a potential political issue following some events including the aftermath of Hurricane Katrina in the United States (Veneema, 2007) and during the Australian Victorian Bushfires Royal Commission (Manne, 2009). Continued competence is a requirement set by many registering authorities, but there is no clear governance over disaster nursing competencies. The question of penalties for failure to meet competency standards has arisen in some settings including criminal charges against clinicians following Hurricane Katrina in 2005 (Gebbie, Peterson, Subbarao, & White, 2009). There is also a reasonable public perception that schools of nursing have a responsibility to adequately prepare their students. This should include assessment of competence and setting expectations that graduate nurses will maintain their own competencies (Veneema, 2007). In addition to the curriculum content, it is essential to identify how the expected learning outcomes can be properly assessed (Chan et al., 2010).

The earliest group formed to clarify nursing disaster competency was the International Nursing Coalition for Mass Casualty Education (INCMCE; later renamed as National Emergency Preparedness Education Coalition or NEPEC) established at Vanderbilt University School of Nursing. This Coalition represented 50 organizations and institutions including some international ones. The stated goals were to

1. Increase awareness of all nurses about mass casualty incidents
2. Provide leadership to the nursing profession for the development of knowledge and expertise related to mass casualty education
3. Identify competencies for nurses at academic and continuing educational levels
4. Establish a clearinghouse of information and web links for professional development of nurses
5. Provide input into policy development relating to nursing practice, education and research at the governmental and institutional levels (NEPEC, 2003).

The competency set published by this group provided a basis for much subsequent competency analysis, training, and research. Slepski and Littleton-Kearney (2010) have contrasted examples of different competency statements and compared the competencies of four groups—INCMCE, Columbia University School of Nursing, Agency for Health Care Research and Quality (AHRQ) and Hsu et al. health care worker competencies. These were designed for different audiences using different approaches, identified few or no outcome measures, and have been applied to varying degrees in a range of settings. Ideally, the conceptual development of competencies would follow a process such as the following:

1. Review the peer-reviewed literature and educational theory.
2. Structure a review of existing competencies, national-level courses, and published training objectives.
3. Synthesize the new competencies.
4. Review by an expert panel
5. Refine new competencies.
6. Develop the stable terminal objectives for each competency using similar processes covering requisite knowledge, attitudes, and skills (Hsu et al., 2006).

Given the frequency of international response to emergencies and disasters, it is important to note that discussions of disaster nursing competencies available in English journals are readily available but "discussions in other languages such as in the Japanese professional nursing journals are tremendously under-investigated" (Kako & Mitani, 2010, p. 162). In the same study, the authors note that many of papers reviewed found the concept of participating in drills to be important, as they did participating in prevention, planning, practice, and response. Participants had low levels of awareness about competencies, with terms such as "practice capabilities" and "preparedness during disasters" were more familiar to them. A 2008 study of Jordanian hospital nurses' preparedness for disaster management found that 17% reported their preparation was good or very good, and 91% wanted to know more about the role of RNs in disaster and knowledge and skills (Al-Khalaileh, Bond, Beckstrand, & Talafha, 2010). From a research perspective, these authors also added to the resources through development of the Disaster Preparedness Evaluation Tool (DPET), an Arabic language tool to measure knowledge, skills, and postdisaster management. Although there is a general perception that most hospitals and nurses are less interested in disaster preparedness, Israeli hospitals are reported to be a notable exception (Bartley and Walsh, 2006). This may be because disaster preparedness practice occurs in countries where terrorist attacks occur frequently (i.e., Israel; Chapman & Arbon, 2008).

The University of Hyogo in Japan, through the College of Nursing, Art and Science, undertook research to develop core competencies for disaster nursing in 2006. This research was undertaken in two stages: the first stage involved the development of a framework of fundamental competencies and the second is identification and structuring of associated curricular content (Yang et al., 2006). The fundamental competencies of integrating knowledge, skills, and judgment are classified into five categories: fundamental attitudes toward disaster nursing, systematic assessment and provision of disaster nursing care, care provision for vulnerable people and their families, care management in disaster situations, and professional development (Yang et al., 2006).

Leaders of the United Nations and WHO began to address the fact that health systems are vulnerable and disaster preparedness and mitigation are essential in reducing the impact of disasters on a worldwide level in January 2005, when 168 governments adopted a 10-year blueprint for disaster risk reduction. Included in the five priorities is to strengthen disaster preparedness for effective response. According to WHO, the most urgent need is for human resources; and nurses and midwives are essential to the response although there is a major gap in their training. This stimulus added to the general level of nursing interest leading the 2009 ICN Framework of Disaster Nursing Competencies, first developed through the WHO Regional Office for the Western Pacific. The ICN framework was developed with the broadest and most formally organized reference group and by that measure can be identified as the current gold standard in nursing. The ICN preparedness competencies are framed in four broad areas: mitigation/prevention competencies, preparedness competencies, response competencies, and recovery/rehabilitation competencies. Within and across these are 10 domains:

1. Risk reduction, disease prevention and health promotion
2. Policy development and planning
3. Ethical practice, legal practice and accountability
4. Communication and information sharing
5. Education and preparedness
6. Care of the community
7. Care of individuals and families
8. Psychological care
9. Care of vulnerable populations
10. Long-term recovery of individuals, families and communities (WHO & ICN, 2009, p. 49).

This version is notated as a first step toward growth of the nursing preparedness and response workforce. In many countries, the ICN and WHO recognition makes it more likely that the competencies will be taken seriously and introduced into education or practice. Because with all newly stated competency sets, they should be revisited for clarification and updating, taking into account all work done in this area to date.

Public Health

The health and safety of communities hinge on the public health workforce, those who extend support for health beyond acute medical care to prevent disease and promote health at the community and systems levels, whether the disaster is caused by natural forces, industrial events, or outbreaks of virulent communicable diseases (Hodge et al., 2008). Most published public health literature focuses on bioterrorism, given the critical importance of epidemiology and public health education in a deliberately caused spread of disease. In emergencies, the competencies serve to identify the expected scope and limits of a person's knowledge, authority, and skills. Within this assessment, competencies serve to highlight where additional resources may be needed and what type of public health information needs to be disseminated (Lichtveld, Hodge, Gebbie, Thompson, & Loos, 2002). Lichtveld et al. (2002) assert that the competencies must be a combination of knowledge, skills, and abilities that are to be demonstrated by members of the organization. In addition, competencies must be observable and measurable and can contribute to the workers' performance and the overall organizations success, highlighting that competencies need to fit the individual as well as the wider organization. In addition, some competencies such as communication are more generic than others because they do not apply to any specific profession or program.

Public health practice encompasses multiple disciplines, including nursing, medicine, environmental science, laboratory science, statistics, epidemiology, health education, public health law, and many more (Gebbie & Merrill, 2002). Competency sets in all disciplines are interrelated and provided a framework for developing preparedness of public health leaders, health care professional law enforcement, and others (Lichtveld et al., 2002). Because the public perception of "health" as personal medical care and the media attention to individual rescue and treatment at the time of disaster, communication of public health activities is critical. Competency research in public health states that each public health worker must be able to describe his or her communication role in an emergency response within the agency they work and understand how that role connects with the general public. Development of related curriculum provides guidance for training and retraining and preparedness for the public health workforce. The knowledge generated from these competencies is important part of the knowledge needed for the preparedness for bioterrorism (Gebbie & Merrill, 2002; Lichtveld et al., 2002).

Law serves as a public health critical function and knowing how to apply the law to competencies is an important element of "knowing one's place" (Lichtveld et al., 2002, p. 186). At the individual level, the public health worker needs to understand and apply state powers, understand the scope of traditional powers versus emergency powers, and be able to distinguish what the duties of the public health agencies are as separate from those of other agencies. As well as upholding the law, having a close relationship with law enforcement is also a crucial part of exercising an effective response. Competencies ensure that staff members possess the necessary skills to do their job effectively to assist in contributing to an effective and efficient public health response (Lichtveld et al., 2002).

In the earliest work to formalize the process of public health competencies (Gebbie & Merrill, 2002), a Delphi survey method was implemented. Initially, 42 statements of competencies were gathered that were determined to be needed by a public health worker. These statements were then surveyed by a panel of experts to develop a consensus opinion on what competencies were necessary. Competencies were then defined by the different category of worker, coupled with levels of experience. Four competency sets were derived from the focus groups and panel interviews from the expert panel, with nine core competencies identified across all roles. This work resulted in the publishing of *Core Public Health Worker Competencies for Emergency Preparedness and Response*. Because a total of 43 competencies were developed through this process, all of these competencies were linked back to the corresponding core competency for clarity. These core competencies and annotated competencies were then validated through allowing public health workers to review them, and then they were finalized (Gebbie & Merrill, 2002).

At approximately the same time, the Michigan Center for Public Health Preparedness (MI-CPHP) undertook a process to integrate competency-based learning and assessment in all its educational and training initiatives (Calhoun, Davidson, Sinioris, Vincent, & Griffith, 2002). MI-CPHP used Bloom's *Taxonomy of Educational Objectives* to create definitions around the many terms to be used when developing competencies and used the domains of cognitive, affective, and psychomotor (consistent with Lichtveld et al., 2002, cited previously) to facilitate a common language. Progressive levels of development within each domain allow the worker to develop several skills and proficiency from novice to expert. Bloom's *Taxonomy* (Bloom, Englehart, Furst, Hill, & Krathwohl, 1956) and the novice to expert paradigm (Benner, 1984) serve as key theoretical underpinnings of all course and competency development. All that is needed for public health workers is divided into three domains: preparedness and planning, response and mitigation, and recovery and evaluation. Across these three domains, nine core competencies were identified with 75 subcategories. These competencies are believed to have allowed for uniform-based learning and assessment processes while increasing faculty or trainer understanding of competency-based training (Calhoun, Rowney, Eng, & Hoffman, 2005). Lastly and perhaps most important, the development of the MI-CPHP has enabled a high-level leadership and created synergies across many partners and departments locally and nationally involved in public health preparedness.

The Centers for Disease Control and Prevention (CDC) and their multi-disciplinary partners have continued to work toward a competent workforce. In 2007, for example, a national meeting focused on ways to assure that those who work within the auspices of public health understand the legal frameworks, which govern their practice and are competent in applying them as required during an emergency. Consensus was reached that continued work was needed in four areas: expanding the role of sectors, improving competency specification, disseminating competency information to target audiences, and improving the measurement of evaluation of practice (Gebbie et al., 2008). Regarding expanding sectors in attainment of competencies, there is quite a long list of other departments and individuals who could benefit from attaining competency in public health emergency preparedness. They include government public health staff working in areas such as epidemiology, disease control, and environmental regulation. In addition, hospital administrators, academics, and legal counsellors of key emergency defense personnel would benefit from understanding emergency competencies. The authors also suggest that law schools should move toward discussing public health emergency awareness as part of their curricula, so that all members have the opportunity to develop competency in this area (Gebbie et al., 2008).

The public health community has also recognized that there is a second phase of competency development that improves on the first phase and should be "ordered, inclusive and technologically sound" (Gebbie et al., 2008, p. 54). It is this type of approach that has been used by the public health community in developing a set of core competencies in public health responsive to the requirements of the PAHPA legislation. This has been done through a transparent process involving a national steering committee, a panel of more than 300 public health practitioners and academics, and regular sharing of draft and intermediate products leading to the model published in December 2010 (Association of Schools of Public Health [ASPH], 2010).

Medical

Developing competencies for disaster health is a challenging task. Disasters happen in disparate settings, vary in their nature, and happen irregularly. Many professions are involved in disasters and perform many different roles, thereby making a draft of competencies for various professions and the multitude of experiences challenging (Daily, Padjen, & Birnbaum, 2010). Although training and education have been long accepted as integral to disaster preparedness, Hsu et al. (2006) developed seven competencies which cut across the needs of all health care workers in response to a disaster (see Figure 8.1).

Cross-Cutting Competencies for Healthcare Workers
1. Recognize a potential critical event and implement initial actions
2. Apply the principles of critical event management
3. Demonstrate critical event safety principles
4. Understand the institutional emergency operations plan
5. Demonstrate effective critical event communications
6. Understand the incident command system and your role in it
7. Demonstrate the knowledge and skills needed to fulfill your role during a critical event

FIGURE 8.1 Cross-Cutting Competencies. Reprinted with permission from Hsu, E. B., Thomas, T. L., Bass, E. B., Whyne, D., Kelen, G. D., & Green, G. B. (2006). Healthcare worker competencies for disaster training. *BMC Medical Education, 6,* 19.

To develop these competencies, current educational theory on training, curriculum, and competency development was reviewed by educational experts. As with the nursing and public health professions, it is recognized by medicine that the highest priority in relation to an effective disaster response is to build standardized guidelines for education and training. Hsu et al. (2006) note that cultural differences among health care workers can affect a successful response—an observation not mentioned in other reviewed literature. However, like many others (Calhoun et al., 2002; Lichtveld et al., 2002), he also acknowledges differences in training, education, and work experience, which can impact on coordinating an efficient disaster response (Hsu et al., 2006). Competency-based training has been widely implemented across the United States in recent years. The Accreditation Council for Graduate Medical Education (ACGME) has implemented a core competency process to facilitate the knowledge and skills of physicians when responding to a disaster. This model has also been endorsed by the American Board of Medical Specialists (Hsu et al., 2006).

In the United States, military physicians who provide medical care as a response during disasters are referred to as tactical emergency medical response (TEMS). The goal of TEMS is to enable law enforcement and others to operate more effectively with reduced risk because of the presence of prepared health professionals. The U.S. Defense Board Committee for Tactical Combat Casualty Care (TCCC) recognized a need for competencies to be developed in this specialized area to facilitate consistent definitions of terms and prioritize skills (Schwartz et al., 2011). In addition, it is recognized that as well as being context dependent, individuals of different ranks will need to meet the same competency to provide safe patient care. Lastly, competencies for this group were seen as a way to standardize training practices and increase accountability of the TEMS teams. Lastly, competencies were seen as a way to define the role and responsibilities of responders and create educational programs of study (Schwartz et al., 2011).

Given the place of the emergency department as the entry point for disaster victims to the hospital, it is not surprising that the American College of Emergency Physicians (ACEP) has been one of the groups active in defining roles and needed competencies. Their work has encompassed not only physicians but also emergency medical technicians and paramedics, and emergency nurses (ACEP, 2009). This work identifies skills and expectations that are common to all professionals in the emergency specialty as well as some that are specific to subgroups. Many of the key participants in this professional group have also been active with other cross-cutting dialogues about emergency preparedness and response.

In 2003, the American Medical Association (AMA) joined with interested educators to create a National Disaster Life Support (NDLS) educational program, designed to assure that physicians and other health professionals who were part of any emergency response would have the necessary competency to provide safe care to those in need (NDLS, 2012). The program includes three levels of course work, with the advanced level including specific, advanced medical interventions in the face of various hazards. The original structure has been expanded into the NDLS Educational Coalition, which states its mission as achieving and promoting excellence in education, training, and research related to disaster medicine and public health preparedness for all health professionals based on sound educational principles, scientific evidence, and best clinical and public health practices. Because courses are updated, they are assessed for consistency with competency-based educational principles and best adult learning practices. Although the original work has been perceived as primarily aimed at physicians, more recent work is attempting to be broadly useful to the health professions.

Finally, the AMA has also taken the initiative to convene a wide range of interested health parties to consider what core competencies might undergird all of the health professions, and thus be essential curricular components for all health professions schools including medical schools. The first iteration of these competencies was published in 2008 and included three levels (student, practitioner, leader) in multiple competencies (Subbarao et al., 2008). As with most beginning iterations of competencies, there were issues of clarity (or lack thereof) and potential overlap with other work. In the interval since that publication, the AMA convened a wide range of experts in emergency preparedness and response, humanitarian response, and competency-based education to develop an updated statement of core competencies for all health professionals

(Walsh et al., 2012). The 11 competencies are that each individual health professional should be able to

1. Demonstrate personal and family preparedness for disasters and public health emergencies
2. Demonstrate knowledge of one's expected role(s) in organizational and community response plans activated during a disaster or public health emergency
3. Demonstrate situational awareness of actual/potential health hazards before, during, and after a disaster or public health emergency
4. Communicate effectively with others in a disaster or public health emergency
5. Demonstrate knowledge of personal safety measures that can be implemented in a disaster or public health emergency
6. Demonstrate knowledge of surge capacity assets, consistent with one's role in organizational, agency, and/or community response plans
7. Demonstrate knowledge of principles and practices for the clinical management of all ages and populations affected by disasters and public health emergencies, in accordance with professional scope of practice
8. Demonstrate knowledge of public health principles and practices for the management of all ages and populations affected by disasters and public health emergencies
9. Demonstrate knowledge of ethical principles to protect the health and safety of all ages, populations, and communities affected by a disaster or public health emergency
10. Demonstrate knowledge of legal principles to protect the health and safety of all ages, populations, and communities affected by a disaster or public health emergency
11. Demonstrate knowledge of short- and long-term considerations for recovery of all ages, populations, and communities affected by a disaster or public health emergency. (Walsh et al., 2012, pp. 50–51)

Thirty-six subcompetencies are included in the discussion, providing a rich beginning for any health professional school or employing agency desiring to build a relevant curriculum.

Humanitarian Relief
There is little formal literature found on the competency needs of public health officials or health workers in a humanitarian context, although the fields are seen as overlapping (Leaning, 2008). Grey literature (Chastonay, Klohn,

Zesiger, Freigburghaus, & Mpinga, 2009) that was sourced suggests that public health competencies are at the core of training needs, however, there is also a need for "know-how" and understanding regarding basic human rights. These authors used a needs assessment approach to assess the educational needs in the field of health and human rights for nursing students in South Africa. To begin this process, they reviewed available data and conducted focus groups followed by distribution of a questionnaire. From this information, an interactive e-training program in the field of health care and human rights competencies was implemented. They further claim that in French-speaking Africa, the most important competencies are the need for basic public health planning as well as the need for project management coupled with human rights knowledge. For nurses in particular, competencies in health and human rights are part of core training programs in natural disasters. However, core competencies such as social mobilization and using research tools were not identified as a priority in this region. From this study, the authors found that the most pressing need for their workers was the integration and identification of basic human rights violations that occur in the current health system (Chastonay et al., 2009).

As humanitarian operations have become increasingly complex, so is the recognition that disaster preparedness is integral for the success of an operation. Elsharkawi et al. (2010) from the Norwegian Red Cross assert that more skills and training are needed for an effective disaster response and propose a Red Cross/Red Crescent training model for responders. The training proposed by the Red Cross is based on a field school training concept where participants are mentored and learn by doing. In this article, there is no mention of competency development to underpin practice, although it is acknowledged that a commitment to developing policies and guidelines needs to be addressed in the future (Elsharkawi et al., 2010).

On a broader basis, individuals involved internationally in humanitarian assistance have argued that professionalizing the field would strengthen humanitarian response generally and be of benefit to the target populations (Walker, Hein, Russ, Bertleff, & Caspersz, 2010). The discussion grows from a scoping study and conference that highlighted the challenges of the largely volunteer humanitarian efforts, and the associated problems (Walker & Russ, 2010). This argument is carried forward in an editorial specifically citing the clarification of competencies needed in the field as a key step in the professionalization process (Hein, 2010). The editorial perspective comments on the overlapping and confusing world of emergency preparedness competencies but suggests that as the field moves toward clarification, humanitarian competencies should be considered a part of the larger whole.

CHALLENGES OF COMPETENCY DEVELOPMENT

Currently, there is a wide array of competencies, coupled with a vast assortment of domains and nomenclature within disaster health care. Daily et al. (2010) reviewed existing disaster literature that focused on competencies to identify common issues and the degree of applicability to emergency and disaster preparedness. Thirty-nine articles were included in this review; 28 of which described competencies targeted at specific professions, whereas 10 described competencies defined for a specific role. Four articles described competencies that related to a skill level and one article discussed skill levels and proficiency. Two articles specifically related to nursing and 14 of the articles cut across all professions and were targeted at health workers.

With this diversity in the literature, Daily et al. (2010) cite the challenges of competency development as many. Disasters happen in various settings at different times. Multiple professions and disciplines are involved, many unique roles are required during a disaster, and different levels of performance and/or competencies may be necessary during a disaster situation. Trying to accommodate this varying need and situations makes developing competencies for disaster preparedness difficult, and there is little documentation of evidence-based practices related to outcomes (Daily et al., 2010; Tsu et al., 2006). With the many different approaches to competency development and the plethora of identified disaster competencies, the lack of consensus and clarity of disaster competencies highlights the evident negative—that an overabundance of competencies may be used to justify slow movement toward implementation of standardized practices. The positive side is that there is a wealth of completed work that can be seen as the solid groundwork for continuing efforts to clarify the common framework for preparedness and response competencies across disciplines and globally (Daily et al., 2010).

It is not surprising that one major challenge identified by Daily et al. (2010) was the variance in terminology that was used within the literature reviewed. Some competency sets divide material into domains, whereas others identify subcompetencies. In addition, not all published competency statements include an action nor a context or an ability to address the required skill, all of which are generally assumed to be minimum requirements of well-stated competencies (Daily et al., 2010). As mentioned previously, it is integral to competency development to include knowledge, skills, and abilities as well as progressive level development (Calhoun et al., 2002; Gebbie, 2004; Gebbie & Merrill, 2002; Lichtveld et al., 2002). Well- articulated competencies define what is required of the individual to fulfill essential core functions, provide educational guidelines, and to provide guides to consistent response performance. In addition, competencies that are endorsed can provide a framework for regulatory bodies through setting standards for practice and accreditation (Daily et al., 2010), which can only lead to the advancement of disaster health care practice.

INVESTIGATION OF COMPETENCIES USED DURING DISASTERS

Two hundred responders (nurses, physicians, dentists) who staffed health facilities during hurricanes Katrina and Rita were asked to respond to a survey to investigate whether these people felt prepared and competent to function during this time. That is, to examine if specific professional competencies were important in the response of health care providers during disaster situations (Slepski, 2007). The origin of the study is the investigator's perspective that the term "preparedness" and how it is measured is inconsistent, with no single authority or approved body or curriculum to standardize competencies, leaving no clear vision between existing competencies and confusion about what competencies are supposed to achieve in this arena (Slepski, 2007).

Responders described a transition or an abrupt change from their everyday environment, with a need to experience a period of acclimatization, although they learned about the environment around them and the people that they were working with. First-time responders felt that they were least prepared in the area of performing skills within systems that were already in place. In addition, first-time responders felt that they did not know when priorities changed, acronyms that were used, or how to document effectively in this setting. Responders also articulated that they did not understand how different groups worked together or what the chain of command was during the disaster response. Furthermore, first- time responders felt unprepared for the level of devastation they experienced, the volume of patients, and the level of acuity they were expected to deal with. Moreover, first-time responders were not prepared for the long hours that they needed to work, coupled working with limited supplies, and having to deal with hostile patients (Slepski, 2007).

Moderately experienced responders (11 to 20 years of experience) were supervising others. They also expressed concerns about the long hours, how to manage the mental ill problems of patients, and the high patient ratio. Other identified concerns were where to transfer patients to and working outside of the own area of practice, for example, pediatrics or orthopedics. These participants cited not being able to take care of their own family as their main personal concern. Regarding professional concerns, they cited poor management, poor communication, and inadequate supplies as the main issues. Interestingly, this group of middle responders looked at opportunities to identify referral sites and other agencies that could help. In addition, they were concerned with ensuing that patients had access to food and water (Slepski, 2007).

The very experienced responders (21–30 years of experience) performed basic clinical care, administrative duties or triage, and were often selected to provide on-the-job training and function as a liaison between different entities involved in the disaster. This group did not have many concerns regarding expectations of what to do but cited concerns around "red tape" disregard for chain of command and ineffective working relationships. Other areas that were identified as difficult were talking to the media, tracing families, supply levels (lack of), and identifying ways to resupply. Recommendations from this group centered on clarifying the goals of the mission and understanding the strengths and weaknesses of fellow team members. Further recommendations focused on improving individual hands-on clinical skills and overall team effectiveness (Slepski, 2007).

The findings from all three groups of responders included the need to be flexible about their roles, schedules, and expectations; working in areas that were outside their normal roles coupled with having to work with little direction created a challenging work environment. At all levels, the need to understand the organization of disaster response and the relationships among organizations was identified as an important need. Slepski (2007) asserts that current training programs generally focus on skills that are often a part of ongoing work in the usual setting rather than preparing responders for the ongoing changes they may face when working during a disaster response. Subsequent studies may address whether or not professional competencies and transitions happen in different emergency responses. Because the topic of disaster research is still in its infancy, there are still many challenges ahead.

EDUCATIONAL PROGRAMS IN NURSING

A prepared and competent workforce can respond quickly and in a timely way for a disaster event. Education in disaster response is an essential part of preparedness (Hsu et al., 2006). There has been a significant rise in the number of educational activities worldwide since the disasters of September 11, 2001, the 2004 Asian tsunami, and 2005 Hurricane Katrina as nurses and health professionals more broadly attempted to address the issues of preparedness and competency of the workforce (Powers & Daily, 2010). The curricula for basic nursing training for nursing and midwifery vary greatly internationally, although minimum requirements were established in 1997 by those countries in the European Union (Principle 13b2 WHO, 2001). Unfortunately, much of the training is neither evidence based nor standardized, at least as described in the work reviewed for this chapter. For example, although nurses are motivated and ready to respond in disasters, many feel they have little to contribute, especially if they are not prepared with critical care or emergency care skills (ICN, 2009). Duong (2009) suggests that confidence in the role of disaster nursing will build when nurses' disaster response education is standardized and freely available.

In the same way that standardization of competencies has not been resolved, standardization for education in disaster response has yet to be agreed upon internationally. Many schools of nursing do not include disaster preparedness in the undergraduate curriculum. In 2003, only 53% of U.S. schools offered content on disaster preparedness with a mean of 4 hours (Weiner, Irwin, Trangenstein, & Gordon, 2005). The most frequently used resources were Websites (48.1%) and journal articles (44%). It was reported that the content for biological and chemical agents improved over 3 years, 2000–2003, but that for nuclear and radiological topics, improvement was slow.

If approximately half of the nursing population do not receive this content in the undergraduate setting (and the quality of that received by the other half is not known), nurses need to be able to receive it in the postgraduate setting or through employer- and private-provided educational packages suitable for the graduate. The current preferred training methods are tabletop exercises, disaster drills, computer simulation, conferences, satellite broadcasts, and continuing education (Slepski & Littleton-Kearney, 2010) but the authors observe that it is unclear which method is the best or how often the training should take place. Nurse educators have a major role in developing competencies and assessing competence, developing teaching materials, and assessing the developing expertise.

An exploration of disaster nursing content in the curriculum for undergraduate nursing students in 19 schools of nursing across Australia identified negligible interest in including such content. The study identified little importance attached to disaster nursing study for undergraduates, with students having little or no knowledge of the area (Usher & Mayner, 2011). The authors suggest that a major push from registration boards would be required to change this situation in the future. They further surmise that their findings are likely to be replicated in other countries, given that the WHO and ICN have been critical of nursing courses for this gap. Disaster nursing content is included in the curricula of a few countries, but it is included in Istanbul University, Hadassah-Hebrew University, and the University of the West Indies, but overall, there are far too few. For example, despite being a country with a history of major earthquakes, 60% of the nursing programs in Japan had no disaster nursing course and had no intention of adding a course in the future (Yamamoto & Watanabe as cited in WHO & ICN, 2009).

The need for standards at both the undergraduate and postgraduate level was identified early (Weiner, 2005). Chan et al. (2010) used the ICN framework to design an introductory training course for undergraduate nurses, postgraduate nurses, and midwives from 44 universities in China, Taiwan, Macau, and

Hong Kong. Greater competence in policy, planning, education, and psychological care and a lower level of competence in ethical practice, legal and vulnerable populations were reported by participants, who also stated that they would continue to update their knowledge and skills. The authors also noted that some of the basic emergency and trauma care prerequisites from the ICN were not included in the undergraduate curriculum in China, and so would be needed in postgraduate courses. A key challenge is providing clinical practice in real or simulated disaster settings (Gebbie & Qureshi, 2002). Student nurses in China, in a curriculum based on the ICN competencies, spent only 5 of 60 hours in the lecture room. The remaining time was spent in interactive workshops, including psychological first aid, wound management, community health needs assessment, and continuous assessment of the learning outcomes (Pang, Chan, & Cheng, 2009).

As has been true in many studies, participants self-rated their competence without validation, thus the acquisition of competency could not be determined (Chan et al., 2010). Existing competency statements have been described as ability-based statements without outcome measures (Slepski & Littlejohn-Kearney, 2010), which may be one reason for the lack of a stronger assessment approach. Another reason may be that faculty feel inadequately prepared to teach this topic (Silenas, Akins, Parrish, & Edwards, 2008; Weiner et al., 2005). Yet undergraduate emergency and disaster preparedness content is now a required curriculum content area according to the American Association of Colleges of Nursing (AACN; Stangeland, 2010), and there is some support for assuring that new graduates should have at least a novice level of capability in this area (Gebbie, 2010).

HEALTH PROFESSIONAL PROGRAMS

Although the discussion thus far has been about programs targeted to nurses, the literature suggests that multiprofessional training programs for disaster situations are preferable (Kennedy, Carson, & Garr, 2009; Silenas et al., 2008). The ACEP (2009) work cited previously has accepted this perspective in establishing standards for preparedness for physicians, nurses, paramedics, and emergency medicine technicians. The CDC work on public health preparedness has been multiprofessional since the earliest work funded at Columbia University (2002), which has looked at roles (administrative, professional, technical, support) rather than the familiar health disciplines. A question frequently asked, however, is how the various training programs, based on a range of competency materials, fit together, as any one individual is both a health professional and a member of a single profession and may be a specialist in some aspect of care, and an emergency volunteer for specific circumstances. The recent publication on common competencies provides some guidance on these intersections in the following figure.

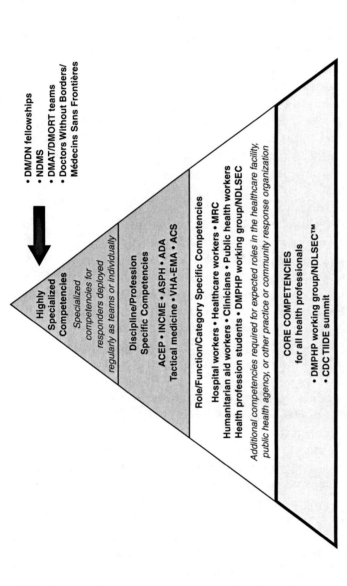

FIGURE 8.2 ACEP = American College of Emergency Physicians; ACS = American College of Surgeons; ADA = American Dental Association; ASPH = Association of Schools of Public Health; CDC = Centers for Disease Control and Prevention; DM = Disaster Medicine; DMAT = Disaster Medical Assistance Team; DMORT = Disaster Mortuary Operational Response Team; DMPHP = Disaster Medicine and Public Health Preparedness; DN = Disaster Nursing; INCMCE = ; MRC = Medical Reserve Corps; NDLSEC = National Disaster Life Support Education Consortium; NDMS = National Disaster Medical System; TIIDE = Terrorism Injuries: Information Dissemination and Exchange; VHA-EMA = Veterans Health Administration-Emergency Management Academy. Adapted from Walsh, L., Subbarao, I., Gebbie, K., Schor, K. W., Lyznicki, J., Strauss-Riggs, K., . . . James, J. J. (2012). Core competencies for disaster medicine and public health. *Disaster Medicine and Public Health Preparedness, 16*(1), 44–52.

Simulated disaster exercises and educational processes for improving hospital preparedness have included medical, nursing, and administrative staff. At an Australian hospital thought to be well prepared, a disaster exercise found that preintervention knowledge was poor and in following drill participation, only 50% passed the postdrill assessment, with no significant increase in the perceived level of preparedness (Bartley, Stella, & Walsh, 2006). Medical, veterinary, public health, and nursing students at a school in Texas were invited to participate in an experiential tabletop exercise in learning core competencies for a project entitled "Training Future Physicians About Weapons of Mass Destruction" (Silenas et al., 2008). It was designed for a multidisciplinary team of 69 students at second year level without a lot of clinical experience, using data about the 2005 Avian influenza experience as though it were a biological attack. The findings were that the 3-hour interactive exercise was sufficient for improving knowledge, highlighting that not a lot of time needs to be spent on improving competence for an effective disaster response.

SUMMARY

The overall conclusion of this update is a simple one; although competency sets continue to be generated and there is agreement that training is needed, there is a decided lack of concurrence regarding the most necessary core competencies and the way to assure that all nurses achieve them. This challenge is not unique to nursing; all health professions are struggling with the challenge of inserting this much-needed area of content into already full curricula. Furthermore, there is awareness that real competence requires continued practice; although most nurses and other health professionals do not engage in emergency or disaster planning, response, or recovery on a routine basis.

The process of assuring that nurses and other professionals practicing in emergency departments or military settings or in countries that experience disasters frequently is somewhat easier because of the overlap with ongoing needs. It is this group of professionals who will most likely be expected to provide the advanced expertise in the management of victims with specific types of injuries, working in collaboration with public health and others with expertise in various disasters. For most nurses (physicians, dentists, pharmacists, others), an emergency means continuing to practice the core professional skills, but in unusual circumstances, under a different management scheme, or with unfamiliar colleagues. The feedback from Hurricane Katrina respondents clearly documents the need, therefore, to focus ongoing competency clarification and subsequent training, on what is needed for the transition from "usual" to "disaster" situations.

Several of the reported studies highlighted the need for a stronger empirical base for accepted competencies, associated with clear, evidence-based standards against which achievement can be measured, with measures that are clearly associated with improved patient outcomes. Most assessments of learning to date have been learner self-report with some observer information. Yet, the limited standardization of desired level of performance makes these data impossible to interpret. The global community deserves a nursing workforce that is well-positioned to contribute to planning for disaster response, responding effectively when a disaster occurs, participating in community recovery, and assisting in assessment and improvement planning postdisaster. It will be essential, then, that the nursing community continue with organized improvements to competency sets (whether nursing specific or general to health professionals) and establish programs of research that provide the evidence for practice standards associated with each competency. Then and only then will it be possible to move to more advanced levels of research on the contribution of competent nurses to systemic capacity to prepare for, respond to, and recover from emergencies and disasters of all kinds.

REFERENCES

Al-Khalaileh, M. A., Bond, E., Beckstrand, R. L., & Al Talafha, A. (2010). The disaster preparedness evaluation tool: Psychometric testing of the classical Arabic version. *Journal of Advanced Nursing, 66*(3), 664–672.

American College of Emergency Physicians. (2009). *Development of a national standardized all-hazard disaster core competencies for acute care physicians, nurses, and EMS professionals.* Dallas, TX: Emergency Medicine Foundation.

Arbon, P., Bobrowski, C., Zeitz, K., Hooper, C., Williams, J., & Thitchener, J. (2006). Australian nurses volunteering for the Sumatra–Andaman earthquake and tsunami of 2004: A review of experience and analysis of data collected by the Tsunami Volunteer Hotline. *Australasian Emergency Nursing Journal, 9*(4), 171–178.

Association of Schools of Public Health. (2010). *Public health preparedness and response core competency model.* Retrieved from http://www.asph.org/document.cfm?page=1081

*Bartley, B. H., Stella, J. B., & Walsh, L. D. (2006).What a disaster? Assessing utility of simulated disaster exercise and educational process for improving hospital preparedness. *Prehospital and Disaster Medicine, 21*(4), 249–255.

Benner, P. (1984). *From novice to expert: Excellence and power in clinical nursing practice.* Menlo Park, CA: Addison-Wesley.

Bloom, B. S., Englehart, M. D., Furst, F. J., Hill, W. H., & Krathwohl, D. R. (1956). *Taxonomy of educational objectives, handbook I: The cognitive domain.* New York, NY: David McKay.

Calhoun, J. G., Davidson, P. L., Sinioris, M. E., Vincent, E. T., & Griffith, J. R. (2002). Toward an understanding of competency identification and assessment in healthcare management. *Quality Management in Health Care, 11*(1), 14–38.

Calhoun, J. G., Rowney, R., Eng, E., & Hoffman, Y. (2005). Competency mapping and analysis for public health preparedness training initiatives. *Public Health Reports, 120*(Suppl. 1), 91–99.

Chan, S. S., Chan, W., Cheng, Y., Fung, O., Lai, T., Leung, A., . . . Pang, S. (2010). Development and evaluation of an undergraduate training course for developing International Council of Nurses disaster nursing competencies in China. *Journal of Nursing Scholarship, 42*(4), 405–413.

Chastonay, P., Klohn, A. M., Zesiger, V., Freigburghaus, F., & Mpinga, E. K. (2009). Developing a human rights training program for French speaking Africa: Lessons learned, from needs assessment to a pilot program. *BMC International Health and Human Rights,* 1–9. Retrieved from http://www.biomedcentral.com/1472-698X/9/19/

Chapman, K., & Arbon, P. (2008). Are nurses ready? Disaster preparedness in the acute setting. *Australasian Emergency Nursing Journal, 11,* 135–144.

Columbia University School of Nursing Centre for Health Policy. (2002). *Bioterrorism and emergency readiness: Competencies for all public health workers.* Atlanta, GA: Centers for Disease Control and Prevention.

Daily, E., Padjen, P., & Birnbaum, M. L. (2010). A review of competencies developed for disaster health care providers: Limitations of current processes and applicability. *Prehospital and Disaster Medicine, 25*(5), 387–395.

Duong, K. (2009). Disaster education and training of emergency nurses in South Australia. *Australasian Emergency Nursing Journal, 12*(3), 86–92.

Elsharkawi, H., Sandbladh, H., Aloudat, T., Girardau, A., Tjoflat, I., & Brunnstrom, C. (2010). Preparing humanitarian workers for disaster response: A Red Cross/Red Crescent field training model. *Humanitarian Exchange Magazine, 46.* Retrieved from http://www.odihpn.org/humanitarian-exchange-magazine/issue-46/preparing-humanitarian-workers-for-disaster-response-a-red-crossed- crescent-field-training-model

Gebbie, K. M. (2004). *Competency-to-curriculum toolkit: Developing curricula for public health workers* (Rev. ed.). New York, NY: Center for Health Policy, Columbia University School of Nursing, Association of Teachers of Preventative Medicine.

Gebbie, K. M. (2010). The current status of nurses' emergency preparedness: A commentary on the development of emergency preparedness and response competency [Letter to the editor]. *Collegian, 17,* 209–211.

Gebbie, K., Hodge, J., Meier, B., Barrett, D., Keith, P., Koo, D., . . .Winget, P. (2008). Improving competencies for public health emergency legal preparedness. *The Journal of Law, Medicine & Ethics, 36*(1 Suppl.), 52–56.

Gebbie, K., & Merrill, J. (2002). Public health worker competencies for emergency response. *Journal of Public Health and Management Practice, 8*(3), 73–81.

Gebbie, K. M., Peterson, C. A., Subbarao, I., & White, K. M. (2009). Adapting standards of care under extreme conditions. *Disaster Medicine and Public Health Preparedness, 3*(2), 111–116.

Gebbie, K., & Qureshi, K. (2002). Emergency and disaster preparedness. *The American Journal of Nursing, 102*(1), 46.

Hein, K. (2010). The competency of competencies. *Prehospital and Disaster Medicine, 25*(5), 396–397.

Hodge, J., Gebbie, K., Hoke, C., Fenstersheib, M., Hoffman, S., & Lynk, M. (2008). Assessing competencies for public health emergency legal preparedness. *The Journal of Law, Medicine & Ethics, 36*(1 Suppl.), 28–35. Special Supplement: The National Action Agenda for Public Health Legal Awareness.

Hsu, E. B., Thomas, T. L., Bass, E. B., Whyne, D., Kelen, G. D., & Green, G. B. (2006). Healthcare worker competencies for disaster training. *BMC Medical Education, 6,* 19.

International College of Nursing. (2009). *ICN framework of disaster nursing competencies.* Geneva, Switzerland: International Council of Nurses and World Health Organization. Retrieved from http://www.icn.ch/publications/free-publications/

Kako, M., & Mitani, S. (2010). A literature review of disaster nursing competencies in Japanese nursing journals. *Collegian, 17,* 161–173.

Leaning, J. (2008). Editors corner: Disasters and humanitarian crises: A joint future for responders? *Prehospital and Disaster Medicine, 23*(4), 291–294.

Lichtveld, M., Hodge, J., Gebbie, K., Thompson, F., & Loos, D. (2002). Preparedness on the frontline: What's law got to do with it? *The Journal of Law, Medicine & Ethics, 30*(3 Suppl.), 184–188.

Manne, R. (2009, July). Why we weren't warned: The Victorian bushfires and the Royal Commission. *The Monthly,* (47), 22–35. Retrieved from http://www.themonthly.com.au/victorian-bushfires-and-royal-commission-why-we-weren-t-warned-robert-manne-1780

National Disaster Life Support Program. (2012). Retrieved from http://www.ama-assn.org/ama/pub/physician-   resources/public-health/center-public-health-preparedness-disaster-response/national-disaster-life-support.page

Nursing Emergency Preparedness Education Coalition. (2003). *Educational Competencies for Registered Nurses Responding to Mass Casualty Incidents.* Retrieved from http://www.nursing.vanderbilt.edu/incmce/competencies.html

Pandemic and All-Hazards Preparedness Act, Pub. L. No. 109-417, 120 Stat. 2831 (2006).

Pang, S. M. C., Chan, S., & Cheng, Y. (2009). Pilot training program for developing disaster nursing competencies among undergraduate students in China. *Nursing and Health Sciences, 11,* 367–373.

Robinson, J. J. (2010). Nursing and disaster preparedness. *International Nursing Review, 57*(2).

Schwartz, R., McManus, J., Croushorn, J., Piazza, G., Coule, P., Gibbons, M., . . . Lerner, B. (2011). Tactical medicine: Competency-based guidelines. *Prehospital Emergency Care, 15*(1), 67–82.

Silenas, R., Akins, R., Parrish, A., & Edwards, J. (2008). Developing disaster preparedness competence: An experiential learning exercise for multiprofessional education. *Teaching and Learning in Medicine, 20*(1), 62–68.

Slepski, L. A. (2007) Emergency preparedness and professional competency among health care providers during hurricanes Katrina and Rita: Pilot study results. *Disaster Management & Response: DMR, 5*(4), 99–110.

Slepski, L. A., & Littleton-Kearney, M. T. (2010). Disaster nursing educational competencies. In R. Powers & E. Daily (Eds.), *International disaster nursing.* New York, NY: Cambridge University Press.

Smith, E. (2007). Emergency health care workers willingness to work during major emergencies and disasters. *The Australian Journal of Emergency Management, 22*(2), 21–24.

Stangeland, P. (2010). Disaster nursing: A retrospective review. *Critical Care Nursing Clinics of North America, 22*(4), 421–426.

Subbarao, I., Lyznicki, J. M., Hsu, E. B., Gebbie, K. M., Markenson, D., Barzansky, B., & James, J. J. (2008). A consensus-based educational framework and competency set for the discipline of disaster medicine and public health preparedness. *Disaster Medicine and Public Health Preparedness, 2*(1), 57–68.

Tsu, E., Thomas, T., Bass, E., Whyne, D., Kelen, G., & Green, G. (2006). Healthcare worker competencies for disaster training. *BMC Medical Education, 6*(19), 1–8.

Usher, K., & Mayner, L. (2011). Disaster nursing: A descriptive survey of Australian undergraduate nursing curricula. *Australasian Emergency Nursing Journal, 14*(2), 75–80.

Veneema, T. (2007). *Disaster nursing and emergency preparedness for chemical, biological and radiological terrorism and other hazards* (2nd ed.). New York, NY: Springer Publishing.

Walker, P., Hein, K., Russ, C., Bertleff, G., & Caspersz, D. (2010). A blueprint for professionalizing humanitarian assistance. *Health Affairs, 29*(12), 2223–2230.

Walker, P., & Russ, C. (2010). *Professionalising the humanitarian sector.* Retrieved from http://www.elrha.org/uploads/Professionalising_the_humanitarian_sector.pdf

Walsh, L., Subbarao, I., Gebbie, K., Schor, K. W., Lyznicki, J., Strauss-Riggs, K., . . . James, J. J. (2012). Core competencies for disaster medicine and public health. *Disaster Medicine and Public Health Preparedness, 16*(1), 44–52.

Weiner, E. (2005). Disaster management and response: A national curriculum for nurses in emergency preparedness and response. *Nursing Clinics of North America, 40*(3), 469–479.

Weiner, E., Irwin, M., Trangenstein, P., & Gordon, J. (2005). Emergency preparedness curriculum in nursing schools in the United States. *Nursing Education Perspectives, 26,* 336–339.

Wisniewski, R., Dennik-Champion, G., & Peltier, J. W. (2004). Emergency preparedness competencies: Assessing nurses' educational needs. *Journal of Nursing Administration, 34*(10), 475–480.

World Health Organization. (2001). *Nurses and midwives for health: WHO European strategy for nursing and midwifery education: Prospective analysis methodology questionnaire.* Copenhagen, Denmark: WHO Office for Europe.

World Health Organization & International Council of Nurses. (2009). *ICN Framework of disaster nursing competencies.* Geneva, Switzerland: Author.

Yang, Y. N., Xiao, L., Cheng, H. Y., Zhu, J. C., Yamamoto, A., & Watanabe, T. (2006). *Disaster nursing competencies.* Retrieved from http://www.coe-cnas.jp/english/group_education/img/group_education_01.jpg

CHAPTER 9

Willingness, Ability, and Intentions of Health Care Workers to Respond

Mary Pat Couig

ABSTRACT

Health care workers (HCWs) are a critical component of the emergency management cycle (prevention, mitigation, preparation, response, and recovery). The potential for large numbers of *injured* from either a man-made or natural disaster has resulted in the development of surge capacity plans and attempts to predict how many HCWs will be available to respond. Since 1991 (with the majority of the research published in 2002 and later), researchers have been conducting studies to learn about the willingness, ability, and intentions of HCWs to respond to disasters. Potential and real barriers to disaster response are being explored as well. This chapter focuses on research authored or coauthored by nurses. Nurse-authored research is just a portion of the growing body of knowledge in this area; however, the findings are consistent with other published works. HCWs are more likely to be willing and able to respond to natural disasters and less likely to be willing and able during infectious outbreaks or incidents with potential exposure to harmful agents (biological, chemical, nuclear, or radiological). HCW concerns include safety of self and family, availability of protective equipment, medicines and vaccines, and caretaking responsibilities (children, elders, and pets).

© 2012 Springer Publishing Company
http://dx.doi.org/10.1891/0739-6686.30.193

Terrorism, natural disasters, and infectious pandemics are a part of man's history. The burning of Rome's harbor Ostia in 68 BC (Harris, 2006), the eruption of Mount Vesuvius in 79 AD (Ball, n.d.), and the bubonic plague of 542 AD (Dennis, Gage, Gratz, Poland, & Tikhomirov, 1999) are respective examples of these events. More recently in the United States, the 2001 terrorist attacks at the World Trade Center towers and the Pentagon, the crash of Flight 93, and the natural disaster Hurricane Katrina were the deadliest and most costly of any disasters (General Accountability Office, 2010). More than 2,981 people died from the terrorist attacks on September 11, 2001 (Kean & Hamilton, 2004) and there were more than 1,200 deaths during Hurricane Katrina; the estimated cost of Hurricane Katrina was $125 billion (Graumann et al., 2005). The United States was unprepared for such large-scale events as evidenced by the loss of lives and property (Townsend, 2006).

As a result of the terrorist attacks on U.S. soil and Hurricane Katrina, new laws, requirements, and funding were enacted to strengthen the public health infrastructure. These included congressional legislation to create a new department (Homeland Security Act of 2002), pandemic and all-hazards management (Pandemic and All-Hazards Preparedness Act, 2006), presidential directives for managing domestic incidents, and establishing plans for coordinated responses (U.S. Department of Homeland Security [DHS], 2010). To help strengthen hospital and clinic preparedness, The Joint Commission (TJC), a nonprofit evaluation and accreditation organization, revised its emergency management standards in 2008 (TJC, 2008). In addition, the Congress increased appropriations for public health emergency preparedness initiatives.

Estimates of total funding for public health emergency preparedness are elusive; it is managed and funded in several federal agencies including the DHS and the Department of Health and Human Services (HHS) with active participation and involvement of other federal agencies during times of need (DHS, 2008a). The revised and enacted 2008 budget for DHS Federal Emergency Management Agency (FEMA) was more than $5,220,000 (DHS, 2008b). The Centers for Diseases Control and Prevention's (CDC) funding for public health preparedness and response activities has been approximately $1.5 billion per year since 2002. This funding supports various activities at CDC and at state and local levels (CDC, 2010).

Despite directives, legislation, and increased funding, there are still questions about the nation's capability and capacity to respond to public health emergencies at both state and national levels. In its 2010 yearly study on state's preparedness, *Ready or not?*, the Trust for America's Health reported more states were prepared than in previous years, based on 10 key indicators of preparedness

(Levi, Vinter, Segal, & St. Laurent, 2010). However, state budget cuts are threatening progress. Since 2009, 33 states and the District of Columbia have cut budgets by $429 billion. The most recent *Ready or not?* report (Levi, Segal, Lieberman, & St. Laurent, 2011) documents further state budget cuts and a number of programs at risk for either elimination or loss of federal funding—research and training programs, medicine and vaccine distribution programs, and epidemiological support. The loss of funding and resultant loss of program support has the potential to reverse recent gains and adversely affect public health emergency preparedness.

At a national level, the General Accountability Office (Jenkins, 2010) reports a continued need for strengthening disaster response planning, including the development of a management plan to ensure the completion of key national policies and planning documents. Ultimately, the U.S. government, health systems, and health and public health professionals must answer the question "Are we ready to prevent, to protect, to respond to and recover from all-hazards?"

The National Response Framework (NRF) is the nation's guiding document that establishes a national, comprehensive, all-hazards approach to domestic incident response (DHS, 2008a). Within this framework is the emergency management cycle—mitigation, preparedness, response, and recovery (FEMA, n.d.). Health care workers (HCWs) are a critical component of this cycle, especially during the response phase when there are injured and/or displaced persons who need care. After the September 11, 2001 attacks on the United States when airplanes were used as weapons of mass destruction and shortly thereafter anthrax was deliberately released via the U.S. postal system to a member of Congress and a national news anchor, there has been increased interest in learning about the willingness, ability, and intention of HCWs to respond to public health emergencies, natural or manmade. The purpose of this chapter is to provide a brief overview of the topic in general and a review of the current state of willingness, ability, and intentions of HCWs to respond research, with a focus on publications authored or coauthored by nurses.

BACKGROUND

One of the first studies to investigate willingness and ability of HCWs to respond in a disaster was conducted in 1991 in Israel by Shapira and colleagues (1991). The researchers provided a scenario of a missile attack and asked a number of questions related to whether or not the responders would report to work. The researchers discovered that overall, 42% of responders were willing to report to work. If guaranteed protective equipment, spectacles fitted to gas mask, an all-clear announcement by an official spokesperson, and transportation to the hospital, 44% of responders would change their mind and report to work for an overall report to work rate of 86%. Not surprisingly, having young children and being female correlated negatively with willingness to report to work.

A study of emergency health care providers at a facility in upstate New York revealed that anywhere from 18% to 84% of providers would be willing to report to work during a mass casualty incident. The variation in willingness to report to work was dependent on several factors including whether or not the cause of the incident was known, a treatment or a vaccine was available, providers became ill, the agent was transmissible, and family members could receive treatment (Syrett, Benitez, Livingston, & Davis, 2007). Another study examined both willingness (the personal decision of the person) and ability (the capability of the person) to report to work in various catastrophic scenarios (Qureshi et al., 2005). The findings evidenced a difference in willingness and ability to respond based on the type of event (ability to respond mass casualty incident (83%) versus severe acute respiratory syndrome (SARS) outbreak (64%), and willingness to respond to mass casualty incident (86%) versus SARS (48%). Obstacles to willingness included personal health problems and concern and fear for family and self. Obstacles to ability included child and eldercare responsibilities, pet care, and transportation.

Chaffee (2009) conducted an integrated literature review of 27 studies published before December 1, 2007. These studies identified many of the same issues with respect to willingness and ability to respond: dependence on the type of disaster, concern for family and beloved others, concern about pets, varies with provision of personal protective equipment, and personal responsibilities (e.g., child and eldercare). Additional findings included a relationship between type of education and willingness, the responder's perception of the significance of his or her role, whether or not basic physiological needs can be met, the ability to maintain contact with the outside world (e-mail and Internet access), and the maximum length of time health professionals would remain on duty to respond.

METHODS

A search of the Cumulative Index to Nursing and Allied Health Literature (CINAHL), PubMed, Web of Science, Embase, and the World Wide Web was conducted using the following terms: *willingness and ability to respond*, *disasters*, *nursing*, *nurses*, *intentions*, *theory of planned behavior*, *duty*, and combinations of the previous terms. The search was limited to articles published in English between the periods of January 1990 and June 1, 2012. Ancestry searching was also performed. Abstracts were reviewed for the previous terms. Publications authored or coauthored by nurses are included in the review.

RESULTS

More than 50 studies were identified from the review of the literature; 21 publications were authored or coauthored by nurses (see Table 9.1). The studies were conducted in at least five states (two of the articles provided only a general description of the area of the country where the study was conducted) and six countries. Specific topics included pandemics; willingness and ability to work during a disaster; willingness to work and risk perception; chemical, biological, radiation and nuclear incidents and terrorism; natural disasters; training and education; and an integrated literature review. Most study subjects were nurses and nursing students. Other group studies include physicians, emergency medical service responders, support staff, administrators, fire rescue workers, public health personnel, police sector workers, and correctional personnel.

Willingness and Ability Depends on Type of Disaster

As evidenced by the review of the literature on willingness, ability, and intention to respond, these findings are consistent with other studies in this area (Adams & Berry, 2012; Chaffee, 2009). Willingness and ability to respond varies by type of disaster. Response rates ranged from a high of 93.0% (willingness) and 90.6% (ability) for a mass casualty incident (Adams & Berry, 2012) to a low of 10% of sampled junior and senior nursing students for an infectious disease outbreak, unless their families were provided protection (Young & Persell, 2004).

Barriers to Responding

Barriers to responding include a broad range of issues and concerns including the following:

1. Concern for safety of self and family (French, Sole, & Byers, 2002; Gershon et al., 2010; Good & Agan, 2011; Smith, Morgans, Qureshi, Burkle, & Archer, 2008; Veenema, Walden, Feinstein, & Williams, 2008; Yonge, Rosychuk, Bailey, Lake, & Marrie, 2010; Young & Persell, 2004).
2. Caretaking commitments (e.g., child, elder, other family member or pet[s]; Adams & Berry, 2012; Considine & Mitchell, 2009; Davidson et al., 2009; French et al., 2002; Good & Agan, 2011; Grimes & Mendias, 2010; Mitani, Kuboyama, & Shirakawa, 2003; Qureshi et al., 2005; Qureshi, Merrill, Gershon, & Calero-Breckheimer, 2002).

TABLE 9.1

*Major Findings in Nurse Authored or Co-Authored Studies of Willingness,
Ability, and Intention to Respond (1990–2012)*

Year	Author(s)	Study Population	Type of Incident	Major Findings
2002	French et al.	Emergency Department nurses in Florida, $n = 30$	Hurricane	Main concern for safety of family. Other concerns—pet care, ability to meet nurse's basic needs, & safety measures to protect nurses.
2002	Qureshi et al.	Public Health Nurses in New York, $n = 53$	Findings from pilot training	90% of nurses had at least one barrier that would prevent them from reporting—child/older adult care, no transportation, health issues.
2003	Mitani et al.	Nurses & nursing students in Japan, $n = 477$	Earthquake & disasters in general	3% would participate in future disaster with no conditions, 84.2% with some conditions, 9.5% would not participate at all.
2004	Ko et al.	Nurses in southern Taiwan, $n = 750$	SARS outbreak	42.7% had a positive intention to provide care to patients with SARS, 25.4% would volunteer to care for patients with SARS, 74.5% felt professional obligation to care for patients with SARS.
2004	Young & Persell	Junior and senior nursing students in Arkansas, $n = 95$	Terrorism—chemical, biological, & nuclear	90% would not care for patients with infectious diseases unless they had safety measures for self & family, 74% selected personal protection as their main concern.

TABLE 9.1

*Major Findings in Nurse Authored or Co-Authored Studies of Willingness,
Ability, and Intention to Respond (1990–2012)   (Continued)*

Year	Author(s)	Study Population	Type of Incident	Major Findings
2005	Qureshi et al.	Health care workers from 47 facilities in New York, $n = 6,428$	Weather related, terrorism (biological, chemical, nuclear), mass casualty, infectious diseases	Ability to work—82.5% for MCI, 80.6% for environmental disaster, 71.0% for chemical incident, 68.6% for smallpox, 63.8% for radiation event, 63.5% for SARS, 48.9% for snow storm Willingness to work—MCI, 85.7%; snow storm, 80.4%; environment, 84.2%; chemical, 67.0%; smallpox, 61.1%; radiation, 57.3%; & SARS, 48.4%.
2006	Kim et al.	Nurses from four hospitals in Korea, $n = 679$	SARS outbreak	Nurses had negative attitude toward care of patients with SARS and most did not intend to care for patients. Negative influences were from family & friends.
2007	Chaffee	Integrated review of literature	Willingness to work in disaster	27 studies; 25 quantitative & 2 qualitative. Findings—willingness decisions based on type of disaster, family & pet responsibilities, prior training & education, professional duty, belief in contribution to response, basic needs met, protective device, and prophylaxis/ treatment availability & how long they would be expected to respond.

(Continued)

TABLE 9.1

Major Findings in Nurse Authored or Co-Authored Studies of Willingness, Ability, and Intention to Respond (1990–2012)   *(Continued)*

Year	Author(s)	Study Population	Type of Incident	Major Findings
2008	Fung et al.	Master's nursing students in Hong Kong, $n = 164$	Disasters	If a disaster happened while on duty, 38.4% would follow the emergency plan, 34.8% would wait for guidance from superiors, 24.4% would inform others before leaving duty, 15.2% would remove patients, and 7.3% would leave immediately.
2008	Smith et al. (Qureshi)	Paramedics in Victoria, Australia, $n = 58$	Transportation incident, explosion, infectious outbreak	Risk perception related to type of disaster, primary concern for self-safety and health, other concerns—duty, training, communication, & lack of trust of ambulance management services.
2008	Veenema et al.	Hospital nurses & a professional nursing association in New York, $n = 668$	Radiation	Most of the nurses were willing to respond to a radiation incident, 15.3% were not willing to work in a severe incident; personal safety was a primary concern.
2009	Considine & Mitchell	Emergency Department nurses in Australia, $n = 64$	Biological, chemical, & radiological incidents	Work after shift over in CBR incident—42.2% "no problem," 31.3% "probably possible," 14.1% "difficult," 1.8% "impossible."
2009	Davidson et al.	Nurses in southern California, $n = 8$	Wildfire	Factors that affected decision to work—professional vs. personal commitments, "caring" organizational culture, wanting to help.

TABLE 9.1

Major Findings in Nurse Authored or Co-Authored Studies of Willingness,
Ability, and Intention to Respond (1990–2012)   *(Continued)*

Year	Author(s)	Study Population	Type of Incident	Major Findings
2009	Pang et al.	Nursing students in China, $n = 150$	Pilot training	After attending a 2-week introduction to disaster course, most students were willing to help in disaster.
2010	Gershon et al. (Qureshi)	HCWs, EMS, fire, police, public health, & correctional personnel in New York, $n = 1,103$	Pandemic	80% able to report to duty, 65% willing to report, 49% willing and able to report to duty. Factors affecting willingness—wearing protective equipment, organizational assistance in obtaining vaccine & protective equipment, & organizational trust.
2010	Grimes & Mendias	Nurses in Texas, $n = 292$	Bioterrorism & other contagious incidents	Depending on type of incident, 8%–20% of nurses are "extremely likely" to respond and 21%–64% are "highly likely" to respond. Of those who provided written comments (253/292), 73 reported they would respond because of professional duty.
2010	Jacobson et al. (Turley)	Nurses in Texas, $n = 941$	Training & readiness self-assessment	32.7% are able & willing to respond for state emergency plans and 28.3% are able & willing to diagnose & treat potential cases of bioterrorism.

(Continued)

TABLE 9.1

*Major Findings in Nurse Authored or Co-Authored Studies of Willingness,
Ability, and Intention to Respond (1990–2012)   (Continued)*

Year	Author(s)	Study Population	Type of Incident	Major Findings
2010	Yonge et al.	Nursing students in Canada, $n = 484$	Pandemic	If healthy & able, 67.9% would volunteer if provided protective equipment, 77.4% would respond if compensated, 55.6% would respond if mandated by government, less than 50% would volunteer.
2011	Good & Agan	Hospital HCWs on 5 urban campuses in southwestern U.S., $n = 1,645$	Pandemic	92% would respond; concerns—availability of antivirals, family caretaking & safety, disease knowledge, coworker trust, & safe work place.
2011	Schmidt et al.	Nursing students in all states & Guam, Puerto Rico, & the Virgin Islands, $n = 1,348$	Disaster response readiness	3% responded they had volunteered to help in a disaster.
2012	Adams & Berry	Essential HCWs & staff in midwestern health care network, $n = 1,342$	Variety of incidents—weather-related, infectious outbreak; chemical & radiological incident; & an explosion with mass casualties	Ability to work—from 71.1% for a weather-related event to 90.6% for the MCI incident. Willingness to report—69.1% for radiologic incident to 93% for MCI. Child/eldercare primary barrier to responding.

Note. Nurse coauthors are listed in parentheses. SARS = severe acute respiratory syndrome; MCI = mild
cognitive impairment; CBR = chemical biological radiological; HCWs = health care workers;
EMS = emergency medical services.

3. Availability of protective equipment, medicines, or vaccines for self and family (Considine & Mitchell, 2009; Gershon et al., 2010; Good & Agan, 2011; Grimes & Mendias, 2010; Ko et al., 2004; Yonge et al., 2010; Young & Persell, 2004).
4. Education and training (Chaffee, 2009; Considine & Mitchell, 2009; Fung, Loke, & Lai, 2008; Good & Agan, 2011; Jacobson et al., 2010).

Nursing Students
In their study of junior and senior baccalaureate nursing students—9 months after September 11, 2001—Young and Persell (2004) found that 90% of the students stated that they would not respond in an infectious disease outbreak unless their families were protected. The student's two concerns were safety and protection for family and self. A study of Canadian nursing students regarding their willingness to respond during a pandemic revealed that 67.9% would respond during an influenza pandemic if they were able and well (Yonge et al., 2010). As part of a course evaluation offered after a 2-week training program for undergraduate student nurses in China, the students were asked if they would be willing to respond to a disaster. Most of the students (144/150) responded positively (Pang, Chan, & Cheng, 2009). Schmidt et al. (2011) surveyed National Student Nurses' Association members (1,107/1,348 [82%]; respondents were prelicensure) about their disaster preparedness. Included in the survey was a question about whether or not they had responded to a disaster; 3% (n = 46) reported affirmatively.

Cultural Perspectives
Kim, Yoo, Yoo, Kwon, and Hwang (2006) conducted a study of Korean nurses to determine their intentions to care for SARS patients. The study was administered from December 2004 to March 2005 in four university-based hospitals in two large metropolitan cities. The time frame for the study was 1.5 years after the disease was declared contained by the World Health Organization (WHO) in July 2003. WHO (2003) reports that there were three probable cases of SARS in the Republic of Korea. The study findings revealed that Korean nurses were unwilling to provide care to patients with SARS and had the belief that family and friends would not endorse their caring for patients with SARS.

Theoretical Models
A theoretical model helps guide research and potentially prevents missing important information during the conduct of a research study. Several theoretical models or adaptations of models were used in the studies presented in this chapter. In Chaffee's (2009) integrated review, two of 27 reports used theoretical concepts or models.

Balicer, Omer, Barnett, and Everly (2006) used risk perception theory to develop their survey of HCWs views of responding in an influenza pandemic. Crisis theory concepts were used to guide a study of student nurses' readiness and concerns related to nuclear, chemical, and biological terrorism incidents (Young & Persell, 2004).

Crane (2005) used a modified theory of reasoned action (TRA) model (Ajzen & Fishbein, 1980). TRA posits that intentions to perform a specific behavior are directly influenced by the "attitude toward the behavior" and the "subjective norm." Attitude toward the behavior is the person's assessment of positive or negative evaluation of conducting the behavior. Subjective norm is the person's discernment of the peer or social pressure regarding the behavior. TRA is a predecessor model to Ajzen's (1991) theory of planned behavior (TPB). TPB adds a concept, which helps account for the fact that behavior is not all voluntary. Perceived behavioral control is the extent to which the person believes they have the skills, knowledge, and resources to perform the behavior. Two studies used TPB to study nurse's intentions to care for patients with SARS (Kim et al., 2006; Ko et al., 2004).

Gershon et al. (2010) used an adaptation of DeJoy's behavioral-diagnostic model. The two components of this model are individual (protective equipment, medicines and vaccines, demographics, and risk perception) and organizational (facility/employer programs and planning, culture of safety and trust) factors. Both of these types of factors influence behavioral intentions (willingness and ability to respond).

DISCUSSION AND RESEARCH RECOMMENDATIONS

In this review of the research on the current state of willingness, ability and intentions of HCWs to respond (focus on publications authored or coauthored by nurses), 21 published reports were located in CINAHL, PubMed, Web of Science, Embase, and the World Wide Web. Most of the reports were available in CINAHL and PubMed. Although direct comparisons cannot be made with other research studies because of differences in research question, study design, methodology, sampling, and/or study populations, the findings of these reports are similar to other published reviews (Adams & Berry, 2012; Chaffee, 2009). This is a growing body of knowledge that provides insight into the reasons for, barriers against, and other factors that influence an HCWs' intention to respond to a disaster. With this knowledge, action can be taken to help address HCWs' concerns.

First and foremost is planning. Guidance and resources are widely available on the World Wide Web and from federal, national, and state organizations to assist facilities, communities, and organizations to prepare for potential disasters/threats specific to their geographic location. Specific recommendations are included in all of the published reports. For general recommendations related to the barriers identified in the review, see Adams and Berry (2012), Gershon et al. (2010), and Qureshi et al. (2005).

Of particular interest are the findings related to cultural perspectives and student nurses. Korean nurses believed that their friends and family would not approve of their caring for patients with SARS (Kim et al., 2006). With the diversity of cultures in the United States and increase of U.S. employment of nurses from other countries, this is an area that would benefit from further research. What are potential cultural influences and how might they be addressed? Young and Persell's (2004) study of nursing students in Arkansas shortly after September 11, 2001 found that 90% would not care for infectious patients unless they and their families were equipped with protective measures. This is one of the few studies to research students and another area that would benefit from research. What are the current perceptions of HCWs and response personnel students? Are their concerns different from HCWs who are already licensed? How are students socialized to their professions? What role or influence does the socialization have on their willingness and ability to respond? How might health professional schools address any concerns identified in the research?

LIMITATIONS
There is a possibility that some studies in this area were not included in this review. Any published studies in a language other than English were excluded from the search. Given the lack of standard terminology in this area, it is possible that articles were missed during the literature search. For example, at least one article included in this review was discovered through ancestry search because neither the title nor key words provided any evidence that the report contained information about willingness and ability to respond (Pang et al., 2009).

CONCLUSION
If society maintains an expectation that HCWs will respond in a public health emergency, then society is obligated, to the extent possible, to provide resources and support before, during, and after an incident to support all HCWs and other response personnel who may be in immediate danger or at risk because of exposure to harmful substances or diseases. With few exceptions, HCWs and response personnel have performed their duties even when they or their families were in danger (World Trade Center, SARS, Fukushima Daiichi nuclear disaster). This evolving scientific evidence base will continue to contribute to the knowledge needed to protect the women and men who respond when others are in need. Nurses are a crucial part of this process.

DISCLAIMER

The views expressed in this article are those of the author and do not necessarily reflect the position or policy of the Department of Veterans Affairs or the U.S. government.

REFERENCES

Adams, L. M., & Berry, D. (2012). Who will show up? Estimating ability and willingness of essential hospital personnel to report to work in response to a disaster. *Online Journal of Issues in Nursing, 17*(2), 8.

Ajzen, I. (1991). The theory of planned behavior. *Organizational Behavior and Human Decision Processes, 50*(2), 179–211.

Ajzen, I., & Fishbein, M. (1980). *Understanding attitudes and predicting social behavior.* Englewood Cliffs, NJ: Prentice-Hall.

Balicer, R., Omer, S., Barnett, D., & Everly, G. (2006). Local public health workers' perceptions toward responding to an influenza pandemic. *BMC Public Health, 6*(1), 99.

Ball, J. (n.d.). Mount Vesuvius—Italy. Retrieved from http://geology.com/volcanoes/vesuvius/

Centers for Disease Control and Prevention. (2010). *2010 Report: Public health preparedness.* Retrieved from http://www.bt.cdc.gov/publications/2010phprep/background/funding.asp

Chaffee, M. (2009). Willingness of health care personnel to work in a disaster: An integrative review of the literature. *Disaster Medicine and Public Health Preparedness, 3*(1), 42–56.

Considine, J., & Mitchell, B. (2009). Chemical, biological and radiological incidents: Preparedness and perceptions of emergency nurses. *Disasters, 33*(3), 482–497.

Crane, J. S. (2005). *Assessment of the community healthcare providers's ability and willingness to respond to a bioterrorist attack in Florida.* Tampa, FL: University of South Florida.

Davidson, J. E., Sekayan, A., Agan, D., Good, L., Shaw, D., & Smilde, R. (2009). Disaster dilemma: Factors affecting decision to come to work during a natural disaster. *Advanced Emergency Nursing Journal, 31*(3), 248–257.

Dennis, D. T., Gage, K. L., Gratz, N., Poland, J. D., & Tikhomirov, E. (1999). *Plague manual: Epidemiology, distribution, surveillance and control.* Retrieved from http://www.who.int/csr/resources/publications/plague/whocdscsredc992a.pdf

Federal Emergency Management Agency. (n.d.). *The four phases of emergency management.* Retrieved from http://emilms.fema.gov/IS10/FEMA_IS/IS10/ADA0304001.htm

French, E. D., Sole, M. L., & Byers, J. F. (2002). A comparison of nurses' needs/concerns and hospital disaster plans following Florida's Hurricane Floyd. *Journal of Emergency Nursing, 28*(2), 111–117.

Fung, O. W. M., Loke, A. Y., & Lai, C. K. Y. (2008). Disaster preparedness among Hong Kong nurses. *Journal of Advanced Nursing, 62*(6), 698–703.

General Accountability Office. (2010). *FEMA has made limited progress in efforts to develop and implement a system to assess national preparedness capabilities.* Retrieved from http://www.gao.gov/new.items/d1151r.pdf

Gershon, R. R., Magda, L. A., Qureshi, K. A., Riley, H. E., Scanlon, E., Carney, M. T., . . . Sherman, M. F. (2010). Factors associated with the ability and willingness of essential workers to report to duty during a pandemic. *Journal of Occupational and Environmental Medicine, 52*(10), 995–1003.

Good, L., & Agan, D. L. (2011). Working during the pandemic: Fears and concerns of health care workers. *Journal of the Association of Occupational Health Professionals in Healthcare, 31*(1), 21–25.

Graumann, A., Houston, T., Lawrimore, J., Levinson, D., Lott, N., McCown, S., . . . Wuertz, D. (2005). *Hurricane Katrina: A climatological perspective*. Retrieved from http://www.ncdc.noaa.gov/oa/reports/tech-report-200501z.pdf

Grimes, D. E., & Mendias, E. P. (2010). Nurses' intentions to respond to bioterrorism and other infectious disease emergencies. *Nursing Outlook, 58*(1), 10–16.

Harris, R. (2006). Pirates of the Mediterranean. *The New York Times*. Retrieved from http://www.nytimes.com/2006/09/30/opinion/30harris.html?pagewanted=all

Homeland Security Act of 2002, Pub. L. No. 107-296, 116 Stat. 2135 (2002). Retrieved from http://www.gpo.gov/fdsys/search/pagedetails.action?browsePath=107%2FPUBLIC%2F[200%3B299]&granuleId=&packageId=PLAW-107publ296

Jacobson, H. E., Soto Mas, F., Hsu, C. E., Turley, J. P., Miller, J., & Kim, M. (2010). Self-assessed emergency readiness and training needs of nurses in rural Texas. *Public Health Nursing, 27*(1), 41–48.

Jenkins, W. O., Jr. (2010, September). *Disaster response: Criteria for developing and validating effective response plans* (No. GAO-10-969T). Washington, DC: General Accountability Office.

Kean, T. H., & Hamilton, L. H. (2004). *Final report of the national commission on terrorist attacks upon the United States*. Retrieved from http://govinfo.library.unt.edu/911/report/911Report_Exec.htm

Kim, C. J., Yoo, H. R., Yoo, M. S., Kwon, B. E., & Hwang, K. J. (2006). Attitude, beliefs, and intentions to care for SARS patients among Korean clinical nurses: An application of theory of planned behavior. *Taehan Kanho Hakhoe Chi, 36*(4), 596–603.

Ko, N. Y., Feng, M. C., Chiu, D. Y., Wu, M. H., Feng, J. Y., & Pan, S. M. (2004). Applying theory of planned behavior to predict nurses' intention and volunteering to care for SARS patients in southern Taiwan. *The Kaohsiung Journal of Medical Sciences, 20*(8), 389–398.

Levi, J., Segal, L. M., Lieberman, D. A., & St. Laurent, R. (2011). *Ready or not? 2011*. Washington, DC: Trust for America's Health, Robert Wood Johnson Foundation.

Levi, J., Vinter, S., Segal, L. M., St. Laurent, R. (2010). *Ready or not? 2010*. Washington, DC: Trust for America's Health, Robert Wood Johnson Foundation.

Mitani, S., Kuboyama, K., & Shirakawa, T. (2003). Nursing in sudden-onset disasters: Factors and information that affect participation. *Prehospital and Disaster Medicine, 18*(4), 359–366.

Pandemic and All-Hazards Preparedness Act, Pub. L. No. 109-417, 120 Stat. 2831 (2006).

Pang, S. M. C., Chan, S. S. S., & Cheng, Y. (2009). Pilot training program for developing disaster nursing competencies among undergraduate students in China. *Nursing & Health Sciences, 11*(4), 367–373.

Qureshi, K., Gershon, R. R, Sherman, M. F., Straub, T., Gebbie, E., McCollum, M., . . . Morse, S. S. (2005). Health care workers' ability and willingness to report to duty during catastrophic disasters. *Journal of Urban Health, 82*(3), 378–388.

Qureshi, K., Merrill, J., Gershon, R., & Calero-Breckheimer, A. (2002). Emergency preparedness training for public health nurses: A pilot study. *Journal of Urban Health, 79*(3), 413–416.

Schmidt, C. K., Davis, J. M., Sanders, J. L., Chapman, L. A., Cisco, M. C., & Hady, A. R. (2011). Exploring nursing students' level of preparedness for disaster response. *Nursing Education Perspectives, 32*(6), 380–383.

Shapira, Y., Marganitt, B., Roziner, I., Shochet, T., Bar, Y., & Shemer, J. (1991). Willingness of staff to report to their hospital duties following an unconventional missile attack: A state-wide survey. *Israel Journal of Medical Science, 27*(11–12), 704–711.

Smith, E., Morgans, A., Qureshi, K., Burkle, F., & Archer, F. (2008). Paramedics perceptions of risk and willingness to work during disasters. *Australian Journal of Emergency Management, 23*(2), 14–20.

Syrett, J. I., Benitez, J. G., Livingston, W. H., & Davis, E. A. (2007). Will emergency health care providers respond to mass casualty incidents? *Prehospital Emergency Care, 11*(1), 49–54.

The Joint Commission. (2008). Emergency management. *Joint Commission Standards*. Retrieved from http://www.jointcommission.org/JointCommission/Templates/GeneralInformation.aspx?NRMODE=Published&NRNODEGUID={A08FCD4F-CB99-4B32-B309-1FF1F51CC6C6}&NRORIGINALURL=%2fNewsRoom%2fhealth_care_issues.htm&NRCACHEHINT=Guest#3

Townsend, F. F. (2006). *Federal response to Hurricane Katrina: Lessons learned*. Washington, DC: U.S. Government Printing Office.

U.S. Department of Homeland Security. (2008a). *National response framework*. Retrieved from http://www.fema.gov/pdf/emergency/nrf/nrf-core.pdf

U.S. Department of Homeland Security. (2008b). *Budget-in-Brief Fiscal Year 2008*. Retrieved from http://www.dhs.gov/xlibrary/assets/budget_bib-fy2008.pdf

U.S. Department of Homeland Security. (2010). *Homeland security presidential directives*. Retrieved from http://www.dhs.gov/xabout/laws/editorial_0607.shtm

Veenema, T. G., Walden, B., Feinstein, N., & Williams, J. P. (2008). Factors affecting hospital-based nurses' willingness to respond to a radiation emergency. *Disaster Medicine and Public Health Preparedness, 2*(4), 224–229.

World Health Organization. (2003). *Summary of probable SARS cases with onset of illness from 1 November 2002 to 31 July 2003*. Retrieved from http://www.who.int/csr/sars/country/table2003_09_23/en/index.html

Yonge, O., Rosychuk, R. J., Bailey, T. M., Lake, R., & Marrie, T. J. (2010). Willingness of university nursing students to volunteer during a pandemic. *Public Health Nursing, 27*(2), 174–180.

Young, C. F., & Persell, D. J. (2004). Biological, chemical, and nuclear terrorism readiness: Major concerns and preparedness of future nurses. *Disaster Management & Response, 2*(4), 109–114.

CHAPTER 10

International Disaster Humanitarian Assistance for Nurses

Andrew C. Stevermer

ABSTRACT

Nurses participate in humanitarian assistance following disasters throughout the world. Many have limited training or experience in this type of humanitarian aid. This chapter provides an overview and foundation of international humanitarian assistance for nurses to build upon to strengthen their participation in and contribution to these efforts. There is a growing sophistication and coordination of humanitarian assistance across many organizations and governments. This chapter reviews the research and resources that promote nurse participation in international disaster humanitarian assistance.

INTRODUCTION

Every year, the world experiences one or more tragic disasters that tug at the heart strings of all compassionate people. These disasters are often catastrophic in scope and have devastating human impacts. The Internet, cell phones, and mass media bring the stark reality of these disasters into the workplaces and homes around the globe. Nurses often react by asking themselves, "What can I

© 2012 Springer Publishing Company
http://dx.doi.org/10.1891/0739-6686.30.209

do to ease the suffering?" It is this caring that is inherent to the nature of nurses. It is also the question that often leads nurses to become personally involved with international disaster humanitarian health assistance.

Disaster humanitarian assistance is aid to a population negatively impacted by a disaster. Its primary purpose is to save lives and alleviate suffering of the affected population (Office for the Coordination of Humanitarian Affairs [OCHA], 2008). Nurses can make huge contributions to humanitarian aid. One only needs to look at the lives of Florence Nightingale or Claire Bertschinger to see how a single nurse can dramatically improve aid.

Many nurses are routinely engaged in international disaster humanitarian assistance through various organizations. Some do this as a full-time career. Others provide intermittent, temporary nursing surge support to address particular disaster needs. Although many nurses are interested in providing this type of assistance, some are uncertain on how to learn about and connect to the international disaster humanitarian response world. This chapter will discuss the resources available to support nurses to participate in international disaster response, the character of international disaster response, and the preparation a nurse must undertake to become an international responder. Professional nursing assistance with any disaster must be done within the context of the existing response systems. Free-form response, regardless of how altruistic and well intentioned, is rarely helpful to anyone and could become dangerous and/or disruptive. This chapter will provide some foundational information and guiding principles for nurses to appropriately engage with the international disaster humanitarian health response system and the research available to support these principles.

DISASTER NURSING

Training

All nurses need a basic understanding of disaster response. In the past several years, the International Council of Nurses (ICN) has prioritized mobilizing resources to support the nursing role in disaster preparedness, response, and recovery (Kingma, 2008). This support is available in the form of training, networks, and research.

For some, their involvement with disaster response will only occur if the disaster impacts the area where they live and work. Knowledge of local facility disaster plans, state and local emergency plans, and the national response framework is essential for those nurses to "automatically" become disaster responders. Unfortunately, too often, nurses do not have this basic understanding of disasters. A 2008 large study in Canada found that fewer than 10% of the nurses had participated in any emergency training or drills, and less than half of the nurses surveyed knew about the existence of a formal emergency plan for a large-scale infectious disease outbreak (O'Sullivan et al., 2008). Clearly, many nurses need to continue training, exercise, and planning for disaster in their everyday work and home environments.

There are several training resources available to support these needs. Nursing schools and local schools of public health offer various disaster training curricula. Many online training programs exist such as the ones offered by the Federal Emergency Management Agency (FEMA; 2011), the Centers for Disease Control and Prevention (CDC; n.d.), and numerous academic institutions (e.g., Yale, Columbia, Vanderbilt, George Washington) and state health departments in the United States. All of these resources are excellent opportunities to help prepare nurses to better respond when disasters touch their lives.

Some nurses will seek out opportunities to provide support to disaster responses in other locations including international disasters. These nurses need a broader training specific to the international response structure and coordination. Training opportunities for this type of international disaster response are more limited. A major step forward in providing this training was achieved in 2010 with the publishing of *International Disaster Nursing* (Powers & Daily, 2010). This is the first truly comprehensive and internationally focused resource to address the diversity of issues that nurses may encounter during international disaster response. In addition, there are academic institutions and international conferences now offering international disaster nursing training. Nurses preparing to become international responders must seek out and take advantage of these training opportunities prior to international response.

International nurse responders must expand their knowledge base to include transportation, logistics, communications, negotiations, security, and international humanitarian law (Burke, 2000).

Networks
Network development for nurses active in disaster response is also important to support nurses in this role. There are several efforts at building such networks. The Asia Pacific Emergency and Disaster Nursing Network (APEDNN, 2011), the International Disaster Nursing Network Project (2011), and the World Society of Disaster Nursing (2011) are a few available nursing-specific network resources. A more established and more broadly focused network is the World Association for Disaster and Emergency Medicine (2011). Although this association focuses on the broad array of disaster and emergency medicine issues across the health

care workforce, it has a dedicated nursing section and an online journal *Nursing Insight*. This online journal reviews all disaster nursing literature three times yearly and is an excellent source for nurses to stay abreast of the current literature and research in the area of disaster nursing.

Responding to international disasters is not something that can be done in a vacuum or on impulse. It must be deliberate and planned. There were numerous international humanitarian responders in Southeast Asia following the 2004 tsunami and a similar outpouring of medical responders following the 2010 Haiti earthquake. Many were not prepared for the challenges of working in austere conditions with a limited health care infrastructure. Well intentioned, compassionate, and capable clinicians that are ill prepared for the environment, untrained in international response, and unconnected to the larger international response community place themselves at risk and fragment the overall response. Interested nurses must become networked with others who are already engaged in disaster nursing response. In advance of any disaster, nurses need to reach out to the network of nurses specific for the desired response organization (e.g., Red Cross, domestic medical response teams, international medical response teams, World Health Organization [WHO]). There are many of these organizations, and each has a Website that provides a process on how to become volunteer nurse responders.

HUMANITARIAN DISASTER NURSING RESEARCH

The body of research on disaster nursing is small but expanding. There are numerous journal reports on disaster response experiences of nurses from across the world in many different disasters. All are important accounts of the value of nurses in these responses, but few provide an empirical and systematic evaluation of the experiences. In addition to capturing the experiences and lessons learned, nurses must begin to systematically examine their collective experiences. For example, many Australian nurses volunteered to support the humanitarian response to the Sumatra–Andaman earthquake and tsunami of 2004. The information on the large outpouring of volunteers was captured and analyzed to create a profile of nurses that are willing to volunteer for humanitarian disaster response (Arbon, Bobrowski, Zeitz, Hooper, Williams, & Thitchener, 2006). Interestingly, 80% had no prior disaster response or military experience, 85% had never visited the impacted countries, and 83.5% did not have relevant language skills. Another similar after-action study was done on U.S. Navy nurses responding to the same disaster in 2004 that systematically assessed the challenges of humanitarian nursing response (Almonte, 2009). These creative pieces of research not only tell the story of nurses' responses but also contribute to the informational knowledge base of nurses engaging in international response. More research like this is needed. Research that characterizes the readiness of nurses to respond, the knowledge, skills and abilities most needed, and measurable impacts of a response are essential. Compassion and courage are the foundation, but objective analysis of these experiences is needed to advance the field.

There is no single journal or Website for publication of disaster nursing research. It is found throughout the various professional nursing, disaster, and emergency management journals. Fortunately, the World Association for Disaster and Emergency Medicine has a "repository of research" in its nursing section that summarizes newly released disaster nursing research from around the world. In addition, the World Society of Disaster Nursing has been sponsoring annual disaster nursing research conferences for the past 3 years (World Association for Disaster and Emergency Medicine, 2011). Nurses with a desire to respond to disaster internationally need to use these resources to stay abreast of the limited research in the field.

INTERNATIONAL RESPONSE

Knowledge of the basics of international disaster response is essential for any nurse wanting to become an international responder. International health responders must recognize that they serve as a part of a much wider package of humanitarian aid (Burke, 2000). This wider package has rapidly grown in recent years from a $6.5 billion activity in 2000 to a $14.9 billion business in 2008. In 2009, some 210,000 people worldwide were employed in humanitarian aid programs (Walker, Hein, Russ, Bertleff, & Caspersz, 2010). This is a very large effort, and nurses need an understanding of the basics prior to response. The following sections provide an overview of the critical elements of international response that nurses must consider in the training and preparation for deployment.

Anatomy of an International Disaster Response

The FEMA (2010), leading disaster response agency in the United States, describes the disaster life cycle as the process of preparing for, responding to, recovering from, and mitigating/preventing the effects of disasters. International disaster humanitarian health assistance is generally provided in the response phase of this disaster life cycle. Some disasters require protracted assistance for many years; however, most is provided in the immediate aftermath of the disaster. Roberts (2005) describes five phases to the response life cycle—warning or threat phase, impact phase, heroic or rescue phase, honeymoon phase, disillusionment phase, and reconstruction or recovery phase. The *warning or threat phase* can be quite short as with earthquakes and tsunamis, or quite long as with civil strife and famine. The near real time world news systems share knowledge of these warnings and threats across the globe; however, it is not until the *impact phase* (the actual disaster) that media really engages the entire world in the suffering and devastation of the disaster. This is the point at which nurses and other health professionals begin to consider providing direct care support to the survivors of the disaster. The *heroic or rescue phase* is usually supported by local responders and well-organized international response teams that can mobilize quickly and have a history of successful support for international disasters (e.g., International Committee of the Red Cross [ICRC], Médecins Sans Frontières [MSF], OCHA). There are many of these types of response organizations that engage in the response at this phase and remain engaged throughout the honeymoon, reconstruction, and recovery phases.

The *honeymoon phase* is when the myriad of international responders finally get coordinated with one another and the national response groups. It is this phase when many nurses opt to volunteer in the response. Roberts (2005) says that there is ultimately a *disillusionment phase* that follows when the reality of the losses and immensity of the tasks ahead become a daunting challenge leading to the long *reconstruction and recovery phases*. Responding nurses must be prepared for the expected changes, which may occur throughout the response life cycle.

CHARACTER OF CONTEMPORARY INTERNATIONAL DISASTERS

There are several characteristics of contemporary international disasters that are much different from the domestic disaster response a nurse would experience in the United States. First, many of the disasters requiring international assistance are complex humanitarian emergencies. A complex emergency is defined by the Inter-Agency Standing Committee (IASC) of the UN OCHA as

> a humanitarian crisis in a country, region, or society where there is total or considerable breakdown of authority resulting from internal or external conflict and which requires an international response that goes beyond the mandate or capacity of any single agency and/or the ongoing UN country programme. (OCHA & IASC, 2008)

OCHA—the UN agency responsible for coordination of all humanitarian responders to ensure a coherent response to emergencies—has observed the changing character of international disaster response over the past several decades and adapted to the complexity of coordinating humanitarian responses to events in Darfur, Haiti, and the Congo. Many of the international humanitarian disaster responses that nurses participate in are complex disasters.

Second, many of the disasters necessitating international assistance will involve multilateral involvement with many different response partners including nongovernmental organizations (NGOs), national militaries and governments, and International Governmental Organizations (IGOs; e.g., UN, and international corporations such as McDonalds, Sony, Toyota). Nurses participating in international disaster response must have an understanding of the diversity of the network of responders that come together to support the response.

Lastly, international humanitarian response involves personal safety risks for the responders that are much different from those in domestic responses. The past 10 years has been one of the worst decades ever in terms of attacks on humanitarian workers. Over the past decade, aid worker casualties have tripled, reaching more than 100 deaths per year (OCHA, 2011). The increasing trends of civilian victims of armed conflicts and the direct targeting of humanitarian aid workers both have contributed to this distressing change. Nurses choosing to participate in international disaster response must be prepared for the increased risks of working in these environments. There are skills that nurses can use to minimize these risks as detailed in the recent UN OCHA report *To Stay and Deliver* cited previously.

ASSESSING THE NEED

Watching reports of international disasters on world news or Internet resources can often be emotionally charged and highly motivating to take action. This is often what inspires nurses to begin thinking about participating in the response. It is also frequently incomplete and lacks the depth and quality of assessment that must be done before taking action. The adage about "only fools rush in" is apropos. Nurses must rely on the experts in international disaster humanitarian assistance to determine what assistance is needed.

Early in the impact phase of the response, there is sometimes considerable misinformation and missing information that limits the response. This is known as the "fog of response." Although there is a sense of urgency to take action during this phase, it must only be done with clarity of understanding about what is needed and desired by the host country. There are several systems of assessment that are used to help define the need for humanitarian assistance following a disaster. The first and most important is the assessment and desires of the government of the impacted area. This government is the only authority to decide if external humanitarian support will be provided by the international community. If assistance is desired, the "host government" must make that request known to the UN, other countries, and the NGO communities. The sovereignty, territorial integrity, and national unity must be respected in accordance with the charter of the UN (1945).

The UN has two powerful emergency response tools to provide disaster assessment and to define the need for external support. First, there are the United Nations Assessment and Coordination (UNDAC) teams. There are three such teams across the globe, each representing multiple countries and disciplines. The teams are constantly ready to respond on short notice to disasters anywhere in the world. The diversity of these teams makes them well versed in the local conditions, languages, and culture. The UNDAC responds quickly to the disaster and begins to assess the damages and threats, in addition to determining the type and volume of support that will be necessary in the response. The assessments of this team are shared back through OCHA who is responsible for regularly communicating the results of the assessment and analysis to interested parties such as emergency responders, donors, and the media (OCHA, 2006). This is done through regular reports and briefings, many of which are posted to the UN ReliefWeb Website (2011) to be shared with the international response community. This information is more informed and reliable than open source media about the status of the disaster and should be used by any nurse to gain better awareness of the situation and possible needs for assistance.

Another powerful tool for gaining situational awareness of the disaster's impact is through the health cluster (WHO, 2009). The cluster approach to disaster response was adopted by OCHA in 2005 after a comprehensive independent review of the international response system recommended designating operational accountability for the various sectors involved in humanitarian response. Health was one of these sectors, and thus the development of health clusters. The health cluster is led by the WHO. The cluster is a way of promoting coordination and cooperation among all the health responders to emergencies. It provides a framework for effective partnership and coordination of the diverse array of humanitarian "health actors" in the response. Health clusters can be initiated during the response or may be established prior to the disaster in areas that have complex emergencies or recent prior disasters. The cluster becomes a valuable source of situational awareness for the health sector within the response. Its situational reports are important tools for maintaining situational awareness and can be monitored through the WHO Emergencies Website (or one of its regional offices; WHO, 2011). This is an important site for nurses to monitor as they consider volunteering for international response.

The third source for assessing the need is through the Websites of numerous NGOs. Most major international health response organizations have active Websites that are used to inform others about their organization and their work on particular disasters. Some of this information sharing is linked to donation appeals—which are to be expected in that most are nonprofit organizations and dependent on donor funding. In general, this information is accurate and timely and can also provide details on the needs and activities of the individual organizations in the response.

The plethora of international health organizations that become involved in disaster responses can be overwhelming. Fortunately, there are three organizations/Websites that provide a collective voice for NGOs working in humanitarian assistance. The Websites provide linkages to the various organizations that are actively involved in a particular disaster response. These are InterAction (2011), International Council of Voluntary Agencies (ICVA, 2011), and OneResponse (2011). All provide awareness of and connectivity to the many agencies and organizations engaged in a particular disaster response. The resources can assist nurses to better understand the complexity of the disaster response and the specific actions each of the humanitarian actors are taking in the response.

COMPLEXITY OF INTERNATIONAL DISASTER RESPONSE

The complexity of international humanitarian disaster response can be difficult to understand and appreciate. There is great diversity in the responders including NGOs, governments, IGOs, and private industry. All come to support the host country, frequently with limited knowledge of the activities of other responders. Nurses must have a basic understanding of the humanitarian actors and response structure of international disaster response prior to volunteering to support the response.

Coordination of this diverse and fragmented response is essential. There are two principle coordination functions. First, all responders are there at the request or with the permission of the host country. Second, the host country is the principal "director" of all incoming response resources. These resources are there to augment and support the host country's organic resources.

Many of the host countries that need international disaster humanitarian assistance frequently have compromised capacity because of financial restraints, political instability, or severe disruptions to the host country's governing capacity as was seen in the Haiti earthquake in January 2010. Many of the Haitian governmental offices were destroyed, and staff were killed in the earthquake. It took time for the national government to recover sufficiently to coordinate incoming response resources. Therefore, the international response community must have a system for coordinating the diverse responder groups who arrive to help.

The UN OCHA is responsible for mobilization and coordination of effective and principled humanitarian action in partnership with national and international humanitarian actors. OCHA uses various tools to achieve this coordination. The OCHA UNDAC provides the initial assessment and coordination for the international response community. Sector clusters (e.g., health, water/sanitation, nutrition, protection) are then established as needed to organize and coordinate the various sector-specific response organizations. These clusters bring together diverse groups including government, NGO, IGO, and private response teams for each sector area. All of this coordination activity is done in close collaboration with the host country and the resident UN Country Team in the host country. All coordination is ultimately under the authority of the UN Emergency Response Coordinator (ERC) who is an Undersecretary-General of the UN. There may be further delegation of this responsibility to a UN Humanitarian Coordinator who is the lead UN official at the country level for the specific disaster response.

In addition to the UN coordinated response, host countries will often ask other nations to support the response through binational aid arrangements. This may involve support from militaries, financial or direct assistance through international aid programs of the donor governments (e.g., United States Aid for International Development, Canadian International Development Agency, and European Community Humanitarian Office), or through the provision of technical assistance. The coexistence of binational and multinational response activities is a reality of international disaster response and must be acknowledged and coordinated.

HEALTH CLUSTERS

The health cluster is the health sector coordination entity within the response. It is led by the WHO. It is responsible to establish a clear system of leadership and accountability for the international response in the health sector. Furthermore, it must provide a framework for effective partnerships among international and national health actors (WHO, 2009). It ensures that the international health responses are appropriately aligned with the health response of the host country.

The cluster is led by a health leader from the WHO region impacted by the disaster. They are responsible to the UN Humanitarian Coordinator for the response, and receive support through the UN Country Team. These leaders are trained in health cluster operations and look to engage all health responders to ensure that needs, risks, capacities, and opportunities are understood and shared across the health sector.

All health responders to a disaster should be participants in the health cluster to share information, highlight needs and gaps, report progress, mobilize resources, and build local capacity. The health cluster also becomes a forum where disparate response organizations can agree to adhere to principles, policies, and standards.

The success and use of health clusters as a response coordination tool is being evaluated. Since its implementation in 2005, the cluster system has been used in about 27 countries. Several evaluative studies have been done or are in process on the effectiveness of the health cluster such as the ones from Zimbabwe (WHO & Zimbabwe Ministry of Health and Child Welfare, 2009), Democratic Republic of Congo (Binder, de Geoffroy, & Sokpoh, 2010), and Haiti (Bhattacharjee & Lossio, 2011). All demonstrate some positive impacts from the use of clusters in promoting coordination of humanitarian response to implement coherent strategies. There are other ongoing evaluations to this approach as the UN gains more experience with using the cluster approach.

HUMANITARIAN ACTORS

Those who work in the humanitarian service sector providing relief in emergencies (acute and chronic) are referred to as humanitarian actors. Most of these responders will be associated with NGOs. The number, diversity, and commitment of these NGOs are truly awe inspiring. This is the foundation of international disaster relief. Most health care provided in the aftermath of a disaster requiring international assistance is provided by the NGO community. The number of international relief and development NGOs now total in the thousands, but a small fraction are consistently the major humanitarian actors in international humanitarian health response. In 2005, it was estimated that 48%–58% of all humanitarian funding to international disasters flowed through NGOs (Walker & Pepper, 2007). These organizations are the backbone of emergency response, and it is important that nurses become familiar with some of the key actors in the NGO community.

NGOs from the United States have a unified voice through InterAction. Many of the 200 NGO members of this alliance provide health services in disasters domestically and around the world. The ICVA represents more than 70 international NGOs that are involved in international response. Many of these also have a strong health focus in their mission. The organizational profiles of these international NGOs can be reviewed on their Websites. A few of the larger, commonly recognized international health NGOs are the ICRC, MSF, Christian Action Research and Education (CARE), International Medical Corps (IMC), International Rescue Committee (IRC), Medecins du Monde (MDM), Merlin, Save the Children International, and International Federation of Red Cross and Red Crescent Societies. There are many other smaller NGOs that also provide humanitarian health care that will be encountered in a response.

FUNDING OF HUMANITARIAN HEALTH ASSISTANCE

Funding humanitarian assistance is as diverse as the humanitarian actors who provide the assistance. As previously discussed, most of this funding ultimately flows through the NGOs who provide the international response services. A highly visible source for this funding includes donations through the UN in the form of flash appeals, consolidated appeals, or voluntary contributions to the Central Response Emergency Fund. These funds are used by the UN OCHA to fund all aspects of the emergency response.

Other disaster funding is given by other governments directly to the host country as a binational contribution. These funds are used by the host country to support the response and may include support to national and international NGOs providing disaster response services.

NGOs also have their own donor base. Additional donations are often solicited during a response by NGOs to further support their activities. Media, Internet, and direct funding campaigns are commonplace for NGOs in the midst of a large response. Nurses should maintain knowledge and appreciation for the breadth of funding strategies that support international response. These funding can often drive response priorities.

INTERNATIONAL STANDARDS OF CARE

Standards of care will be different in many international disaster responses from the standards known to most U.S. trained nurses. The international response community has developed some of their own standards. The Sphere Project is one such example. The international response community came together in 1997 to develop a minimum set of standards for saving lives in a humanitarian response (SPHERE Project, 2011). In addition, some NGOs such as MSF (2012) have published clinical guidelines for their health professionals. This is not only for use in MSF programs but also for other programs in similar context and who may be using WHO emergency health kits and the WHO essential drug list. Nurses should have familiarity with these standards before engaging in the international response environment.

In addition to the standards of care developed by the international response community, nurses must be aware of the standards of care in the host country. These are best learned quickly upon arrival with the assistance of local health providers. Expatriate nurses need to learn local practices, standards of care, and health systems as quickly as possible to ensure that the emergency response augmentation harmonizes with the local system and standards of care.

The ICN (2012) can be a helpful resource for nurses pursuing a better understanding of nursing across the globe. The ICN leads and connects nurses internationally to promote quality nursing care and promote sound health policies globally. Through this network, nurses can learn about nursing care from more than 130 member countries.

NURSES AS INTERNATIONAL RESPONDERS

This article began by describing the typical scenario that precipitates a nurse's decision to become an international disaster responder. The motivations of those nurses are complex and multifactorial. Although the underpinning of the decision is most often compassion and concern for others, curiosity, quest for new knowledge/skills, exposure to new challenges, adventure, belief that the work is inherently worthwhile, guilt, and a sense of accomplishment all can serve to motivate nurses in this direction. Each nurse should identify his or her unique motivators to ensure that he or she is consistent with the response organization of his or her choosing.

The decision to become a responder must be planned well in advance of the response. Nurses must be networked, trained, and preregistered with a response organization. There is no place for lone wolves or heroes in a response. It only places the individual at risk and fragments the cohesiveness of the medical response.

There are personal risks in all disaster response and particularly in international responses where there may be coexistent civil unrest or armed conflict. In addition, the living and working conditions for responders in the international environment are often austere. Nurses must assess their willingness and ability to accept these risks and hardships. Some of this ability cannot be fully determined until the nurse is "field tested"; however, to the extent possible, nurses should understand what to expect and gauge their ability to live with these realities.

Collaboration is the key to success of all disaster response. This was emphasized in the UN pillars of reform for humanitarian aid in 2006. This reform was built on a foundation of strong and consistent partnerships between all humanitarian partners. This reform created the Global Humanitarian Platform (2011) that endorsed the *Principles of Partnership* (Global Health Partnership, 2007) in July 2007. This document describes the goals and principles of how the diverse international response community will work together. Nurses engaging in international response need to be aware of and agree with these principles. Even though most nurse responders will not be leading organizations during the response, the principle of effective, collaborative work among all humanitarian responders is essential.

Volunteering for humanitarian disaster assistance can be a long-term or short-term commitment. These are personal decisions that are negotiated with the response organization. Given the protracted nature of responses to the complex and acute disasters in the world, many of the humanitarian medical aid organizations remain in the host country for a long time. Minimum deployments are two or more weeks, and some deployments can last for years.

Selecting a response organization is similar to developing an association with any civic or social organization. Nurses must share common values, goals, and health care ideals. There is great variation in the many organizations that provide humanitarian health aid. Some have religious, academic, or governmental affiliations. Nurses should select an organization with a kindred philosophy prior to committing to a deployment. This is best done by first exploring the organization. Use InterAction or the ICVA as a springboard to find the organizations of greatest interest. Research the organization through the Internet and by reaching out to prior volunteers with the organization. There is a strong informal communication network among volunteers that can be easily tapped by just talking to colleagues. These contacts can be important in helping to determine if the organization is a good match for the nurse.

Finally, contact the organization directly to ask specific questions that are not contained in the organization's public literature. If the nurse and organization match, it is then time to register with the organization and begin whatever training and orientation is expected. This is a critical step that cannot be done at the time of an emergency response when the focus is to rapidly mobilize assistance. Nurses must be already registered in the system, trained, and networked prior to activation.

SUMMARY

There is a clear need and role for nurses in international disaster humanitarian assistance. The training and networking of nurses in this role is developing. All nurses need to be trained and prepared to participate as disaster responders in their communities. Some will choose to do so for other communities and some across the world. The international disaster response world is significantly different from and often more challenging than typical domestic disaster experience in the United States. Nurses choosing this role must prepare themselves personally with knowledge of the international emergency response community and awareness of what will be expected of them in an international disaster response. This article provides some of the basic information and resources that will guide these nurses along the path to becoming capable international disaster humanitarian aid providers.

Additional research is needed to support the ongoing participation of nurses in international disaster humanitarian assistance. Transitioning from individual or group experiential accounts of humanitarian missions to empiric assessment and analysis is critical. Nurses need to define response readiness indicators. This includes both professional skills and knowledge of the international humanitarian response world. Defining these will be an important step forward in making nurses more successful and safe in international humanitarian response.

DISCLAIMER

The views expressed in this manuscript do not necessarily represent the views of the U.S. Department of Health and Human Services, U.S. Public Health Service, Office of the Assistant Secretary for Preparedness and Response, or the U.S. government.

REFERENCES

Almonte, A. (2009). Humanitarian nursing challenges: A grounded theory study. *Military Medicine, 174*(5), 479–485.

Arbon, P., Bobrowski, C., Zeitz, K., Hooper, C., Williams, J., & Thitchener, J. (2006). Australian nurses volunteering for the Sumatra-Andaman earthquake and tsunami of 2004: A review of experience and analysis of data collected by teh Tsunami Volunteer Hotline. *Australasian Emergency Nursing Journal, 9*(4), 171–178.

Asia Pacific Emergency and Disaster Nursing Network. (2011). Retrieved from http://www.apednn .org/default.aspx

Bhattacharjee, A., & Lossio, R. (2011). *Evaluation of OCHA response to the Haiti earthquake: Final report.* New York, NY: United Nations Office for the Coordination of Humanitarian Affairs.

Binder, A., de Geoffroy, V., & Sokpoh, B. (2010). *IASC cluster approach evaluation, 2nd phase country study: Democratic Republic of Congo.* Berlin, Germany and Plaisians, France: Global Public Policy Institute and Groupe URD.

Burke, F. M. (2000). Lessons learned from and future expectation of complex emergencies. *Western Journal of Medicine, 172*(1), 33–38.

Centers for Disease Control and Prevention. (n.d.). *Emergency preparedness and response.* Retrieved from http://www.bt.cdc.gov/training/

Federal Emergency Management Agency. (2010). *What we do.* Retrieved from http://www.fema.gov/ about/what.shtm

Federal Emergency Management Agency. (2011). *Emergency management institute.* Retrieved from http://training.fema.gov/is/crslist.asp?page=all

Global Health Partnership. (2007, July). *Principles of partnership.* Presented at the meeting of Global Humanitarian Platform, Geneva, Switzerland.

Global humanitarian platform. (2011). Retrieved from http://www.globalhumanitarianplatform.org

Interaction. (2011). Retrieved from http://www.interaction.org/

International Council of Nurses. (2012). Retrieved from http://www.icn.ch/about-icn/about-icn/

International Council of Voluntary Agencies. (2011). Retrieved from http://www.icva.ch/

International Disaster Nursing Network Project. (2011). Retrieved from http://www.coe-cnas.jp/english/ group_international/index.html

Kingma, M. (2008). International Council of Nurses: Disaster nursing. *Prehospital and Disaster Medicine, 23*(3), s4–s5.

Médecins Sans Frontières. (2012). *Clinical guidelines: Diagnosis and treatment manual*. Geneva, Switzerland: Author.

Office for the Coordination of Humanitarian Affairs. (2005). *Humanitarian response review*. New York, NY and Geneva, Switzerland: United Nations.

Office for the Coordination of Humanitarian Affairs. (2006). *UNDAC handbook*. New York, NY: United Nations.

Office for the Coordination of Humanitarian Affairs. (2011). *To stay and deliver*. New York, NY: United Nations.

Office for the Coordination of Humanitarian Affairs & Inter-Agency Standing Committee. (2008). *Civil military guidelines and reference for complex emergencies*. New York, NY: United Nations.

O'Sullivan, T., Dow, D., Turner, M., Lemyre, L., Corneil, W., Krewski, D., . . . Amaratunga, C. (2008). Disaster and emergency management: Canadian nurses' perceptions of preparedness on hospital front lines. *Prehospital and Disaster Medicine, 23*(3), s11–s18.

OneResponse. (2011). Retrieved from http://oneresponse.info/Pages/default.aspx

Powers, R., & Daily, E. (Eds.). (2010). *International disaster nursing*. New York, NY: Cambridge University Press.

ReliefWeb. (2011). Retrieved from http://reliefweb.int/

Roberts, A. R. (2005). *Crisis intervention handbook: Assessment, treatment, and research* (3rd ed.). New York, NY: Oxford University Press.

SPHERE Project. (2011). *Humanitarian charter and minimum standards in humanitarian response* (3rd ed.). Rugby, United Kingdom: Practical Action.

United Nations. (1945). Charter of the United Nations. San Francisco, CA: Author.

Walker, P., & Pepper, K. (2007). The state of humanitarian funding. *Forced Migration Review, 29*, 33–35.

Walker, P., Hein, K., Russ, C., Bertleff, G., & Caspersz, D. (2010). A blueprint for professionalizing humanitarian assistance. *Health Affairs, 29*(12), 2223–2230.

World Association for Disater and Emergency Medicine. (2011). Retrieved from http://www.wadem.org/

World Health Organization. (2009). *Health cluster guide*. Geneva, Switzerland: WHO Press.

World Health Organization. (2011). Retrieved from http://www.who.int/topics/emergencies/en/index.html

World Health Organization & Zimbabwe Ministry of Health and Child Welfare. (2009). *Evaluation of the health cluster response to cholera outbreak in Zimbabwe*. Geneva, Switzerland: World Health Organization.

World Society of Disaster Nursing. (2011). Retrieved from http://wsdn2010.umin.jp/

Index

Note: Page references followed by "*f*" and "*t*" denote figures and tables, respectively.

Disillusionment phase, disaster response, 214

Dissertation research, 34–36

Duty to report or respond, 58–62, 194

Duty to treat, 57–58

Economic theory, 9

Education, 169–192
  nursing programs, 184–186

Emergency Management Assistance Compact (EMAC), 81

Emergency Preparedness Resource Inventory, 154

Emergency response, legal issues in, 67–88

Ethics
  allocation of resources, 144
  nursing disaster, 47–66
    concerns of professionals, 62–63
  overview, 51–52

Ethnic minorities, 103–104

Facilitated discussion, crisis response leaders, 38–39

Federal Civil Defense Act of 1950, 28

Federal Emergency Management Agency (FEMA), 7–8, 28
  special or functional needs, 127–129, 128t

Federal Nursing Service Council (FNSC), 32

Federal Public Relations and Emergency Preparedness Act, 79

Federal Volunteer Protection Act, 79

Fidelity, in nursing ethics, 50

Framework of Disaster Nursing Competencies (ICN & WHO), 33

Framework of Disaster Nursing Competencies(ICN), 174

Fukushima Daiichi, informatics in, 156

Future nursing research, 15–17, 16t, 39–41

General Accountability Office, disaster response and, 195

Geographical information systems (GIS), 158

Global Outbreak Alert and Response Network (WHO), 157

Global Public health Intelligence Network, 157

Good Samaritan statutes, 82

Guidance for Establishing Crisis Standards of Care for Use in Disaster Situations (IOM), 75–77

Guidance on Planning for Integration of Functional Needs Support (FEMA), 129

Haddon's matrix, 14

Health clusters, 218–219

Health information exchange (HIE), 152–154, 163

Health Information Technology for Economic and Clinical Health (HITECH) Act, 152

Health insurance, lack of, 131–132, 131t

Health Insurance Portability and Accountability Act (HIPAA), 2–3

Healthcare workers (HCWs), 193–208
  background, 195–196
  cross-cutting competencies, 178f
  methods, 196–197
  professional programs, 186–188
  research recommendations, 204–205
  results, 197

HealthMap (Boston Children's Hospital), 158

Heroic or rescue phase, disaster response, 214

H1N1 flu virus, 30, 155–156

Homeland Security Presidential Directive (HSPD) 21, 157–158

Honeymoon phase, disaster response, 214

Hospital emergency preparedness, 69–70

Hospital Incident Command System (HICS), 70

Hospital Preparedness Program (HPP), 32

Humanitarian actors, 219

Humanitarian response
  competency needs, 180–181
  disaster nursing research, 212–213